"A scholarly yet poetically sensit[...]
symbols. It provides a many-laye[...]
will bring one back for rereading and rereading and
rereading."   —Selma Hyman, M.D.

"An arresting book of unique value for our time . . . of
first importance for all those concerned with symbolic
or imaginal healing, be they physicians seeking cures for
cancer or psychotherapists seeking cures for neuroses."
                          —Katharine Whiteside Taylor, Ed.D.

"A highly original study . . . a unique and comprehensive picture of the Navaho ritual."
                          —Joseph L. Henderson, M.D.

The medicine man, Natani Tso, at work on the third figure of a sand painting of the Star People from Big Star Way.
(Donald Sandner)

Navaho Symbols of Healing

A Jungian Exploration of Ritual, Image, and Medicine

DONALD SANDNER, M.D.

Healing Arts Press
Rochester, Vermont

Healing Arts Press
One Park Street
Rochester, Vermont 05767

LIBRARY OF CONGRESS CATALOGING-IN-PUBLICATION DATA
Sandner, Donald
Navaho symbols of healing : a Jungian exploration of ritual, image, and medicine / Donald Sandner.
p. cm.
Includes bibliographical references and index.
ISBN 0-89281-434-9
1. Navajo Indians—Religion and mythology.
2. Navajo Indians—Medicine. 3. Healing—Southwest, New.
4. Symbolism (Psychology) I. Title.
E99.N3S22 1991
299'.782—dc20
91-11867
CIP

Printed and bound in the United States.

10 9 8 7 6 5 4 3 2 1

Healing Arts Press is a division of Inner Traditions International, Ltd.

Distributed to the book trade in the United States by American International Distribution Corporation (AIDC)

Distributed to the book trade in Canada by Book Center, Inc., Montreal, Quebec

Distributed to the health food trade in Canada by Alive Books, Toronto and Vancouver

Contents

Dedicated with loving gratitude to
Joe and Jane Wheelwright
and
Natani Tso
three great medicine persons

Then go on as one who has long life,
Go on as one who is happy,
Go with blessing before you,
Go with blessing behind you,
Go with blessing below you,
Go with blessing above you,
Go with blessing around you,
Go with blessing in your speech,
Go with happiness and long life,
Go mysteriously.

from the Emergence Myth
Wheelwright and Haile, 1949: 54

Note

The sand paintings referred to in this text will be identified by the reference work in which they are found, or by their number in the collection of the Wheelwright Museum in Santa Fe. All the prayer and song translations are taken from original works or from tapes made in the field. In the latter case I have used Navaho translators, fluent in both languages, to produce intelligible English versions.

All Navaho sand painting and "poetry" have their place within a ritual context, and whenever possible I have tried to to keep them within that framework. To dispense with the need for footnotes, all references will be in parentheses, giving (if necessary) the last name of the author, the year of the work, and, when appropriate, the page number of the reference.

I wish to thank the C. G. Jung Institute of San Francisco and Joe and Jane Wheelwright for a grant to aid this research. David Jongeward for assistance in the early field work; Jim Peterson, who took the black-and-white photographs; and Bill Blick for careful pruning of an otherwise overgrown garden.

Acknowledgments

For permission to reprint parts of their published works, I wish to thank the following sources: Harvard University Peabody Museum, publisher, Mary Wheelwright, author, and the Wheelwright Museum in Santa Fe, N.M., for *Texts of Navaho Creation Chants* collected from Hosteen Klah, 1929; University of Arizona Press, Tucson, for various quotes and songs from *Blessingway* by Leland C. Wyman, copyright 1970; Wesleyan University Press for quotations from *A Magic Dwells: A Poetic and Psychological Study of the Navaho Emergence Myth*, by Sheila Moon, copyright 1970 by Wesleyan University; the University of Washington Press for quotations from *Prayer, the Compulsive Word* by Gladys A. Reichard, copyright 1944; Aldus Books Limited for quotations from "Ancient Myths and Modern Man" by Joseph Henderson, in *Man and His Symbols* by C. G. Jung, published in 1964; Princeton University Press for quotations from *The Hero with a Thousand Faces,* by Joseph Campbell, Bollingen Series XVII, copyright 1949 by Princeton University Press, renewed copyright 1976, and for Table I from *Navaho Religion: A Study of Symbolism* by Gladys A. Reichard, Bollingen Series XVIII, copyright 1950 and 1963 by Princeton University Press; Basic Books, Inc., for quotations from *The Interpretation of Cultures* by Clifford Geertz, copyright 1973 by Basic Books, Inc.; Beacon Press for quotes from *Navaho Witchcraft* by Clyde Kluckhohn; Cooper Square Publishers, Inc., for quotes from *An Apache Lifeway* by Edward Opler; Macmillan Publishing Co., Inc., for quotes from *Magic, Faith, and Healing* by Ari Kiev, copyright 1964 by the Free Press of Glencoe, a division of Macmillan; and Harper & Row, Publishers, Inc., for quotes from *Myth and Reality* and *Rites and Symbols of Initiation* by Mircea Eliade.

Navaho
Symbols
of
Healing

Introduction

This book is about the general principles governing the process of symbolic healing. To appreciate that process it is necessary to describe a specific example, and no better example could be found than the Navaho religion. When I first read about Navaho ceremonies and saw their sand paintings, I was struck by the intensity and vividness of the symbols. As a psychiatrist, it seemed to me that a study of the process of healing, which is the main substance of their religion, might reveal something about the ancient roots of our own healing disciplines. For the Navaho, healing is not directed toward specific symptoms or bodily organs, but toward bringing the psyche into harmony with the whole gamut of natural and supernatural forces around it. I saw that their use of striking symbolic images could create harmony-giving changes in their patients, and that, from the psychiatric point of view, we might learn much from their skill in this area.

In the classical Navaho religion the priest and the doctor are one and the same person. Religion, medicine, and art are inextricably intertwined in an astonishing unity of purpose. Almost all their religious ceremonies are also healing ceremonies designed to restore health and harmony within and without. Here we can study the symbolism of healing in one of its original forms, in a culture that gives it paramount importance.

The plan of this book is as follows: the first chapter gives a condensed explanation of some modern views of symbolism, and how they relate to cultural systems and the art of healing. I define what I mean by symbolic healing as contrasted with other kinds of healing, and explore in some detail the difference between them. The second chapter introduces Navaho medicine men, and presents information that I gathered while talking to them in their homes and offices (ceremonial hogans). Their training, their professional methods of healing, and their attitudes toward their profession are described. The third and fourth chapters are a more formal description of Navaho religion and the way it is oriented toward the symbolic healing process. This is illustrated by describing the ritual procedure of the Night Chant and how it follows the stages of symbolic healing.

The fifth chapter is an examination of the importance of cultural bias in the manifestation of disease, its diagnosis, and the methods employed for its cure. This leads in the following three chapters to an account of four central principles basic to healing in the Navaho culture, and perhaps in other cultures as well. The first is *return to the origins;* the second, *confrontation and manipulation of evil;* the third, *death and rebirth;* and the fourth, *restoration of the universe.* The ninth chapter deals with the Navaho sand paintings as healing mandalas, and the esoteric meaning of the pollen path. The tenth relates the Navaho chant system to other preliterate healing systems, and finally, in the eleventh chapter, to the fundamental principles of modern psychotherapy.

I based this study on ethnological data drawn from the life's work of a small but distinguished group of anthropologists who, since the late nineteenth century, have lived and worked on the Navaho reservation. Several of them have learned the Navaho language—no easy matter—and have become almost as intimate with the chant practice as the chanters themselves.

Washington Matthews, an army surgeon, was the first to study the chant practice in detail. He was on the Navaho reservation from 1880 to 1884, and again from 1890 to 1894, and he continued to write articles on Navaho religion until his death in 1905. He studied the famous Night Chant under the tutelage of Laughing Doctor, who was reputed to be one of its greatest practitioners. When Matthews suffered a paralytic stroke while studying the chant, the Navahos felt that it was due to the chant's powerful influence. Matthews belonged to the old tradition of descriptive anthropology and presented his observations straight, with little tampering to prove a particular theoretical bias. He is a constant delight to read, and his translations of Navaho songs and prayers are a contribution to world literature.

One of the finest old-school scholars among students of the Navaho was Father Berard Haile, a Franciscan missionary at St. Michael's, Arizona. He was sent to the Navaho reservation at the age of twenty-six, and stayed there for fifty-four years. He was extremely fluent in Navaho, and through his missionary work made many close friends among the Navaho medicine men. From these friends he obtained the finest versions of many Navaho myths. Because of the respect they had for him, they did not withhold important parts, as they often did when giving information to outsiders. His definitive texts of the Blessing Way myth (published posthumously by Wyman) are brilliant examples of the results of devoted scholarship in uncovering wide areas of mythic material easily overlooked by others. He presented the material but did not interpret it: he left that to others.

The greatest of these was Gladys A. Reichard, a tough field worker and student of Franz Boas. She spent thirty years studying the Navaho religion, and was even adopted into the family of her teacher, Red Point. She specialized in the study of the Male Shooting Chant, and was perhaps the only non-Indian who could have given the chant, sand paintings and all, almost as well as any chanter. She was the first to see that Navaho religion embraced a unified symbolic system which integrates each separate chant into a general framework: "Once the symbolic connotation of a number of other elements is understood, they are found to be an interlocking whole which amazes, not because of the uniqueness of any one element, but because of the careful dovetailing of each part, not only with others, but with all the others" (1944b: 5). She was surprised to find that the Navaho themselves were not consciously aware of this. A detailed survey of this symbolism was presented in her comprehensive work on Navaho religion published in the Bollingen Series XVIII (1950). This now stands as the authoritative reference work in that area. Her short monograph, *Prayer, the Compulsive Word* (1944), is a minor masterpiece, and her longer books, *Navaho Medicine Man* (1939) and *Sandpaintings of the Navaho Shooting Chant* (1937, with Franc Newcomb), contain some of the most beautiful reproductions of sand paintings to be seen. Her more personal works, *Spider Woman* (1934) and *A Navaho Shepherd and Weaver* (1936), are loving accounts of life with her Navaho family.

Clyde Kluckhohn and Leland Wyman, both distinguished American behavioral scientists, contributed dozens of articles and books on every aspect of Navaho life and religion. Kluckhohn, with Dorothea Leighton, wrote the best general overview of Navaho culture (1946). Wyman specialized in the chants and gave invaluable documented accounts of several specific chantways (Beauty Way, 1957; Red Ant Way, 1965; Wind Way, 1962; Blessing Way, 1970). He is at present the greatest authority on Navaho religion outside the Navaho themselves, who know it in a different way.

Surprisingly, several nonprofessional persons not specially trained in scientific field work contributed greatly to our knowledge of Navaho religion. Mary Wheelwright, a Boston society woman, was captivated by Navaho chant practice on one of her trips to the Southwest. She came back again and again to encourage permanent collection of sand paintings and myths. In partnership with the Navaho's greatest medicine man, Hosteen Klah, she founded the Museum of Navaho Ceremonial Art, now the Wheelwright Museum, in Santa Fe, which keeps in its archives copies of hundreds of sand paintings and texts on Navaho religion and related subjects.

Maud Oakes, an American artist, went into the Navaho reservation on her own and collected myths and sand paintings which would otherwise have been lost. She was the first to show, with Joseph Campbell, how Jungian concepts of symbolism could be applied to Navaho material. *Where the Two Came to Their Father: A Navaho War Ceremonial* (1943) is a thoroughgoing presentation of the myth, the sand paintings, and symbolic interpretation of a particular ceremony.

There was also Franc Newcomb, wife of a trader on the Navaho reservation, who became very interested in the chantways, and was able to record sand paintings and witness ceremonies that were rarely performed. When she attended the chant performances, she had to memorize exactly all the sand paintings she saw, for no notes or sketches were permitted during the ceremonies. Her work grew over a period of twenty years into an irreplaceable collection of more than five hundred sand paintings.

Hosteen Klah himself did more than anyone else to make Navaho religion available to outsiders. He opened his ceremonies to interested observers, and even supervised and corrected some of the earliest sand-painting sketches. He took the unprecedented step of weaving fine rugs into sand-painting reproductions. What was once produced only in perishable sand now became permanent tapestry. Later all his rugs and ceremonial equipment, as well as many manuscripts of the chant myths, were preserved at the Museum of Navaho Ceremonial Art. At his own request, he was buried in an unmarked grave on museum grounds.

In dealing with the complex symbolism of the Navaho chant system, I have offered interpretations beyond the literal descriptions of the ethnographic material. In doing so, I have used the concepts of several prominent thinkers from other fields. The philosophical background of my work is based on the writings of Ernst Cassirer and Susanne Langer on symbolic forms. In applying theories of symbolism to anthropological material, I have been guided by the work of Paul Radin, Victor Turner, and Clifford Geertz, among others. In the field of comparative mythology I have often quoted Mircea Eliade and Joseph Campbell.

Finally, in applying these symbolic concepts to the process of healing, I am guided—as in my daily work with patients— by the pioneer work of Carl Jung. He was the first to show that the symbolism produced by his patients, and the symbolism found in mythologies and cultures from various parts of the world, have basic similarities.

My own work on the Navaho reservation (from 1968 on), interviewing medicine men and going to whatever chants were available, was not meant to add to the vast store of ethnological data already assembled on the Navaho. I have had no formal training in that area, and all my findings and general statements have been carefully checked with the standard works on Navaho culture. It was the healing process that interested me; as a Jungian-trained analyst, I was especially drawn there by the healing symbols I had read and heard about. I wanted to see them alive and in their cultural context, in the active healing of patients, and I wanted to see and talk with the men who knew and used them. Some of this I was able to do, but I was acutely aware that the cultural context of the Navaho religion was rapidly passing. The traditional half-nomadic, half-agricultural way of life, which developed and maintained this beautiful symbolic healing system, is rapidly giving way on all sides to the encroaching demands of modern technological society.

Whether that society and traditional Navaho religion can find common ground depends largely on the initiative and judgment of the small group of Navaho medicine men who have spent their lives immersed in their religion. Their thoughts are deep and searching, and their speech carefully weighed. They do not give easily, but also they seldom entirely withhold. They have lived lives of hardship and poverty, yet many of them have attained that goal which is the crowning jewel of a life spent in service. They have become the embodiment of the wise old man and woman who are thoroughly at home in their own culture, and yet universal in the depth of their vision. Such wise old men and women are rare in our own society, in spite of the comparative ease and comfort we enjoy. Perhaps that is just what has made us blind to the path that has always been there—the path to inner wisdom. Perhaps a life of hardship and ascetic living makes that path plainer and more acceptable. Whatever the reason, these old singers of the desert have preserved the visions of the past which can still form the basis for the wisdom of the future.

CHAPTER ONE

Symbolic Healing

Suffering is an integral part of human life. The process of growth from infancy to childhood, from childhood to adolescence, and on to adulthood, old age, and death, involves inescapable suffering. If the process is blocked at any level, the suffering increases to the point of acute and painful symptoms. To a doctor or medicine man who works with people in distress, this has an immediate daily reality. He learns that man can accept a tremendous amount of legitimate suffering; what he cannot accept is suffering that has no purpose. To be endured and accepted, suffering must be given a meaning.

Therefore the heart of all cultural-psychological methods of healing, whether they occur in literate or preliterate societies, is a symbolic structure that explains, or at least provides a context for, the sufferings of its members. There is much to be endured: the dreary monotony of everyday life, the apocalyptic appearance of illness and misfortune, and the painful result of man's own ignorance and malice. Within the symbolic structure of his culture, man attempts to create a satisfying meaning for these afflictions and a method for curing them.

LIFE SYMBOLS

Anyone who writes about symbols should define what he means. Philosophers, anthropologists, psychologists, and theologians all have differing ideas about the nature and function of symbols. To tackle the theoretical difficulties involved in reconciling all of them would lead us into a bramble from which we would never emerge. Fortunately, many of these wordy conflicts have been squarely faced by Susanne Langer in *Philosophy in a New Key* (1942). In that book, as timely now as when it appeared, she presents a theory of symbolism elegant in its simplicity yet all-embracing in scope. If it fails to satisfy everybody, it at least includes everybody. The part relevant here is summarized as follows.

A symbol is any *thing* which may function as the vehicle for a conception. Such a *thing* may be a word, a mathematical notation, an act, a gesture, a ritual, a dream, a work of art, or anything else that can carry a concept. The concept may be a rational-linguistic one, an imaginal-intuitive one, or a feeling-evaluative one. It makes no difference as long as the symbol carries it effectively. The concept is the symbol's meaning.

Language is the first kind of symbolism Langer discusses; she shows that it has a specific sequential structure which she has termed discursive, so as to set it off from a second kind. Of this second kind she says: "The meanings of all other symbolic elements that compose a larger, articulate symbol are understood only through the meaning of the whole, through their relations within the total structure. Their very functioning as symbols depends on the fact that they are involved in a simultaneous, integral presentation. This kind of semantic may be called 'presentational symbolism,' to characterize its essential distinction from discursive symbolism, or 'language' proper" (p. 97). Examples of presentational symbols would be a musical composition, a painting, a dream, a myth, or a healing ritual with prayers, songs, and sand paintings. All these are complex structures made up of thousands of interrelated parts, but the concept— the meaning and feeling—is carried by the whole. Presentational symbols may "carry" their meaning from one person to another, from a larger group to a single person or vice versa, or from one part of the psyche to another, as in the case of unrecorded dreams. Sometimes, as in Navaho healing rituals, they may carry the ethos of an entire culture. Those symbols which shape the psyche and culture and bind them together, Langer terms *life symbols*.

Life symbols are the stock in trade of anthropologists. Cassirer called them "organs of reality," and Leslie White said they were "basic units of all human behavior and civilization. All human behavior originates in the use of symbols. It was the symbol which transformed our anthropoid ancestors into men and made them human. All civilizations have been generated, and are perpetuated, only by the use of symbols" (1949: 22).

Life symbols make of a culture what it is specifically, and govern the thoughts and feelings of the people who are part of it. By means of origin myths and cosmogonic myths, a picture is built up of what the world is, how it came to be, and how it may be expected to function in the future. It makes no difference whether the facts on which this world view are founded are true or not. The myth makes do with what "facts" it has, and goes about its business of creating an intuitive emotional interpretation of them. The rituals embody sacred action appropriate to the structure of the world built up by the myths. They go hand in hand, completing and complementing each other—the mythic reality and the ritual response.

Not only ritual, but the entire life style of a culture, is built upon its mythic view of reality. As Clifford Geertz put it for the Navaho: "The sort of counterpoint between style of life and fundamental reality which the sacred symbols formulate varies from culture to culture. For the Navaho, an ethic prizing calm deliberateness, untiring persistence, and dignified caution complements an image of nature as tremendously powerful, mechanically regular and highly dangerous" (1973: 130). Theories of disease, methods of healing, and the disposition of evil make up a large part of this great counterpoint. They too must fit into the prevailing ethos created by the myths. In order to perform their functions they must make use of the symbols, full of numinous energy, that are provided by culture. Again it is Geertz who describes this function of the Navaho chants.

> The sustaining effect of the sing (and since the commonest disease is tuberculosis, it can in most cases be only sustaining), rests ultimately on its ability to give the stricken patient a vocabulary in terms of which to grasp the nature of his distress and relate it to the wider world. Like a calvary, a recitation of Buddha's emergence from his father's palace, or a performance of *Oedipus Tyrannos* in other religious traditions, a sing is mainly concerned with the presentation of a specific and concrete image of truly human, and so endurable, suffering powerful enough to resist the challenge of emotional meaninglessness raised by the existence of intense and unremovable brute pain.
>
> (1973: 105)

Yet symbols do more than that. They may not only provide a vocabulary and an explanation, but also change the psyche by converting energy into a different form, a form that can heal. As Jung said: "The symbols act as transformers, their function being to convert libido from a 'lower' into a 'higher' form. This function is so important that feeling accords it the highest value" (1956: 232). In the act of healing, symbols work upon the patient who is vulnerable, open, and ready to experience them. He identifies with them in the form of the sacred images and the person of the medicine man. They transform him and allow him to partake of their hidden power. Under such conditions he may be not only persuaded by their suggestion or reconciled to his fate, but cured.

The validity of that cure is the main subject of this book. The cure comes about in response to the presentation of a symbol from within or without, and it may happen slowly or immediately. It is an experience which, like many inner experiences, must be known to be appreciated. But it can be demonstrated clinically in modern psychological analytic work with patients. When it occurs, the patient feels different. It is as if two compartments in the psyche are forcefully brought together: there occurs a release of energy and a feeling of relief. Jung once said that the appropriateness of a dream interpretation could be judged by the release of tension it brought about in the patient. It may be a relatively weak but still perceptible experience, or it may come with the force of revelation. In the latter case it might be felt by the patient to occur at the center of his psyche, and gradually work its way out into the feelings and actions of everyday life.

I once had a patient who produced very few dreams, and could make almost nothing out of those that he did. All attempts at interpretation seemed to him merely interesting; no release of tension, no symbolic healing was taking place. Then suddenly out of the blue he had a "big dream"—a mandala that showed the whole of his inner universe; on it his place was marked with an X, and although it was not clear in the dream just where the X was, it was most certainly there and belonged there. This satisfied him in a manner which I found astonishing, and the troublesome symptoms for which he was driven to consult me seemed no longer to oppress him.

Such symbolic manifestations as these, when they come with strong, inner certainty, can exert lifelong influence and lead one down pathways where otherwise one might never have ventured. Is this true healing? I shall assume that it is, and that this is what a Navaho patient experiences when conditions are right, and when he is presented forcefully and vividly with a sacred symbol pregnant with meaning and imbued with numinous power. Such an experience is complete and sufficient as a healing technique in its own right.

SCIENTIFIC AND SYMBOLIC HEALING

There are many ways to classify the arts of healing in various cultures, but the ones I have found most useful are the two broad categories of scientific and symbolic healing. The two overlap to a certain extent, and there is always a little of each in every healing act; but generally one is clearly emphasized and highly valued, and the other relegated to an inferior status. In this respect, our own and the Navaho positions are polar opposites.

Scientific healing might also be called objective or rational healing. It makes use of empirical facts and builds a base of sound anatomical, physiological, and pharmacological knowledge. It focuses on specific organs, rarely on the body as a whole, and is based on tested and verified procedures. It has in its repertoire a wide spectrum of highly skilled techniques ranging from surgical operations and complex biochemical laboratory determinations, to internal and external medication of experimentally proven worth.

Because the biology of man is roughly alike throughout the species, scientific medicine is genuinely cross-cultural. It will work as well, within limits, on an Australian aborigine as on an American office worker. When the appendix is inflamed, an appendectomy is the best procedure no matter to what culture the patient belongs. Penicillin and related antibiotics combat infection wherever they are judiciously administered. The practitioners of scientific medicine work with principles and facts, not beliefs. That is their strength and also their limitation because this type of healing, though often effective, is not enough. Scientific fact can never "prove" human values. It may restore the specific organ (and we are grateful for that), but it does not satisfy the individual in his quest for harmony with his surroundings and for peace of mind within.

Therefore every culture has another kind of healing which is symbolic and does not rely on detailed scientific knowledge of bodily organs. It might be called cultural healing, for it derives its symbols from a specific culture, and relies for its effect on identification of the patient with supernatural (or intrapsychic) power through the mediation of the symbol. All phases of medical care—nosology, etiology, diagnosis, therapy, prognosis—are based on that symbolic identification.

This kind of healing is regarded by the Navaho as the heart of their system, and is given first importance. It is based on ritual and myth, not on physiological principles. The cause and cure of disease are connected to the greater mythological whole, and are seen against the supernatural background of man's life. The "doctor" is the shaman or medicine man who is trained in the specific beliefs and rituals of his culture.

Therefore this method is culture-bound: it cannot be extended from one culture to another except under special conditions. In a culture unlike his own, the medicine man's painfully acquired fund of special knowledge and practice would be virtually meaningless; worse still, it would be misunderstood and berated. The patient must share in most of the basic beliefs of the medicine man and his culture, or symbolic healing cannot work. One of the medicine men I interviewed said exactly that in his own way: "If the patient really has confidence in me, then he gets cured. If he has no confidence, then that is his problem. If a person gets bitten by a snake, for example, certain prayers and songs can be used, but if the patient doesn't have enough confidence, then the cure won't work." The patient shares the responsibility for his cure. In symbolic healing the social function is usually large, because it depends on the consensus of the community as a cultural unit to give validity to its symbols. If skepticism and conflict with other systems caused the symbols to fall into disrepute, then the core of the healing system would collapse.

Besides their considerable differences (see Table I on page 19), scientific and symbolic healing have certain aspects in common. They both accord great respect to the healer and allow him to collect a considerable fee. They both demand that he go through a long and arduous period of training and apprenticeship, and be in some way recognized or "licensed" by the community. Not just anyone can set himself up as a medicine man: he has to earn the approval of his teachers and demonstrate that he can perform the rites successfully.

Both systems have serious drawbacks. Scientific healing often ignores the patient's humanity: I have heard an illness referred to as a "beautiful case of bleeding ulcer"—sometimes in front of the patient. Yet even in the most scientific culture, there is a symbolic system of values operating in the background. Thus the patient is evaluated as a biochemical machine, and the sick and dying are placed in barren white-walled rooms surrounded by machines and penetrated by tubes that have no relevance to the patient's tremendous emotional experience. There is indeed a value system in operation, but it is largely unconscious and no longer in the best interests of the patient.

On the other hand, symbolic healing often ignores the patient as a biological organism, and fails to observe the simplest rules of bodily care and hygiene. To be sure, the Navaho system of healing does contain some rational elements. One of the medicine men I interviewed was a specialist in setting broken bones in a true scientific manner. Hot earth

TABLE I

	Scientific Healing	Symbolic or Cultural Healing
Classification of illness (nosology)	Based on empirical facts and scientific principles; rational.	Based on the mythology or belief system of a particular culture; not rational.
Healing technique	Based on anatomical and physiological principles; can be effectively applied transculturally.	Based on cultural values and beliefs; can be used only in the area of cultural influence.
Healer	Physician or other scientifically trained personnel.	Shaman, medicine man, or priest grounded and trained in cultural lore (myth and ritual).
Patient	Must passively follow directions; doctor is responsible for the cure.	Must actively *believe* in the therapy, carries most of the responsibility for the cure.
Social function of healing	Small; sometimes almost nonexistent.	Large; many persons may actively participate.
Prestige of the healer and size of fee	Relatively large.	Relatively large.
Drawbacks	Ignores the patient's humanity; neglects the effects of cultural symbols on the harmony of mind and body.	Ignores the patient as a biological organism; neglects the simplest rules of physical therapy and organic cause.

trenches and sweat baths are often used to relieve the pain of injuries and rheumatic joints. Herbal remedies used during the ceremonies may have some physiological effects. However, the cleansing of wounds and the basic methods of dealing with infection are seldom comprehended. Reichard once described how an elderly Navaho woman was subjected to the prolonged exertion and chilling exposure of a rigorous chant ceremony lasting several days, in spite of the fact that she was suffering from severe pneumonia.

There is no question that often the time and resources necessary for a chant have delayed or prevented the timely use of a specific, effective scientific remedy. If I had tuberculosis or appendicitis, or cancer in its early stages, I would be quick to avail myself of modern medicine. But if I had one of those maladies for which science has no specific cure, like cancer in its later stages or some psychiatric illness, I would prefer the symbolic healing of the Navaho. On both sides there is ample room for tolerance and understanding. A lot of careful introspection and willingness to see the other side is needed for the two systems to work together.

THE STRUCTURE OF SYMBOLIC HEALING

Even though symbolic healing is not scientific, it is much more than vague and exotic fantasies jumbled together. It has a definite structure, and follows well-defined rules and procedures. There are certain stages through which it proceeds, though these are neither strictly chronological nor mutually exclusive: often they blend one into the other, and more than one stage may be in progress simultaneously. In some cultures certain of these stages may be brief or almost entirely omitted. But usually the stages proceed in a given order, each one leading to the next in a necessary transition. The following outline presents a conceptual framework for understanding and comparing the symbolic healing ceremonies in various cultures.

Stage one: Preparation or Purification. Before the vital symbols are presented and utilized, the medicine man or shaman, as well as the patient, undergo purifying rituals to prepare themselves for the occasion. Often the spectators, the room, or the ceremonial grounds are purified as well. Purification is achieved by washing, sweating, taking emetics, dressing in special clothes, and abstaining from certain everyday activities such as eating specific foods, sexual intercourse, or certain kinds of work.

Stage two: Presentation or Evocation. After the purification the pertinent symbolic images are made and presented in visible or audible form. Taste, smell, and touch may play a part in this stage. The symbols must be presented in a vivid and dramatic manner, as for example through icons, statues, prayer sticks, or sand paintings, or in the rhythmic chanting of songs and prayers. Fumigation with special incense, and the eating of special herbs or foods, are also possible. In this way the symbolic presence becomes *real*. Once evoked, the supernatural powers or divine beings invest the symbols, the medicine man, and the patient with their numinous presence. The way is prepared for the culminating action.

Stage three: Identification—the high point of the ceremony. The medicine man or shaman and the patient—and sometimes even the spectators, too—become identified or intimately invested with the powers that have been evoked and reified. The medicine man symbolically becomes the supernatural power, and at the same time may take into himself the evil or bad part of the patient that is causing the sickness. The medicine man is exalted into a powerful being, what Jung called the mana personality. If the ceremony miscarries at this time, both doctor and patient risk being harmed by power that is no longer under ritual control.

Stage four: Transformation. The healer uses the extraordinary power he now has in the eyes of the patient and the onlookers to bring about the desired good results. He wins the battle, banishes the disease, expels the evil, counteracts the sorcery, or recovers the soul. Symbolically transformed, the patient believes that actual restoration to health and harmony will soon follow.

Stage five: Release. Finally there must be rituals to release the patient, the medicine man, and the audience from the powerful symbolic force they have activated, and to return them to a normal state of being. Having experienced the transforming power of the symbol, the patient must divest himself of it. This may be done by special songs or prayers, or by restrictions against sleeping or cleansing himself until a certain time has passed. This brings the cycle of symbolic healing to a close.

Similar scenarios of healing could be found in the ethnographic literature from other cultures. The content would be different, but the symbolic structure remains similar. As Cassirer says, "Over and over again we find confirmation of the fact that man can apprehend his own being only in so far as he can make it visible in the image of his gods" (1953: 204). By the presentation of these symbols man is put in touch with his inner resources. If the healing images are strong enough, if the medicine man is skillful and unwavering in his purpose, and if the patient's involvement is deep and urgent, then healing can be confidently expected to occur.

CHAPTER TWO

Guardians
of the Symbol

The Navaho live on a high plateau covering much of northeastern Arizona, overlapping into New Mexico and Utah. It is a land of immense proportions, mostly arid and desertlike, covered with small stands of piñon pine, juniper, and sagebrush. The Chuska mountain range runs through the center, on whose western slopes grow well-watered forests of ponderosa pine, spruce, and aspen. Canyon systems, like Canyon de Chelly and Canyon del Muerto, branch for miles in the great stretches of tableland. Brilliant rock formations—red-orange, gray-blue, deep black—rise out of the land like outsize monuments put there by an ancient race of giants. At first the land seems empty and friendless; one's attention is drawn to the sky. There, swift storms sweep in on curtains of rain, then suddenly end in sun and rainbow, leaving an expanse of cloudless blue. The works of man seem not to have touched this place. Only later does one notice that the apparently empty land is really densely populated: small hogans nestle in hillsides and hollows on every side, and flocks of sheep materialize out of an empty desert. One is surprised to come upon a solitary Navaho standing motionless, gazing out into the distance far from any visible habitation. Actually, there may be a well-camouflaged hogan only a short distance away.

This is Dinetah, the ancient Navaho homeland, and the Navaho call themselves Dineh, the People. Today the reservation is bounded on the north by the La Plata Mountains, on the west by the San Francisco Peaks, on the south by the great highway that passes through Winslow and Flagstaff, and on the east by the desert expanses stretching away from the Chuska and Lukachukai ranges. Here, in shades (temporary structures with pole frameworks covered by leafy branches) and hogans hidden far back in the canyons, or standing solitary on the high plains, the last medicine men live and work. They are by far the largest body of active indigenous medicine men in North America. Some have considerably altered the old ways, but most still practice the traditional religion, unadulterated by peyote rites or Christian dogma. All along, of course, foreign influence has entered into the making of the Navaho religion, but only in the Navaho way and with the subtle nuances of the Navaho mind. Originally the Navaho were a nomadic, hunting culture who came late into the Southwest, where they changed gradually through centuries of contact with the quiet village life of the Pueblo agricultural communes. Nevertheless, they have kept their love of solitude and their invincible individualism. The rites they perform are, with a few exceptions, for the benefit of the single individual who feels the need for it, consults his relatives, calls the medicine man, chooses the ceremony, sets the date, and pays the fee. Yet it is true, as Reichard says, that "every rite, every ceremony, includes an underlying factor for the good of the tribe, a feeling of power directed toward blessing all who come even remotely in contact with it" (1945: 206).

In the Navaho ceremonials social healing has an important

place. Kaplan and Johnson (1964: 228) noted that there is a reaffirmation of community solidarity which surrounds the patient with concern and good will, and places him at the very center of the social group. The performance of a large ceremony is so expensive and difficult that the contributions and labor of many relatives are involved. The ceremony draws together the social network and allows gestures of affection to be made to the patient. But the social or emotional background of the patient's illness is given no public airing: there is no open confession of guilt by the patient or his relatives, as sometimes happens in the healing ceremonies of other cultures. Little emotionality or cathartic ventilation is displayed at the healing ceremonies; restraint and dignity characterize the whole proceedings. Both from observation and from the native informants themselves, it is evident that the greatest effectiveness is ascribed to the prayers, sand paintings, songs, and rituals—the symbolic elements which are the backbone of chant practice.

Traditionally there were no supreme tribal chiefs among the Navaho. As doctor and priest, the medicine man was the prime carrier of culture and enjoyed the highest esteem, as he still does. In the Pueblo villages adjacent to the Navaho, the situation is different: the medicine men are not as important as the clan chiefs, who direct the great annual ceremonial cycles for good crops and abundant rain. Until the recent establishment of the tribal fair, the Navaho had not a single annual ceremony. Their ceremonies are performed spontaneously when the need arises, although many of the larger chants can be held only in the winter. Healing was and remains one of the foremost concerns of the Navaho, among whom physical healing is not so important as bringing the patient into a strong, symbolic relationship with his social, cultural, and natural environment. This is the time-honored task of the medicine man, or hatali.

The medicine man accomplishes this mission by the skillful manipulation of a medley of symbolic elements. Later we shall consider each of these separately, but in practice they are intimately and inseparably fused. Anyone following a ceremony can readily see that the paintings, songs, and prayers refer constantly to the central myths. The rites serve to manifest the latent power of all the other constituents. The curative effect is cumulative, and the whole is learned and used as a single entity by the Navaho chanters, who are the masters and guardians of these symbolic forms.

The medicine men I interviewed were all actively practicing in the vicinity of Lukachukai, Arizona, in the east-central part of the reservation. I wanted to see how these men conducted their practices and used their symbols in a healing context. Most of them consented to an extensive interview, several on more than one day, and one of them, Natani Tso, has been a co-operative informant for several years. The interviews were structured not to obtain secrets (most of which are long a matter of record), but to elicit typical attitudes in matters of medical concern. Being a medical man myself was a distinct advantage in approaching them, as most are quite eager to co-operate with Anglo medicine and appreciate its efficiency. None of them admitted speaking more than rudimentary English, and since my Navaho was equally rudimentary, the interviews were conducted with the help of the best interpreters available and recorded verbatim.

TRAINING AND APPRENTICESHIP

Learning to become a medicine man is a painstakingly difficult process. So much is required in the way of detailed knowledge, special equipment, and exact memorization of songs, prayers, and paintings, that a single medicine man can usually learn only a few major chants in his lifetime (three or four would be outstanding). The more ambitious chanters learn at least parts of several more. The effort necessary to learn one major chant has been compared to obtaining a degree in a modern university.

The most common chant in general use is Blessing Way, because it is short and inexpensive, and can be given any time for many reasons. Some of the long chants can be given only when the snakes are in winter hibernation. Many of them, such as the famous Night Chant and Mountaintop Way, are now given much less often; the Male Shooting Chant is the most frequently performed long chant in the Lukachukai area.

I heard of one chanter who knew the Plume or Feather Chant, and one who knew the Coyote Chant. The Coyote chanter could not be tracked down, and when I visited the Plume chanter he was seriously ill with a high fever and swollen joints. When I came back at a later time, he had been taken out of his hogan to a place farther along the road to die. Sometimes the last thing an old Navaho can do for his relatives is to die outside the family hogan, thus sparing the family the expense of purification rites. In olden days a death inside it necessitated the destruction of the hogan, and the transfer of the entire household to another site.

Two of the oldest chanters interviewed were Denet Tsosi, eighty-four, once a member of the tribal council, and Alan George, seventy-eight, who knew the Night Chant. Both were active, busy men. When I interviewed Denet Tsosi he was returning from an all-night sing, but without any great fatigue he spent the morning answering my questions. He had begun learning chant practice in his early teens from his brother, Red Mustache. He followed his brother around, watching him perform the Male Shooting Chant, and after six years he felt he could do it himself. He also had the ceremony sung over himself as patient four times, and had to pay for it each time. Later he learned Evil Ghost Way and Mountaintop Way.

Alan George, on the other hand, did not start learning until he was about fifty. He started then because the chant had helped him twice, once as a child when he had been gored by a goat, and once as an adult when he sprained his back lifting heavy logs. He said, "I was treated by the medicine man with chants and herbs and I got better. I got a feeling about the chants that if nobody knows and learns them, they will die out. I came back then and joined my people to be a medicine man. Later the doctors, hospitals, and clinics came. I respect that, I hold nothing against that, but I still feel that my medicine should be kept up."

Two of the medicine men learned what they knew from their fathers. One of them started to learn the Blessing Way from his father when he was only sixteen. He told me: "When I was learning, I accompanied my father wherever he was called. I memorized the songs and prayers. Finally later on I substituted for him. He encouraged me to sing the songs. Then, if it was not all right, he would correct me. Sometimes he said, 'You say the prayers for me while I watch you.' After I got it pretty well lined up, he polished it up for me. He told me how to conduct the ceremony in certain cases and which songs to use. That's the way I got instructed." He was also the only one who was frightened the first time he performed the ceremony, perhaps because he was still so young. "Yes, naturally I got scared [the first time]. It worried me. My father told me to substitute for him. I wanted him to be present, but I went alone since he told me I had to. Later on he became ill. He said, 'My son, I've been doing this all my life, saving people from illness. Now I'm sick myself, and it overburdens me, all the people I've sung over. I've come to the decision that you should sing over me now. You come over tonight and offer prayers for me. Get the soapweeds and bathe me. Then bless me and sing over me all night.' That's the first time I did that for my father. When I was performing I was nervous and worried, especially about the first twelve songs, the Hogan Way songs. That worried me, because if you miss a word in one of those songs you spoil the whole ceremony. Before I started off I was shaking like a leaf. I wondered how I would do with my instructor as my patient.

I sang and sang all night long. He would tell me to put in a prayer here and another there, and I would do it. Later on in the night I got relaxed and it didn't bother me anymore. He was giving me a good test. When it was over he told me that it was done properly, and that I would live to be an old man. He said I didn't need to worry about sickness, and that's the way it's turned out."

The general pattern of apprenticeship is that the instructor is a relative or fellow clan member, but sometimes only a friend. There always seems to be a close relationship between the two, pupil and instructor, unless something goes wrong and the teaching is broken off; then there might be considerable enmity. To learn any of the important chants, several years are necessary; payment is usually made in livestock, food, and lodging, or the proceeds from the first performances. If the instructor is a close relative, sometimes no payment is necessary. Most of the learning is done at the actual performance, although private instruction is sometimes used as a supplement. Often the instructor sits beside the novice at his first performance to guide and correct mistakes, and to offer moral support. Even though mistakes are not treated lightly, most apprentices feel they have learned their chant well and are confident they can perform it.

The main qualifications for a prospective medicine man are interest and patience. Natani Tso said: "He has to have interest. He must not be too lazy. He's got to have patience. If he gets easily discouraged, there's no use starting. Young men when they are drunk often ask me what a particular song or prayer means, but there is no use telling them. Their mind is not clear. You really have to be serious to learn the chants." In response to the important question whether medicine men have to have special dreams or visions, his answer was: "It is not necessary to have a vision or a dream. He just has to want to learn." The other medicine men were in unanimous agreement: *no special visionary or mystic gifts are necessary to become a good chanter.*

In fact, only one of the chanters could remember having any visionary experience of his own. He related that when he was very sick and about to die, a little bear came down the trail from the mountains and licked him; then he got well again.

DIAGNOSTICIANS

Whenever there is doubt about the cause of an illness or the type of chant to be prescribed for it, another class of medical specialists is consulted, most often called diagnosticians. They are able to place themselves in a state of trance at will, and diagnose illness by divination—hand trembling, star gazing, crystal gazing, or "listening." These persons are not trained, but have a gift which comes upon them spontaneously. Many of them are women, but sometimes the medicine men do their own divination. Because of the altered state of consciousness in which divination is performed, these techniques are more reminiscent of the shamanistic practices of the Plains Indians than any of the ordinary ceremonies in the more formal curing rituals. Also, these diviners do not enjoy the prestige or high status in the community that is accorded the medicine men.

I witnessed a performance that a young woman diagnostician held for an elderly Navaho woman. She was asked to diagnose what was wrong with the patient, and what curing ceremonies would be necessary to correct it. The diviner seemed nervous before the performance, and shy in the presence of strangers—in marked contrast to the usual stoical dignity of the singers. She did not question the patient, saying it was best not to, but she knew the patient well, since they were both members of the same small community. She said that everything she needed would come to her in the trance state. Her fee was ten dollars, which was probably high because she permitted us to attend, take notes, and ask questions before and after. The usual fee is small—a ring or a bracelet, perhaps a dollar or two.

The patient sat on the floor with her legs straight out in front of her. Kneeling on the patient's right side, facing her, the diagnostician assumed a serious expression and began to concentrate. She took out a small bag containing pollen, the sacred substance of life renewal, and touched the patient with a pinch of it on the soles of the feet, the legs, the hands, and the top of the head. Then a little was put inside the patient's mouth. The diviner made an outward gesture and blessed herself with the pollen in the same way. She made a path with the pollen down her right forearm from the elbow to the wrist on the ventral surface, and fanned out the path across the palm to the little finger and thumb. There were little arrows drawn on the line down the arm.

The diagnostician then addressed a prayer to her arm which translates roughly as: "I want you to tell me everything. Don't hide anything from me." The nature of the prayer implies that during the performance the arm functioned autonomously as in automatic writing. Sometimes this prayer is addressed to the gila monster spirits who are supposed to know everything and see into the future. The motion in the hand is said to come from the gila monster, because he shakes his front foot when he raises it from the ground.

After the prayer the diagnostician deepened her concentration, and her hand began to tremble with a to-and-fro motion wider and slower than the motion ordinarily associated with tremors or shaking. Sometimes the hand moved back and forth in the air, and sometimes it struck the body of the patient lightly on the head, arms, shoulders, forehead, legs, ankles, and feet. Sometimes the index finger seemed to point at various parts of the body; sometimes the hand motioned as if gathering something in. As the ceremony proceeded, the hand stayed longest near the chest area and began pointing there most often. The procedure lasted fifteen to twenty minutes. At the end there were more frequent pointing motions, and the trembler was sweating from her exertions.

When the motion stopped, the trembler relaxed and told the patient: "You look healthy all the time. Still you have something wrong with your eyesight, and sometimes you don't feel well for no good reason. Also you don't feel well in the chest." The trembler went on to infer that these troubles could be corrected by the Shooting Chant, which the patient had had twice before but might need again. Since she was not seriously ill at the moment, this could be deferred.

Talking to us afterward, the diagnostician said she had been practicing for fourteen years. She learned it when she was attending a similar ceremony for a relative. Suddenly she felt her own hand trembling in a manner similar to the performer's. Later the man came over and showed her how to use the pollen, then told her she could start practicing; no more training was necessary.

Natani Tso, one of the medicine men who did his own hand trembling, gave a more subjective account: "The corn pollen in the hand-trembling ceremony is an offering to Gila Monster. You put the pollen down your arms with two branches like Gila Monster. I start praying, then singing. Then I work my mind very hard. Then I notice shocks running through my fingers. My hand starts shaking and away I go." When asked how he knows what the diagnosis is, he said: "This depends on what sign your hand is making. I work my mind. I wonder what the hand is referring to. It shakes, sometimes at the patient, sometimes at the ground, until you guess the right answer with your mind. Then when it's done, it stops shaking."

Sometimes this is done by crystal gazing. One medicine man said: "I am a crystal gazer, too. People will come to my place to find out about the patient and ask me why he isn't getting well. They want me to find out. Sometimes I can tell what the trouble is. I make a sand painting. It's not a regular sand painting, but made with white and yellow corn meal.

Then I surround myself with crystals and church candles. I don't know why that is, but they have a greater effect. If I look at the stars it is more doubtful, just guessing. But crystal gazing is pretty sure. I just look at the crystal and see what is wrong with the patient."

ETIOLOGY OF DISEASE

Some of the chants have definite, rational indications. For instance, in past times the Flint Way was performed for persons suffering injury or broken bones. Neal Totsoni, who still knew this chant, although he no longer practices it, recalled how it was done: "Sometimes a man breaks an arm or leg, and may have a broken bone sticking out of the flesh. You can't go in and set it without preparation. You have to use the ceremony. You have to have herbs and bathe the injury. While you or your assistant sings the songs, you begin to set the bone. You have to be careful and do it properly. It's a very delicate thing to do."

Most of the chants, however, are directed toward what Kluckhohn and Wyman (1940) have called the "etiological factors" which cause disease by a process of "infection." This infection destroys the natural harmony between the individual and his surroundings, and the chant is prescribed to restore it. The most prominent source of infection is from powerful animals. According to one of their informants, there were once thirty-two different diseases caused by different animals. The cause involved some sort of improper contact with the animal: being injured by it, trapping it, killing it, eating it, or even dreaming about it. Perhaps the most powerful in causing disease are the bear, deer, coyote, porcupine, eagle, and snake.

Exposure to dangerous natural phenomena such as lightning, strong winds, or whirlwinds may also cause disease.

One of the practitioners of the Wind Chant gave these indications for its use: "You may be injured by cyclones, tornadoes, whirlwinds, or even ordinary winds. If it runs over you and twists your mind, you need the Navaho Wind Way."

Ceremonials, because of their inherent power, may cause infection. This may come about prenatally when a pregnant woman or her husband looks upon the sacred parts of a ceremony or its paraphernalia, or transgresses upon any of the ritual restrictions imposed upon participants in a chant. For four days following a ceremony a patient must remain in isolation. Touching him or any of his personal belongings may cause disease. Natani Tso said: "Several things may affect a person with bad headaches, crippled or paralyzed limbs. His mouth might twist up, or his eyes get crossed. These things might happen if a chant gets violated. I observe the patient. I look at him, at his eyesight, his breathing, his mouth movements. From these I can tell if he needs the chant."

Contact with the dead, or spirits of the dead, is especially dangerous. When asked what complaints patients have who want the Big Star Chant, Natani Tso said: "You see, the main thing is after a death the patient may see the dead body. The body has to be handled in a certain way or else it causes harm. Later on this may worry him. Maybe he feels he left tracks by the dead body. All the tracks must be erased. Maybe dirt sticks to his skin when he handles the body. He needs the ceremony to cleanse him of this." Juan Sandoval enlarged on this: "When you bury a dead body you shouldn't leave tracks. Sweat shouldn't be dropped on the burial place. If you scratch yourself on a rock, blood shouldn't fall on this place. Also you shouldn't talk at the burial. When a person dies, only two people should wash and dress the body. Everybody else goes to another hogan while those two bury the body. They wear only moccasins and are covered with ashes. If you don't follow these rules there is sickness later, and you know it is because something was done wrong at the burial."

One of the commonest causes of illness recognized by the Navaho is witchcraft. Witchcraft is strongly associated with fear of ghosts and of the dead, and a great deal of chant ritual is directed toward turning the evil back upon the witch or sorcerer, and away from the patient. Witches are persons who violate the natural social order by engaging in incest, robbing the dead, and amassing too much personal power. Foreigners and strangers are viewed with the same suspicion, and medicine men, because of their great power, are often suspected of using witchcraft to injure those they hate.

It is up to the diagnostician, the patient, his family, and the medicine man to determine the cause of illness, and then to decide on the proper chant and supplementary ceremonies to use. Sometimes the medicine man plays only a small part in the diagnosis, and does only what he is instructed to do by the diagnostician and the family. Strictly physical illnesses, including injuries and fractured bones, are usually sent to a nearby clinic or hospital. When the patient returns from the hospital or from any prolonged stay with foreigners, a chant may still be deemed necessary. Whatever the particular cause, in general it is always a feeling of being out of harmony with himself and his society that motivates the chant patient.

FEE SETTING

Fee setting is discussed ahead of time with the patient and his relatives, and is usually a hard-headed, realistic process. No good results can be expected from the ceremony if the fee is not right. Natani Tso said in 1968: "There is no standard rate for the Big Star Chant. If someone comes to me who I know is wealthy, he will offer more than a poor person might. A wealthy person might pay me forty or fifty dollars, when a poor person will give me beads or a sheep. I'll do the ceremony anyway." Over and above the fee of the medicine man, there is great expense in collecting all the special gifts for those involved in the performance, and furnishing food for the entire assemblage during the whole period of the chant. It seems clear that a five-night chant might cost from $50 to $100 or more, and a nine-night chant with many visitors as much as $500 to $1,000. The family of the patient is expected to pitch in and help with the cost as well as the kitchen work. The food and the animals for butchering are largely obtained in that way. Great effort and careful planning are involved.

EFFECTS OF CEREMONIALS

When asked whether they felt their ceremonials were successful, the medicine men often responded—like doctors everywhere—with an anecdotal example of a cure they had performed. Natani Tso said: "There was a woman from Red Mesa who was in the hospital in Albuquerque. She had a gall bladder operation. After she came home she still wasn't feeling well, but after I did Blessing Way for her she felt fine." He also remembered a woman who was shot and wounded in the neck as a result of going around with another woman's husband. They took her also to the hospital. The doctors said she had only a fifty-fifty chance of recovery. Even though the patient was in the hospital, he performed the ceremony with the mother acting as ceremonial stand-in for her daughter. After the sing the patient regained consciousness and got well.

Neal Totsoni said: "Once a woman came to me who had a nosebleed for seven days. She went to the clinic and got shots, but it didn't help. They didn't know what else to do for her, so she went to a hand trembler who told her she needed Wind Way. So I went to work on her. On the last day of the chant, the bleeding slowed down. I used baths on her. That night during the final sing, the bleeding stopped altogether."

The effects of the ceremonials are not reckoned entirely in terms of a physical cure. That may happen and it is greatly to be desired, but the true purpose of the chants is to put the patient in a calm and peaceful state, free from evil of all kinds, so that he may accept with equanimity whatever may befall him. Even if he has had surgery and may be already cured, he still needs the chants to restore his harmonious balance.

DREAMS

Dreams are not used in the ritual proper of the Navaho chant ceremonies, but they are important as a diagnostic aid and for a timely warning. Alan George said: "Dreams are very important. That is because they tell you something that is ahead of you. You whites don't pay attention to that, but we Navaho think it is important. We take it pretty seriously. For instance, if I have a relative or friend who dies, and I dream about that person in good health and walking around, it is a warning that his ghost has come back to affect me. I need prayers."

The actual interpretation of dreams is simple. Dreams of falling off a cliff, drowning in deep water, or being burned in a fire are bad dreams. Dreams of your own or someone else's death, or being bitten by a bear or snake, are very bad. Dreams of good crops, lots of rain, or horses and sheep in good condition are good dreams. These meanings are predictable, but there are some exceptions. If you dreamed you were rich, you might suppose this to be a good dream. But if you knew it would not come true, then the meaning is reversed and it is seen as a bad dream. The requisite ceremony for a bad dream is in most cases part or all of Blessing Way.

Confession to the medicine man about the breaking of taboos and other misdeeds is an informal part of the curing, and something held back or left out is often blamed for the chant's lack of success. When asked the reason for their failures, the medicine men—again, like doctors everywhere—rarely mentioned the inadequacies of their practice. It might be thought that the patient was directed to the wrong chant or failed to follow the medicine man's instructions. Many things can hamper the cure.

The medicine men were generally wary of the use of peyote, as practiced in the Native American Church, but toward the orthodox Christian religions they had a friendly and tolerant attitude. Neal Totsoni said: "These don't interfere with one another. I talked to Father B. and he was very good to me. When my son was called to go into the army, I went to him to have him say a prayer for my son. He said, 'You have a pollen bag, don't you?' I said yes. He said, 'Go to the altar and use your pollen and say a prayer for your son.' I did that. As far as I know there is only one supreme God. We call him different things. You call him God, we call him Begochidi or Begotsoi."

Another chanter drew an even closer connection: "My late father, who was a singer, had a house near here, and Father W. would come over with his interpreter. They came to see us quite often. My father would recite his origin stories and then Father W. would recite his. There are many connections between the two. The Joseph story and the story of the Visionary [from the Night Chant] are similar, for example. Also the story of the flood is in Navaho myth and in the Bible. Also there are twelve Holy People in Navaho myth and twelve disciples in the Bible."

Toward modern medicine the medicine men were even more positive, perhaps because it too stresses knowledge and exact procedure, though for different reasons. One chanter said: "As far as I'm concerned, white doctors are just about equal to us. If I became ill and couldn't treat myself or cure myself, I'd fall back on white doctors. I don't think one is higher than the other. When people come back from the hospital, they often like to have a chant performed. I often use my Blessing Way for people who have been advised to go to the hospital, just as I do for boys who have been called into the army. It protects them while they are away."

Denet Tsosi said: "Sometimes Navaho people need treatment in a hospital. In your practice of medicine you operate, you cut him with a knife. When he comes back he feels he should have a Life Way to help heal the wound. We Navaho would like to have co-operation with white men to help preserve the Navaho traditions. If we can hold together, the whites and the Navaho, that is the best for the Navaho people."

All the medicine men recognized that the chant practice was declining, and felt it to be a tragedy for the Navaho people. All the medicine men I interviewed were getting old. There were some younger chanters in the area who did not wish to be interviewed, but none of the older chanters had any serious apprentices, and that was a matter of great concern for them. The young men were more interested in finding jobs and fitting into the surrounding American culture, than in putting forth the time and energy necessary to learn the old chants. Alan George said: "I'm very eager to have new singers trained, but I know it's declining. It worries me sometimes. What happens if it dies out? We will be no-account people."

Until recently it seemed inevitable that the chant system would eventually be lost, but there have been some surprising developments lately. The Navaho are beginning to open schools of their own—as at Rough Rock and the Navaho Community College at Tsaile—where regular college courses are offered in ceremonial rites, the Navaho language, and related subjects. They have begun to meet the challenge of subsidizing young men while they are learning the sacred knowledge. The Ned A. Hatathli Cultural Center on the Tsaile campus is a six-story building that combines the very best of tradition with modern technology. It has clean lines and bright walls that reflect light from the surrounding sky, but it is built in the shape of a hogan, with its main entrance facing the morning sun in the ancient way. It contains classrooms, meeting rooms, storage vaults for the collected chant material, audio-visual recording rooms, a sanctuary, and several chant rooms.

With such modern facilities, and with the co-operation of psychiatrists like Robert Bergman, who taught courses combining traditional chant practice and modern medicine at the Rough Rock Demonstration School, the Navaho are attempting to find a practical meeting ground for modern and traditional healing methods. They may yet find a way to integrate their chant system into modern consciousness.

CHAPTER THREE

Navaho Religion:
The Constituent Parts

Navaho religion is a nature religion. Gladys Reichard said of it: "The Navaho religion must be considered as a design in harmony, a striving for rapport between man and every phase of nature, the earth and the waters under the earth, the sky and the land beyond the sky, and of course, the earth and everything on and in it" (1939: 14). All the parts of nature work together, and the small and seemingly insignificant beings may become as important as the large and mighty ones. There is a Navaho pantheon, but no true hierarchy. The high gods are sometimes eclipsed by small, humble creatures who can do what the great gods cannot. All the powers, with the possible exception of Changing Woman, are both good and bad, depending on their intrinsic nature, the way they are approached, their mood and condition of the moment, and the context of their operation. "Through human exertion neutral power becomes positive, goodness becomes holiness. Evil is the residue unreduced by control which existed before there was any knowledge of the world at all" (Reichard, 1945: 208).

Most of the ceremonies are designed to persuade the gods to bestow good upon mankind, banish evil, and establish the natural harmony. "Ultimate harmony is in itself an abstraction understood only by the most analytic chanters. The attainment of this goal is never in doubt even if all its aspects are not thoroughly understood. The way to it deals with goodness, a more or less natural and expected condition in which most things exist, but which may by manipulation be attracted or distilled to produce holiness. . . . Goodness may not be sufficient to drive off evil, but holiness is" (*ibid.*).

If the ritual is performed with precision, holiness is produced and the gods must comply. There is no humble petitioning or prayerful remorse; correct knowledge and precise technique are the things that count. There are many taboos, ritualistic requirements, and proper behaviors, but there is no concept of sin as we know it. The Navaho confronts a world in which God is not thought of as absolutely good—a concept which has given Christianity no end of trouble. The gods are ambivalent: evil in the form of hostile power is inextricably mixed with good. They function according to their nature, and man must rely on his own knowledge and hard-won skills to turn the balance in his favor.

But he must have techniques. Therefore, by means of masked dancers, prayers, and painted sand figures, he pictures and impersonates symbolic manifestations of the inner forms of these powers, and then identifies with them. This is by far the most important healing device used by the Navaho. Methods of diagnosis, myth-telling, impersonation, dramatic performance, singing, praying, dancing, sand painting, and even herbal medication are all ways of bringing about identification. Finally, with the identification comes the moment of psychic union through the medicine man with the god, supernatural animal, or tutelary hero, bringing the hoped-for healing influence.

THE CHANTWAY SYSTEM

When it suffered the profound shock of contact with Western influence, Navaho religion was probably in a state of gradual syncretization. The various chant myths were being linked together around the central core of the origin myth and Blessing Way, like the books of any sacred text before they become standardized. Now many chants have become extinct and others have been shortened, but it is still a unified system.

Each chant is a complex pattern of ritual actions, songs, prayers, and sand paintings centering loosely around a myth of origin which describes how the hero or heroine made a journey to the land of the gods to acquire special knowledge and healing power. Every one of the chants is a catalogue of symbolism. The symbolic use of geographical place names, of the timing and sequence of events, of color and direction, number and repetition, perceptual events involving light and sound, and key word formulas have all been described in great detail and subtlety (Reichard, 1950). Everything, even things that are left out, has a meaning and fits into the pattern as a whole. A single medicine man can know only a small part of this vast interconnected whole.

According to the classification of Kluckhohn and Wyman (1938), there were about twenty-six different chantways, some with many variations and branches (see Table II, pp. 44–46). Of these, Wyman says that nine are probably extinct and only ten are performed regularly. Besides these, there are various shorter Blessing Ways, hunting and war rites (now obsolete), short prayer ceremonies, and minor rites for special occasions such as the girls' puberty ceremony.

Blessing Way is the shortest (two nights), least expensive, and most popular ceremony. One chanter described it as "the main beam in the chantway house." Parts of it are included in most of the other chants because it is wholly good. It is given for good fortune, good health, and blessing. It is used to correct mistakes made in ceremonial procedures, dispel

TABLE II

CHANT CLASSIFICATION AND SOME TYPICAL INDICATIONS FOR THEIR USE

Chants	Some Indications for Their Use Mostly Derived from Events in the Myth
GROUP I BLESSING WAY, several branches	Used to invoke good luck, good health, and blessing, to obviate the bad effects of mistakes in ceremonials, to dispel fear from bad dreams, for protection of flocks and herds, to cure insanity, to consecrate ceremonial paraphernalia, to cure the prenatal effects of an eclipse, or to install a chief or head man. From it are derived the girls' puberty rite, the house-blessing rite, and the seed-blessing rite.
GROUP II HOLY WAY: The chants in this group are used to counteract offenses against the Holy People and contact with dangerous forces. They mainly promote goodness and attract holiness.	
Hail Way (probably extinct)	Used for persons injured by water, for frozen feet, for muscle soreness, tiredness, lameness.
Water Way (probably extinct)	Used for promoting rain, for paralysis, for resuscitation from drowning, for deafness.
Shooting Way, Male and Female Branches	Used to counteract infection from lightning, snakes, and arorws. Used also for colds, fevers, rheumatism, paralysis, and abdominal pain.
Red Ant Way	Used to counteract diseases said to be caused by red ants. Urinating on an anthill might cause anuria, hematuria, bladder stones, pelvic pain, venereal disease, or other kidney and bladder troubles. Swallowing an ant might cause stomach or intestinal distress or fever. An ant bite might cause itching, skin sores, rashes, boils, swellings, or other skin diseases. Spitting on an anthill might cause a sore throat. Used for the bite of any venomous insect or spider, and also for rheumatism, stiff joints, and bent back.
Big Star Way	Uses not given.
Mountaintop Way, several branches	Used for "porcupine sickness" (constipation, anuria, gall bladder trouble), internal pain, and "bear sickness" (mental illness).

GROUP II HOLY WAY (cont). Prostitution Way, Male and Female Branches	Used to counteract mania and prostitution.
Beauty Way, Male and Female Branches	Used for snake bite, rheumatism, sore throat, stomach trouble, kidney and bladder trouble, abdominal trouble, aching feet, legs, arms, back, or waist, swollen ankles and knees, itching skin, painful urination, dry throat, mental confusion, fear, or loss of consciousness.
Night Way, many branches	Used for diseases of the head, such as blindness, deafness, or insanity. Also for cases of "deer infection," which may cause a kind of rheumatism.
Dog Way (extinct)	Uses unknown.
Big God Way (probably extinct)	Used for blindness and stiffness.
Plume Way (Feather Chant)	Used for diseases of the head, similar to uses of Night Way.
Coyote Way	Used to counteract prostitution, mania, rabies, sore throat, and stomach trouble.
Navaho Wind Way Chiricahua Apache Wind Way	Used for any disease caused by "wind infection" (especially heart and lung trouble); "snake infection," characterized by stomach trouble; and "cactus infection," characterized by general body itching and eye trouble.
Hand-Trembling Way	Used for hand-trembling sickness, nervousness, and mental disturbance.
Eagle-Trapping Way Bead Way	Used to counteract "eagle infection," head diseases, boils and sores, sore throat, swollen legs, vomiting, and itching.
Awl Way (extinct)	Used for headaches, baldness, and for those who have violated restrictions on making baskets.
Earth Way (extinct)	Used to counteract "earth infection" or bad dreams involving the earth.
GROUP III LIFE WAY: The main chant is Flint Way, which has several branches. The uses are quite specific for injuries resulting from accidents: sprains, strains, fractures, swellings, cuts, and burns.	

TABLE II (cont.)

GROUP IV EVIL WAY: All ceremonies in this group are used to exorcise evil spirits.	
Moving Up Way (Upward Reaching Way)	Probably directed against native ghosts.
Red Ant, Evil Way	Used for diseases of the kidney and bladder.
Big Star, Evil Way	Used for persons breaking taboos in handling the dead, to exorcise evil power, or for fear of darkness.
Evil Way, Male and Female Shooting Branches	Used for ghost sickness, dreams of ghosts or evil spirits, venereal disease, fear at night.
Hand Trembling, Evil Way (extinct)	Uses unknown.
Reared-in-Earth Way (extinct)	Uses unknown.
Enemy Way	Used for infections from aliens, for marriage or contact with foreigners (including Anglos and Mexicans).
Two-Went-Back-for-Scalp Way (extinct)	Uses unknown.
Ghosts-of-Every-Description Way (extinct)	Uses unknown.
GROUP V WAR CEREMONIALS: This group consists of chants and prayers used in raiding and warfare. Not in use at present.	
GROUP VI GAME WAY: This group consists of rituals used in hunting the four sacred animals, bear, eagle, deer, and antelope. Not in use at present.	

Sources: Kluckhohn and Wyman, 1938
Oakes, Haile, and Wyman, 1957
Wyman, 1962, 1965, 1970

fear from bad dreams and omens, protect flocks and herds, promote good mental health, and other general purposes. From it derive other special blessing ceremonies such as the girls' puberty rite, the house-blessing rite, and the seed-blessing rite. Even though it is said that Blessing Way is not given for illness, it can be seen from the list of its uses that it does correct disharmony, and the line between disease and disharmony—especially for the Navaho—is never distinct. The content of Blessing Way is discussed in more detail in Chapter Six.

Stemming from Blessing Way, the chantways are divided into three large groups (following Kluckhohn and Wyman, 1938). The Holy Way group is the largest of these and includes the most famous chants. Most of these chants have three- and five-night forms, and some have nine-night forms. The five-night form may be the basis from which the longer and shorter forms derive. It is expected that any of these chants will be repeated four times within the patient's lifetime (four is symbolic of completion and fulfillment for the Navaho). This is not always done, or years may elapse between the chants. Theoretically, they must all be done by the same chanter. The over-all emphasis in the Holy Way chants is to promote goodness and harmony, to summon the Holy People, and to restore health.

The symptoms for which a given chant is prescribed are based on loose connections with the specific chant myth. For instance, Hail Way is said to be good for muscular soreness, tiredness, and lameness because the hero, Rain Boy, suffered from these symptoms when he was attacked by his enemies. Night Way is said to be good for diseases of the head—insanity, deafness, and blindness—because these are dangers which threatened the Night Way hero. Shooting Way is used to counteract the effects of lightning, snakes, and arrows, because these figure prominently in its sand paintings. Beauty Way is said to be good for snake infection, which may include rheumatism, sore throat, stomach trouble, kidney and

Ceremonial hogan where most rituals are performed

bladder trouble, and skin diseases—many of which symptoms troubled the heroine of this chant on her arduous journeys. Thus even the symptoms of the illness itself are used to promote identification of the patient with the chant hero.

Evil Way chants form the next group. They are mainly exorcistic in nature and are directed against the attacks of evil spirits, ghosts, witches, and foreigners. Blackening of the patient is one of the chief rites. The main symptoms involved seem to be sudden weakness, giddiness, or loss of consciousness. Moving Up Way is concerned with the emergence of the Navaho from the lower worlds, and is directed against ghosts. Red Ant Evil Way is used for diseases of the kidney and bladder, which may be caused by red ants. Big Star Way protects against the night and the powerful influence of the stars. Enemy Way protects against infection from aliens.

The last group comprises the Life Way chants, of which the main one is Flint Way. This chant is specific for injuries resulting from accidents, sprains, fractures, swellings, cuts, and burns. The Flint Chant has no definite duration. One medicine man said, "It depends on the condition of the patient: sometimes a week or nine days, sometimes two to four days." Chiefly involved are herbal medicines and songs. The theme of the songs is the sprouting and growth of herbs, which are ground up to make the medicine; many different herbs are used.

THE MYTHS

The myths provide a loose background for the chants. Each chant has an associated myth which describes the origin of that chant, and the adventures of the hero or heroine in obtaining the chant from the gods. At times the prayers, songs, and sand paintings, as well as the ritual actions, refer to the myth, but there is no one-to-one correspondence. The myth could not be reconstructed from the ceremony. It is not even required that a medicine man know the myth of the chant he directs, although he must know everything else in detail. However, it is considered a mark of distinction if he does know it in full.

In an analysis of the plot construction of chant myths, Spencer (1957: 86) found several important value themes: the acquisition of supernatural power, especially for the maintenance of health; the preservation of harmony in family relationships; and the achievement of adult status by the young man. These themes run like leitmotifs throughout the myths, and the best way to appreciate them is to analyze one of the chant myths. I will use the Hail Chant for this purpose. There are two slightly different versions published, both given by Hosteen Klah, once to Gladys Reichard (1944c) and once to Mary Wheelwright (1946a). I present my abstract of the Reichard version, which seems more complete.

The Hail Chant is connected with four other chants: Water Way, Plume (or Feather) Way, Shooting Way, and Wind Way. All are concerned with the control of powerful meteorological forces. Hail Way, which may now be extinct, was one of the ceremonies given by Hosteen Klah.

The myth is concerned with the hero, Rain Boy, who in the beginning of the story is an excessive gambler. He loses all his family's possessions and finally even his father's token of leadership. The people are extremely angry and decide to whip him severely with all the group as witnesses. Bat Woman comes to him the night before the punishment and puts over him her cloak of invisibility, enabling him to escape.

In most of the myths the hero is antisocial at the start—lazy, careless, or a dreamer. Nobody expects he will amount to anything. Rain Boy is worse than most, but still he is favored by a feminine element, Bat Woman, who is associated with darkness. She is also associated with sexuality, since she is said to have a "vagina wing" by which she clings to rocks and makes an embarrassing noise (Reichard, 1950: 383).

> After that he lives off the land; one day he comes upon a beautifully furnished house and finds a beautiful girl inside with a white face and dark eyes. She smiles at him seductively. He tries to leave—perhaps not very hard—but she draws him back with zigzag lightning, rain streamers, forked lightning and rainbow. The fourth time he has to stay. They are caught by her husband, Winter Thunder, one of the most powerful and irascible of all the gods. He immediately loses all control and invokes a hail storm that shatters Rain Boy completely.

This part of the myth lends itself to three levels of interpretation. The first level is the obvious, straightforward attempt to invoke natural forces. The girl symbolizes nature in a gentler mood, and Winter Thunder, the avenger, represents the destructive power of winter storms. He is like thunder gods all over the world: difficult to manage, easily disposed to wrath, and liable to invoke terrible punishments on transgressors. Such power must be brought under control, and this is the avowed purpose of the entire chant and one of its foremost themes.

The second level is one of psychological relationship, the "family romance" scenario peculiar to the Navaho. The young hero would like to marry the forbidden woman (mother, sister, beloved) who belongs to someone else. He is not strong enough to make good his conquest of her, so he must face the wrath of her husband (father, guardian). This mythical scenario fits in with the old Navaho system of residence, in which the young man went to live with his wife's family. Thus he was easily in position to come into conflict with the wife's father and other family members. Since the women own or control most of the property and valuable goods, he must stay and face the conflict or go back to his mother's home.

The third level is the relationship of the hero to his own inner world and his attainment of full power. Here is the anima quality (his feminine side), which is seductive and alluring but not to be trusted, as he has not yet learned to master his own aggression and destructiveness. His own intense masculine rage, still largely unconscious, is symbolized by Winter Thunder.

News of Rain Boy's destruction is carried by Big Fly to the other thunders and winds and a great council of the gods is called. With the eventual help of many of the gods, including Talking God, Calling God, Thunder and Wind People, ants, bees, cornbeetle, Pollen Boy and Begochidi, all the parts of his body are found and ritually restored.

This is the theme of death and rebirth which is characteristic of the symbolism of all initiations, whether into adulthood or mystical vocation (Eliade, 1958). Such an initiation requires a great effort on the hero's part, and every bit of supernatural power he can muster.

Because Winter Thunder has uttered that which is evil the other Thunders organize a war party against him. Changing Woman and her hero sons are notified, but when she enters the council she refuses to participate in this war, saying: "Surely I bore my children to subdue monsters, not to be in the midst of it." So her hero sons cannot participate. Nevertheless the war is staged, and there are a series of terrible battles in which many of the Thunders are killed and wounded. Finally, in the last battle, worm and wood beetle with "something like an ice pick" puncture Winter Thunder's armor and put him in retreat.

Here the decision-making power of the Navaho woman is exercised by Changing Woman, the great Navaho earth goddess. Even for the great heroes, if she says no, it is no; they do not object.

Changing Woman remains peaceful, but a costly sacrifice is required of the other gods to conquer either the harsh destructive power of nature outside or aggressiveness within. In the end it is two small and seemingly insignificant creatures who swing the balance against Winter Thunder.

There is a great desire to make peace but only bat and Black God (the primordial Fire God) will attempt the journey to meet with Winter Thunder. It is Black God's threat to use his firebolt which frightens Winter Thunder into acceptance. Then there is a great peace ceremony, and a healing ceremony is given in which Rain Boy is the patient and Winter Thunder acts as the medicine man with Black Thunder as assistant. Winter Thunder is still very angry at Rain Boy and plans to kill him during the ceremony. However, Rain Boy is forewarned and begins to sing. In a certain part of the ceremony he substitutes the words: "We are in great peace" for Winter Thunder's version: "We are in great danger." Winter Thunder is surprised and ashamed, and instead of killing the patient he merely shows his anger by whirling around holding his obsidian knife.

To ensure peace among the gods, Winter Thunder must be controlled. It is the primordial Fire God who finally subdues him. Then it is shame, a powerful force in Navaho culture, which prevents Winter Thunder from killing his trusting patient. Winter Thunder is still full of wrath which is just barely contained. He is very seldom evoked in the prayers or depicted in the sand paintings, because he is so hard to control.

After the ceremony Rain Boy is restored, but on the way home he visits Rough Frog in his corn patch. Frog taunts him and challenges him to a race around the mountain. Rain Boy accepts, thinking Frog's legs are too weak to win. Frog defeats him by witchcraft, shooting sharp hail into Rain Boy's body, slowing him down. Frog wins the Boy's body parts, and the hero is transformed into a frog. The gods again have to be called to rescue him and they have to look all through Frog's house to find his body parts and restore him to his proper form. In a second race, Rain Boy wins; this time with the help of the gods he is able to avoid Frog's witchcraft. As a prize he takes only the feet, legs and gait of the frog and offers them to the gods. After four days they return these to Frog and put him in charge of cloud, rain and fog for Earth People.

Rain Boy still has not learned his lesson. His encounter with Frog indicates, as so often in the chants, the ever-present danger of psychological inflation. Rain Boy believes himself to be in every way superior to lowly Frog: in bodily form, speed, swiftness, and intelligence. But Frog proves to have unexpected powers arising from cleverness and witchcraft. He defeats Rain Boy in spite of his vaunted superiority, and Rain Boy becomes that which he loathed—Frog. This is a frequent device to identify the hero with some despised enemy. Frog is partly Rain Boy himself, and must be recognized and given due respect. Rain Boy has engaged in this foolish contest in spite of warnings against it, but the gods take pity on him, and everything is put in its rightful place through the ordering power of the chants. Frog becomes a beneficent power of nature.

At the end Rain Boy wants very much to visit his home. He cries in loneliness. Gopher tries to comfort him but fails so Talking God takes him to the home of Dark Thunder, where he is given a test of his fitness to return. He will be allowed to go home only if he agrees to take charge of dark clouds, rain, and snow and ice on his return. Reluctantly he agrees so the gods allow him to depart.

He is received with acclaim; the past is forgotten and everyone is eager to hear his story. He teaches his ceremonial healing knowledge to his older brother who is then able to use it for the benefit of the people. He cannot stay, because he is now partly divine, and he finally wishes to rejoin the gods. His sister wants to accompany him because of all the wonderful things she has heard. His family is sad at his departure but they are reassured that the trip is necessary, and finally Talking God takes them to the sky on dawn light. The hero has a joyful reunion with the gods, and his sister, at first a little shy, is soon made to feel at home. For the benefit of the people he is in charge of rain, and she of plants.

Now the three levels of symbolism in the myth have worked themselves out. On the first level Rain Boy has become a master of the forces of nature. He is in charge of rain and snow that bring fertility to the Navaho land. He has acquired powers of healing through the performance of the chant, which he teaches to his people. On the second level he has won his maturity by confronting and defying the terrible father, Winter Thunder, even without the help of the great mother, Changing Woman. He has gone through a ritual initiation in which he has been torn apart and killed. He has been restored by the positive forces of the natural world and so has attained the powers of heroic manhood. Finally, on the third level his confrontation with Winter Thunder means that he has faced the rage and hatred within himself, of which the terrible anger of Winter Thunder is a projected form. He has survived that onslaught and thus completed what Jung called the shadow work of personal growth—facing what is most dark and terrible within oneself.

He has also met his inferior side in the personage of the lowly, contemptible Frog. Only by becoming Frog temporarily could he appreciate who Frog really is, and gain the humility to accept Frog as part of himself. Then he is ready to confront the feminine component of his nature, the anima, which is at first seductive and dangerous, but then becomes a helpful partner in the person of his sister. At the end of the myth Rain Boy and his sister are a deified pair sharing the powers of fertility and healing.

RITUAL ACTIONS

The myths by themselves have no substance unless they are embedded in the ritual action of the chant. The five-night chant is often thought to be the basic form, of which the two-night chant is a condensation and the nine-night chant an elaboration. Each chant has its own ritual specialties and variations, but a typical five-night chant, described by Kluck-hohn and Wyman (1940), begins at sundown, that night being counted as the first night, and the following day as the first day. On the first evening after sundown there is a consecration of the hogan. The medicine man applies corn meal and sometimes an oak twig to the four roof beams of the hogan, so the gods will know that a chant is being held. It also protects the hogan from lightning and big winds.

On the first four evenings an unraveling ceremony and a short sing are held. An unraveling bundle consists of a small bunch of herbs or feathers tied together by yucca fibers or wool string. The patient undresses, and unraveling bundles are applied to various parts of his body and then quickly untied, letting the contents slip free. This symbolically releases the pain and evil influences held within the patient's body. Infusions and chant lotions are given. The bull-roarer is sounded, the patient is brushed and fumigated, and the unraveling items are disposed of outside. During the short sing about ten to twenty of the special songs of the chant being given are sung with or without the accompaniment of drumming on an inverted basket.

On the first four mornings a setting-out ceremony, a sweat and emetic ceremony, and an offering ceremony are held. The setting-out ceremony is performed before dawn. The patient and the medicine man proceed to an earth mound prepared about six feet east of the hogan doorway. There they sing, set up prayer sticks on the mound, sprinkle corn meal, and intone the special prayer. The prepared mound on which the prayer sticks are set out is a symbol that the chant is in progress, and also an invitation for the gods to attend.

Navaho medicine man chants songs from Blessing Way

*As an act of purification medicine man washes his hair
before the Blessing Way ceremony*

Immediately after this, a sweat and emetic ceremony is held to purge all evil from the participants. A hot fire is made in the hogan and four small sand paintings, usually of snakes, are made around the fire. Then the participants undress and enter the hogan. The bull-roarer is sounded and the patient is given chant lotion. A hot, herbal concoction is prepared and passed around. Everyone washes with it and then drinks some of it. If anyone vomits, the medicine man brushes him off and vigorously slaps him on the back with the brush. Other exorcistic ceremonies may be performed such as application of pokers to the patient's body, fire jumping (in which everyone present steps over the fire), and fumigation. After this purification, everyone is ready for breakfast.

After breakfast there is an offering ceremony in which special prayer sticks, reed "cigarettes," or jewel bundles are prepared and deposited some distance from the hogan. The jewels are small bits of valuable stones wrapped in a cloth. These are meant as gifts to attract and purchase the services of the supernatural powers.

On the fourth and last morning the patient is given a ritual bath. He is washed ceremonially by the medicine man in soapweed suds and dried with corn meal. Pollen is then applied.

Sand paintings specific to the chant are made on the first four afternoons. When the painting is finished, the prayer sticks are brought in and set up around it. Corn meal is sprinkled on it by the chanter and the patient. Then the patient sits on the painting, and the chanter applies sand from the figures in the painting to parts of the patient's body. The prayer sticks may also be applied. On the last day the patient's body may be painted with symbolic designs. A feather plume or bead token is then given to the patient to keep. When these rites are completed, the patient leaves and the sand is carried out and dispersed.

After the sand-painting ritual in some Holy Way chants, unseasoned corn-meal mush is brought to the patient. The mush is blessed with pollen and the medicine man feeds the patient four bites. The patient eats the rest himself. This commemorates food eaten in ancient times and symbolizes the patient's weakness, which is like a baby's.

The ceremony of the fifth and final night begins in the late evening. The traditional First Songs of the chant start off, and song sequences are sung with only short rest periods until dawn. Pollen may be administered from time to time to the patient and the spectators. In the longer nine-night chants all-night dances may be held with a large audience in attendance.

At the first light of day the Dawn Songs are sung, and the patient goes outside to breathe in the dawn four times. A final prayer and song closes the ceremony. There may be many special restrictions which the patient is expected to follow for four days after. He must stay at home and be careful not to touch living things. He must not wash, comb his hair, change his clothes, or do any work.

THE SONGS

The songs contain the great body of chant imagery. They accompany ritual action during the chant, or are sung by themselves in long, loosely knit sequences. Nearly every chant has its unraveling songs, fumigation songs, poker songs, etc. Each chant also has special song groups or sequences which reflect part of the myth of the chant.

The songs are sometimes accompanied by the drum or rattle. The rattle, made of gourds or animal hides, is a distinguishing feature of the chantways. Drumming is done on an inverted basket which commemorates the drums used by the supernaturals. It makes the patient's body "come to life," and also symbolizes pounding evil out of the patient's body.

On the last night the singing lasts until dawn. Therefore

more songs would be necessary on a long winter night than on a short summer one. The first and last songs are the most important, but at least one song from each group must be recapitulated on the final night.

Each chant has hundreds of songs associated with it, but not all of them are used on every occasion. For the Night Chant, Washington Matthews recorded twenty-four sequences containing a total of 324 songs. Of one of these he said:

> One song I may mention is that of the first dancers, which is sung at the beginning of the work on the last night of the great ceremony of the night chant. . . . It has lasted eight days before the four singers, after long and tedious instruction by the shaman [Matthews's term for the medicine man], come out to sing this song. Five hundred people are, perhaps, assembled to witness the public ceremonies of the night; some have come from the most distant part of the wide Navaho territory; all are prepared to hold their vigil until dawn. A score or more of critics are in the audience who know the song by heart and are alert to discover errors. It is a long song and consists almost exclusively of meaningless or archaic vocables, which convey no idea to the mind of the singer. Yet not one syllable may be forgotten or misplaced. If the slightest error is made, it is at once proclaimed by the assembled critics, the fruitless ceremony comes to an end, and the five hundred disappointed spectators disperse. But fortunately they are not as particular with all their songs as they are with this.
>
> (1894b: 185)

To unaccustomed ears the songs sound repetitious and monotonous, especially as they drone on through a long night. But the monotony itself, by lowering the threshold of consciousness, allows the constantly repeated images to register on the deeper subconscious layers. Though no one takes any notice of it, everyone is in an altered state of consciousness, and no one is allowed to sleep. At this time the symbolic imagery may have its greatest effect.

The songs are related to each other by means of a loose myth or scenario which describes the actions of the gods or of the chant heroes, or sets the stage for the events and atmosphere necessary for the patient's recovery. Even more than the other chant elements, they identify the patient with the ongoing action. I will give a few examples of some of the more striking songs, usually in Matthews's translations, to illustrate these points. The first is from the Night Chant, and gives a part of the myth, and the song sung by Dawn Boy as he enters the presence of the gods at Canyon de Chelly.

There was a black kethawn [prayer stick] at each side of the door and a curtain hung in the doorway. When he entered the house, he walked on a trail of daylight and he sprinkled pollen on the trail. The people within became aware of the presence of a stranger and looked up. Talking God and Calling God, who were the chief gods there, looked up angrily at him and one said: "Who is this stranger that enters our house unbidden? Is he one of the People of the Earth? Such have never dared to enter this place before." Dawn Boy replied: "It is not for nothing that I come here. See! I have brought gifts for you. I hope to find friends here." Then he showed the precious things he had brought and sang this song:

Where my kindred dwell, there I wander.
I am the Child of the White Corn, there I wander.
The Red Rock House, there I wander.
Where dark kethawns are at the doorway, there I
    wander.
With the pollen of dawn upon my trail, there I
    wander.

. . . .

In the house of long life, there I wander.
In the house of happiness, there I wander.
Beauty before me, with it I wander.
Beauty behind me, with it I wander.
Beauty below me, with it I wander.
Beauty above me, with it I wander.

Medicine man conducts an all-night sing to conclude
Blessing Way ceremony

Beauty all around me, with it I wander.
In old age traveling, with it I wander.
I am on the beautiful trail, with it I wander.
                    (Matthews, 1907: 27–28)

This example illustrates the power of the songs. After he had
sung his song, the gods were moved to accept him and to begin his instruction.

The next example, from Matthews also, is in a different
style. It includes the first and twelfth songs of a sequence of
Thunder Songs from Mountaintop Way. In it one can see the
vivid natural imagery of many of the songs:

FIRST SONG OF THE THUNDER

Thonah! Thonah!
There is a voice above,
The voice of the thunder.
Within the dark clouds,
Again and again it sounds,
Thonah! Thonah!

Thonah! Thonah!
There is a voice below,
The voice of the grasshopper.
Among the plants,
Again and again it sounds,
Thonah! Thonah!

TWELFTH SONG OF THE THUNDER

The voice that beautifies the land!
The voice above,
The voice of the thunder
Within the dark cloud
Again and again it sounds
The voice that beautifies the land.

The voice that beautifies the land!
The voice below,
The voice of the grasshopper
Among the plants
Again and again it sounds,
The voice that beautifies the land.
(Matthews, 1887: 459)

Not all the songs are poetic descriptions of nature and its workings. Some are full of emotional intensity, like this one, sung by the hero of the Mountaintop Way as he crosses into unknown territory, leaving his homeland behind him to the north.

But instead of looking south in the direction in which he was going he looked to the north, the country in which dwelt his people. Before him were the beautiful peaks of the Dibenca, with their forested slopes. The clouds hung over the mountain, the showers of rain fell down its sides, and all the country looked beautiful. And he said to the land, "Aqalani" (Greeting!), and a feeling of loneliness and homesickness came over him, and he wept and sang this song:

> That flowing water! That flowing water!
> My mind wanders across it.
> That broad water! That broad water!
> My mind wanders across it.
> That old age water! That flowing water!
> My mind wanders across it.
>
> (Matthews, 1887: 393)

Most of the songs accompany ritual action and place the action in its supernatural context, as in the song from the Night Chant which identifies the patient with Dawn Boy. This song accompanies the holding of sacred objects—prayer sticks or kethawns—as is often done during the rites, so as to partake of their power.

> Held in my hand, held in my hand, held in my hand, held in my hand.
> Now with it Dawn Boy I am. Held in my hand.
> Of Red Rock House. Held in my hand.
> From the doorway with dark kethawns. Held in my hand.
> With the pollen of dawn for a trail. Held in my hand.
> At the yuni, the striped cotton hangs with the pollen. Held in my hand.
> Going around with it. Held in my hand.
> Taking another, I walk with it. Held in my hand.
> I arrive home with it. Held in my hand.
> I sit down with it. Held in my hand.
> With beauty before me. Held in my hand.
> With beauty behind me. Held in my hand.
> With beauty above me. Held in my hand.
> With beauty below me. Held in my hand.
> With beauty all around me. Held in my hand.

Now in old age wandering. Held in my hand.
Now on the trail of beauty. Held in my hand.
(Matthews, 1907: 31–32)

It is easy to see that the songs promote intense participation at every stage of the ceremonies, but one cannot escape the impression that the songs are secondary. They set the stage, paint the scene, propel the action, create the mood, but it is the prayers and sand paintings that carry the strongest healing power.

THE PRAYERS

There are several kinds of prayers used in the chants. Some are very informal, such as brief pollen blessings and silent prayers occurring at various points in the proceeding. There are also the word formulas, specific for each chant, such as the one given for the Hail Chant. These formulas consist of words repeated in exact order, before the singer turns over his basket to use it as a drum for the night's singing. The words used are: Earth, Sky, Mountain Woman, Water Woman, Darkness, Dawn, Talking God, Calling God, White Corn, Yellow Corn, Pollen, Corn Beetle (Reichard, 1944b: 10). Also there are certain sound symbols, usually the cry of some supernatural associated with the chant, which the singer utters as he performs ritual acts. Thunder sounds are used for Shooting Way, wind sounds for Wind Way, and the cry of Talking God for the Night Chant.

The most important kind of prayer is the chant litany recited by the singer at the crucial points in the ceremonies. He may chant it for himself as a blessing or to correct mistakes, or he may chant it over the patient while the patient holds a sacred object in his hand. The patient repeats the prayer line for line after the medicine man—sometimes in a mood of reverence or sometimes mechanically.

The prayers must be word perfect. The patient may slip

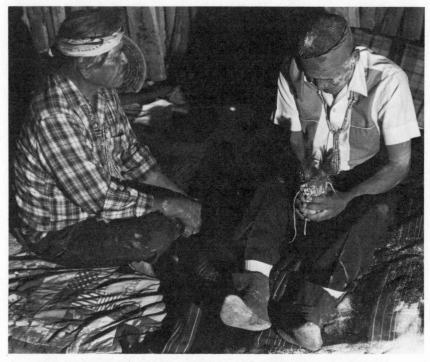

*Medicine man and his patient intone a long Blessing Way prayer
—patient holds sacred objects from medicine bundle*

and stumble through the prayer, but the medicine man must continue with sureness and confidence no matter what happens. Some of the prayers are so sacred that they must never be repeated in part, or twice on the same day. They must always be given in full and with total concentration. Their purpose is "compulsion by exactness of word" (Reichard, 1944b: 10); they are structured on the theory that if the offering is exactly right, the gods must grant the petitioner's request. "The attitude of reverence, as we should interpret it, is at this point apparent, but it is reverence for order and form, not humility before deity" (*ibid.*, p. 14).

The prayers fall mainly into two categories. They either seek to attract good, seek blessing, and evoke kindly supernaturals, or they exorcise evil, restrict its action, destroy the malevolent sorcerer. Most prayers have some of each, but the emphasis is usually one or the other.

There are also great prayers of invocation and liberation which describe journeys for sacred knowledge and power, such as one from the Big Star Chant "which requires a day and a night for its recitation [in the myth] and 'takes you down under the earth, up to the sky and back again' and thus recapitulates the over-all theme of the myth of the Great Star" (McAllester, 1956: 87). There is a famous prayer from the Night Chant which narrates the rescue of the patient by the Warrior Twins and Talking God from the land of the dead, and his restoration to normal life (see Chapter Eight).

THE SAND PAINTINGS

An equally effective and even more dramatic device for identifying the patient with healing powers is the use of the sand painting. There are over a thousand sand paintings known to the Navaho and associated with their ceremonies. About half of these have been recorded, and copies of many can be seen at the Wheelwright Museum in Santa Fe, where large permanent reproductions made by a special technique are on display.

Although the term "sand painting" is generally used, it is not quite correct, as they are not all made of sand. Some, especially those associated with Blessing Way, are made of corn meal, charcoal, and ground-up flower petals spread on buckskin. Most of the big paintings are made with colored sands on the floor of the ceremonial hogan. In diameter they may be only eighteen inches or as much as twelve feet. The medicine man and several assistants may work for several hours to complete one. The assistants work under the direction of the supervising medicine man, and the responsibility to see that all details are correct is always his alone.

There is no pattern or guide for the painting except in the mind of the medicine man. No preliminary sketch is made; only a batten is used to smooth the sand on the floor, and a taut string to make straight lines. Only a few colors are employed, of which most are pulverized sandstone. Black is made from charcoal mixed with sand; white is gypsum or white sandstone; blue may be a mixture of white and black, or ground-up bluish stone; yellow is yellow ocher or yellow sandstone; red is red sandstone. There is no separate color green; blue is used instead. All the materials are ground up finely, and then the ground sand is held in the right hand and allowed to run between the thumb and flexed index finger in a smooth, even trickle to form the design. The technique looks deceptively simple, but anyone who tries it will see how difficult it is to get just the right amount. When finished, the painting is strikingly beautiful, and has the appearance of a fine velvet texture as the figures stand out on the sand background.

The sand painting is supposed to be a reproduction of the painting acquired by the chant hero from the gods on one of his adventurous journeys. Spontaneous originality is allowed only in the decorations on the kilts of the figures or on the medicine pouches. Otherwise they are supposed to be exact copies, and most observers have agreed that they usually are.

In a long ceremony like the Night Chant there may be four small paintings used in the emetic rites on the first four mornings, and four large sand paintings on the four last days. Though masterpieces, the paintings are allowed to remain intact only an hour or so while the ceremony takes place. Most of the Holy Way paintings are made in the afternoon and destroyed before sunset, while some evil-chasing paintings such as those used in the Big Star Chant are made at night and destroyed before dawn. (A more thorough discussion of the sand paintings as healing mandalas will be found in Chapter Nine.)

When the painting is finished the floor becomes a holy altar upon which "the gods come and go." The patient is then allowed to enter and sees the completed painting all at once. Here is a description of what usually happens in a typical sand-painting rite (there are many variations):

Before the Event

The painting is finished.
Prayer sticks are set around it.
Herb infusions in bowls are set inside by the guards.
Women bring food.
The men eat.
The medicine man blesses the painting with pollen.
A caller announces the ceremony.
The patient enters carrying a basket of corn meal.
He scatters it as food to the painting.
The patient removes his clothing.
The medicine man guides the patient to the painting.
The patient sits on the painting facing east.
The medicine man sings with a rattle.
Medicine bundles are pressed to the patient.
Herb infusions may be drunk.

Main Event

The medicine man puts the herb infusion on his hands.
He touches the head of the sand figures.
He touches the head of the patient.
He makes special sounds as he does so.
Power is transferred.
He does this for the patient's neck, chest, arms, and legs.

After the Event

The patient and spectators are fumigated.
A bunch of eagles' wings is used to brush sand off the
    patient.

He leaves.
Spectators may apply sand to their bodies.
Sand is put in a blanket and carried off to the north.

NAVAHO MEDICINE

Besides the medicine men and diagnosticians, the Navaho have another class of informal healers called herbalists. These people need not be versed in chant lore, but they gather herbs and make medicines for general use. Many of these are probably palliatives and placebos, but there are indications that some are surprisingly effective. Such remedies are not based on careful scientific experimentation, nor are they part of the general symbolic system expressed by the ceremonials. In them effective ingredients are unwittingly mixed with many inert substances whose medical action is minimal or nonexistent. When needed, these remedies are usually applied freely with little ceremony. They have no special songs or prayers to accompany their use, and no myths of origin.

The medicine men also use herbal medicines as part of their chant practice. These medicines are therapeutic primarily because they are alluded to in the myths, or have been used by the gods in the original ceremonies to heal the chant heroes. They are gathered with special precautions, sometimes with special prayers. In the Night Chant, for example, there is one plant ingredient gathered only when lightning flashes. The medicines are prepared only by authorized persons and at certain times of the year. They are primarily symbolic, and are used in much the same manner as other chant symbols, to foster identification with the supernatural powers evoked in the ceremony. But in the hundreds of ingredients in these "symbolic medicines," there might be some with true physiological effectiveness.

Kluckhohn and Wyman (1940: 48–57) have given a general description of the use of these medicines in the chant practice. Each chant employs fumigants, emetics, and a chant lotion along with its other ritual procedures. They are mainly for purification, since fumigation is often the concluding act of a ceremony. Two live coals are placed before the patient and other participants. The chanter sprinkles the coals with fumigant and all inhale the vapor and rub it on their arms and legs. The emetics are used with the sweat bath to bring about purification for later rituals. At various times during the rituals the singer applies chant lotion to the patient and other participants, who drink it and bathe in it. It is supposed to be effective for allaying headache, fever, and general bodily discomfort. In the Holy Way chants some chant lotion ingredients are mint, pennyroyal, and horsemint.

Each chant also features a herbal remedy called an infusion specific. "The infusion specific," Kluckhohn and Wyman tell us, "is definitely restricted to a single ceremonial. It seems indeed to be considered the most important actual therapeutic agent of most ceremonials" (ibid., p. 51). The ingredients are a carefully guarded secret. They are sometimes prepared in a turtle or abalone cup and placed on the sand painting between the Rainbow Guardian's hands. When the chanter gives this medicine to the patient he first thrusts the cup toward the major figures of the sand painting, indicating that it is they who are giving this remedy to the patient. He then passes the cup sunwise over the painting and gives it to the patient to drink. This may be done four times.

In Holy Way chants a pollen ball is fed to the patient during the sand-painting rites. The pollen ball is about three-quarters of an inch in diameter and contains pollen, water, corn meal, consecrated sand, and bits of many things mentioned in the chant. For instance, a bit of fish blood is included in the pollen ball given in the Shooting Way chants, to commemorate Holy Boy's journey to the Fish People. Before he gives it to the patient, the singer thrusts the ball toward the sand painting and toward the sun. Then he puts it in the patient's mouth with four swallows of water. The ball is supposed to stay in the patient's body like a spirit, and carry with it the blessings of the chant deities.

Besides herbal remedies the Navaho, like other Indian tribes, make wide use of the sweat house, the sweat bath, hot springs, and hot earth trenches for the alleviation of muscular and skeletal injuries and illnesses. They are reported to be extremely effective.

THE NAVAHO PANTHEON

In many of the chants, Sun (Tsó Hanon, the Sun Bearer) is recognized as the ultimate source of power and light. There is general agreement with Reichard when she says: "Navaho rituals center around the Sun cult. Because of the Navaho idea of conception, the belief that it is due to a union of light (heat, warmth) and water (semen, fluids, dampness, mists) Sun, as a symbol of light, heat and warmth, dominates in a way all other deities or spirits. Since all things are paired— there being a dominant and a subordinate, a stronger and a weaker—Changing Woman is the balancing component of the pair. Her power is quantitatively perhaps as great, though qualitatively different from that of Sun" (1945: 211). Changing Woman (Istsá Natlehi) is the great symbol of earth with all its seasonal variations, a woman's power of renewing life and maternal love. She seems to be consistently well disposed to mankind.

Thus Sun and Changing Woman form the central axis around which all the other powers and beings revolve. They are the ultimate source of health and harmony; they have the power to strengthen and rejuvenate. Out of their union came the Warrior Twins, Monster Slayer (Nayenezgáni) and Child of the Water (Tobadsistsíni), who made an arduous journey to visit their Sun-Father and win the power from him to slay the monsters and liberate the People (described in Chapter Eight). They and their parents, Changing Woman and the Sun, are the "holy family" of Navaho theology. Changing Woman and the Sun are each also linked with a weaker supernatural being of the same sex who completes or extends their nature: the Moon (Kléhanoai) is the weaker brother of the Sun, and White Shell Woman (Yolkáiestsan) the weaker sister of Changing Woman. White Shell Woman is a little more dubious and undependable than her sister.

This "holy family" was a late development in the mythical history of the Navaho. In the lower worlds of the origin myths, First Man and First Woman were the main protagonists, and they were enmeshed in witchcraft and evil. Coyote, Begochidi, Black God (or Fire God), Salt Woman, and insect and other animal people were there from the beginning, and played major roles in the long upward climb to light and consciousness.

Besides the universal figures, every chant seems to have a mini-pantheon of its own. The Hail Chant features Thunder People, with White Thunder and Black Thunder as major deities. Big Star Chant introduces the Star People, with Big Star as the wise chief. In the Night Chant there are special holy people, usually called Yei, who on the final night are impersonated by dancers wearing blue masks with evergreen collars, and singing in an eerie, falsetto voice. The Yei are led by Talking God (Hastyéyalti), who is like a Dutch uncle to the chant heroes, guiding and directing them in their exploits and rescuing them from all manner of predicaments. He is often identified with the east and the rising sun. His cry *Wu hu hu hú* is similar to the dawn call of the Pueblo rituals (Bierhorst, 1974: 334). He is usually paired with Calling God (Hastyéhogan), or Home God as some like to call him, who seems to symbolize domesticity, peace, and fruitfulness, and is associated with the west and the setting sun. Thus they are both part of the solar symbolic complex.

The Navaho world is thick with deity. Every natural force, every geographical feature, every plant, animal, or meteorological phenomenon has its particular supernatural power, and may be represented by a personified image in the sand paintings.

Then there is Begochidi! He is different from all the others and embodies the essence of paradox (Reichard, 1950: 386–90). On the one hand he is the son of the Sun, associated with light and fire, a solar deity, creator of life who had "intercourse with everything in the world." In this benign aspect he is a patron of domestic and game animals: one would pray to him for an especially fine horse. He is pictured as a solar figure with blond or red hair and blue eyes. Natani Tso said of him: "Begochidi made all the living things on earth. When he gets old, he gets young again. There are two of them (two in one), white and yellow, Begochidi and Begotsoi. He knows everything. He gave us all the ceremonials that we have." I could never clarify with him the difference in the two deities, except that the Navaho always have their gods in pairs.

But on the other hand Begochidi is a great mischief-maker and gambler. He can change at will into any other form: rainbow, sand, water, wind, insects, etc. He makes fun of the other gods, sending swarms of insects to bite them unmercifully until they meet his demands. He sneaks up behind young girls and twitches their breasts, shouting "Bego, bego." (His name is said to mean "one-who-grabs-breasts.") When a young hunter is aiming to shoot, he grabs his testicles and spoils his aim. He does the same when a man and woman are having intercourse.

Sometimes Begochidi appears as a worm or insect crawling in the dust and representing something obscene. He favors sex and procreation, but he is also a patron of the berdaches (transvestites) and dresses like a woman. In the Moth Way myth (Spencer, 1957: 148–50) Begochidi lives with the Butterfly People as a berdache. He is always putting his hands to their crotches and saying "Bego, bego." He will not let them marry as long as he is taking care of them. One day when he is gone they practice brother-sister incest with disastrous consequences. They all become "moth crazy" and jump into the fire in a mad rush. They have to be forcibly separated. Finally a cure is found by using medicine from the genitals of a single litter of coyotes, blue foxes, badgers, or bears. As the medicine is given, the brother and sister sit back to back, and butterflies come out of their mouths and vanish through the smoke hole.

If one seeks a parallel to Begochidi's nature one thinks of Mercurius, who was so necessary to the work of the old alchemists. Mercurius could be associated with fire, "the universal and scintillating fire of the light of nature, which carries the heavenly spirit within it" (Jung, 1967: 209). He could also be lascivious, and was sometimes pictured "in continuous cohabitation" (*ibid.*, p. 217). In the *Rosarium Philosophorum*, an alchemical text from the sixteenth century, his dual nature is shown first in cohabitation, then as the fusing or melding of the masculine and feminine sides, associated with the sun and moon. "He is the devil, a redeeming psychopomp, and evasive trickster, and God's reflection in physical nature" (*ibid.*, p. 237).

Thus both Mercurius and Begochidi combine the lowest and highest, the lascivious trickster and the mystic unity with god, a connection with the sun and moon, rampant sexuality and sexual transcendence. Both can help or hinder, depending on how they are approached. In his later versions of the myths, Hosteen Klah may have been trying to identify Begochidi with the Christian image of God's Son. But Begochidi could never be only the good God of the Christians, just as he is never entirely the mischievous trickster. In him the Navaho have created a true union of opposites, of which Jung said, "Psychologically this means that human wholeness can only be described in antinomies, which is always the case when dealing with a transcendental idea" (1954: 312).

Begochidi is a reconciling symbol which brings together good and bad, high and low, pure and impure, male and female, and as such he is one of the most daring intuitive concepts of American Indian religion—an ingenious attempt to express the basically paradoxical nature of man in the image of a god. Klah once described him as a blond or red-haired god with blue eyes, dressed like a woman (Reichard, 1950: 387).

CHAPTER FOUR

Navaho Religion:
The Whole in Action

How do all these disparate elements work together in the over-all task of healing? To gain an idea of the process at work, one must follow one of the nine-day chant ceremonials in its day-by-day operation. For that purpose none could be better than Matthews's detailed account of the ritual ceremony of the Night Chant (1902). The first four days are devoted largely to purification and evocation (stages one and two), which give over in the next four days to rituals of identification and transformation (stages three and four). The last or ninth night is spent summarizing all that went before and releasing the patient from the chant (stage five).

THE FIRST FOUR DAYS

After sundown on the first day there is a consecration of the hogan; the chanter, moving sunwise around the hogan, rubs sacred corn meal on the four main supporting timbers. Then a rite of exorcism is held. Assistants of the medicine man dressed as gods (called god-impersonators) come into the hogan, touch the patient with closed hoops of bent sumac, and then quickly open them. The god-impersonators utter cries and perform characteristic motions of the gods to heighten the effect. This symbolizes freeing the patient from his illness, which is imagined to be blown away by the wind. The same rite is then performed with collapsible quadrangles of willow wands, a sacred talisman of the chant.

As part of the purification of the first four mornings, a sweat-bath ritual is held. Water is thrown on heated stones in a small, specially built sweat house, and the patient enters. The god-impersonators appear again and with a loud whoop call the patient out. They massage him vigorously with prayer wands, paying special attention to the diseased parts, and howl in his ears.

On the second night the patient is dressed in evergreen branches, symbolizing the constrictions which hold him prisoner. Then men impersonating the Warrior Twins, Monster Slayer and Child of the Water, come in brandishing flint knives. Songs announce their coming:

> *In a land divine he strides,*
> *In a land divine he strides,*
> *Now Monster Slayer strides,*
> *Above on the summits high he strides,*
> *In a land divine he strides.*

> *In a land divine he strides,*
> *In a land divine he strides,*
> *Now Child-of-the-water strides,*
> *Below on the lesser hills he strides,*
> *In a land divine he strides.*
>
> (*ibid.*, p. 84)

They cut the patient loose with loud cries.

On the fourth night a mask is placed over the patient's head. A young tree is planted in the center of the hogan and bent over to hook under the mask. When the tree is released it springs upright, pulling the mask from the patient's face. At the end of the fourth day the purifying and exorcistic rites are almost complete. By these methods the patient is freed from the bonds of his illness. In this the medicine man has been aided by his assistants as god-impersonators, a special feature of the Night Chant not found in most other chants.

Rites of evocation (stage two) are going on at the same time. On the first four mornings particular sets of kethawns (prayer sticks) are made and set out to invite the gods to attend. If the procedure has been followed correctly, the gods cannot refuse. While the prayer sticks are being made, songs are sung like this one:

> *A little one now is prepared; a little one now is prepared.*
> *For Calling God, it now is prepared.*
> *A little message is now prepared.*
> *Toward the trail of the he-rain, now it is prepared.*
> *As the rain will hang down, now it is prepared.*
>
> (p. 71)

Painted reeds called cigarettes are made and filled with native tobacco. These are sealed with moistened pollen, and figuratively lit at one end with sunlight passing through a piece of rock crystal. These sacred objects are then placed in the patient's hands and a long prayer is intoned, calling the gods' attention to the offering and describing what is expected in return:

> *I have made your sacrifice.*
> *I have prepared a smoke for you.*
> *My feet restore for me.*
> *My legs restore for me.*
> *My body restore for me.*
> *My mind restore for me.*
> *My voice restore for me.*
>
> *Today take out your spell for me.*
> *Today your spell is removed for me.*
> *Away from me you have taken it.*

> *Far off you have done it.*
> *Today I shall recover.*
> *Today for me it is taken off.*
>
> (p. 73)

This is a short excerpt of a long prayer, but the part quoted implies that the deity had something to do with the working of the spell in the first place, and thus can do evil as well as good.

After the setting out of the sacred objects, songs are begun in the hogan which imply that the gods have heard and are on their way. To reach the patient they must traverse a slender bridge across Canyon de Chelly:

> *Across the Chelly Canyon from the other side he crosses,*
> *On a slender horizontal string of blue he crosses,*
> *For his kethawn of blue, upon the string he crosses.*
>
> *Across the Chelly Canyon from the other side he crosses.*
> *On a slender horizontal string of white he crosses.*
> *For his kethawn of black, upon the string he crosses.*
>
> (p. 74)

During the fourth night a special vigil of the gods begins. During the entire night no one sleeps and the gods come to partake of a communal meal with the people. The patient enters and applies pollen blessing to all the sacred masks of the gods, which are laid out in the medicine hogan. Then the women enter bearing bowls of Navaho food made from traditional recipes. A sacred gruel is prepared, and a virgin boy and girl help to feed some of it to the masks. Then everyone present eats some.

After the gruel is eaten there is a general banquet; anyone who wishes may eat from the traditional Navaho dishes. Other songs are sung until about midnight, when the medicine man goes up to the masks and shakes them to awaken them, while he sings the waking song:

> *He stirs, he stirs, he stirs, he stirs.*
> *Among the lands of dawning he stirs, he stirs;*

The pollen of the dawning he stirs, he sti
Now in old age wandering he stirs, he sti
Now on the trail of beauty he stirs, he stir
He stirs, he stirs, he stirs, he stirs.

(p.

This is repeated with variations several times.
masks have been shaken, the medicine man repeats a prayer
to himself in a low tone:

In beauty may I dwell.
In beauty may I walk.
In beauty may my male kindred dwell.
In beauty may my female kindred dwell.
In beauty may it rain on my young men.
In beauty may it rain on my young women.
In beauty may it rain on my chiefs.
In beauty may it rain on us.
In beauty may our corn grow.
On the trail of pollen may it rain.
In beauty before us, may it rain.
In beauty behind us, may it rain.
In beauty below us, may it rain.
In beauty above us, may it rain.
In beauty all around us, may it rain.
In beauty may I walk.
Goods may I acquire.
Precious stones may I acquire.
Horses may I acquire.
Sheep may I acquire.
Cattle may I acquire.
In old age
The beautiful trail
May I walk.

(pp. 111–12)

The rest of the night is spent in uninterrupted song until
dawn. By now the patient has been well emptied of evil
power, and a great concentration of healing power has been
evoked, ready for use.

In a first-day ritual featuring a small sand painting of the ur sacred mountains, the process of identification (stage three) has already begun. As the patient follows the trail around the mountains, the singers intone:

> *In a holy place with a god I walk,*
> *In a holy place with a god I walk,*
> *On the sacred mountain with a god I walk,*
> *On a chief mountain with a god I walk,*
> *In old age wandering with a god I walk,*
> *On a trail of beauty with a god I walk.*
>
> (p. 81)

As the patient goes to the sweat house carrying twelve plumed wands and led by the singer, the identification is even more definite:

> *This I walk with, this I walk with.*
> *Now Talking God I walk with.*
> *These are his feet I walk with.*
> *These are his limbs I walk with.*
> *This is his body I walk with.*
> *This is his mind I walk with.*
> *This is his voice I walk with.*
> *These are his twelve plumes I walk with.*
>
> (p. 76)

THE FIFTH DAY

The patient bathes and offers more kethawns, and the fourth and last sweat-house ceremony is held. Afterward there is more singing and fumigation, and the medicine man prays. In the afternoon a sand painting is made called the Picture of the Trembling Place. The patient is stripped to a loincloth (a female removes only outer clothing), and a single feather taken from the shoulder of an eagle is tied to his hair. He begins to shake violently, as if in a spasm. Trembling, he walks along tracks of corn-meal footprints leading to the sand painting. He sits on the picture and turns to the east with his limbs flexed. As the song continues, the medicine man reaches behind him and gives loud taps on a hidden drum. At this signal the god-impersonators waiting outside rush in. Everyone acts alarmed when the gods approach the patient and touch him with their talisman. Then the gods leave and the act is repeated three more times. After the ceremony the patient stops trembling and leaves the hogan. The more the patient trembles, the more certain it is that the sickness was caused by the gods of the Night Chant and that it will now be cured.

The fifth night is the night of initiation. This is the Navaho tribal initiation for both girls and boys, and is incorporated into the Night Chant. On that night the drum is "turned down," meaning that drumming is to be a part of the ritual. After the preparations the god-impersonators leave the lodge to return with the initiates. This part of the ceremonial is not only for the patient, but for any person of the tribe who wants to be initiated into the mysteries. A god, in this case Talking God, and a goddess arrive escorting the initiates before them. Talking God carries two large yucca leaves, and the goddess carries a spotted fawnskin containing pollen. The male candidates sit to the north and the girls to the south. The males disrobe under screening blankets while the gods emit occasional whoops.

When they are ready, Talking God approaches the one sitting toward the north. The goddess gives a loud whoop, and the candidate rises, throwing off his blankets. The goddess applies meal to his shins, and Talking God strikes him with the yucca leaves. The goddess then applies meal to several parts of the body, each of which is then struck with the yucca leaves. This happens to all the candidates. The girls do not have to rise and undress, nor are they struck, but they must keep their heads bowed. Instead of the yucca whip, an ear of yellow corn is pressed to parts of their body, and they are sprinkled by the goddess with corn meal.

Then the gods take off their masks and the secret of the Yebitsai is revealed. From their earliest years Navaho children are taught to fear the masked gods. Now they see that the masked persons are not gods, but only people they know who have dressed for the part. This is the secret knowledge they are privileged to learn. The candidates themselves don the masks and look out through the eyeholes. The masks are sprinkled with pollen. Each person prays silently for what he desires most.

THE SIXTH DAY

The great sand painting of the Whirling Logs is made. The painting represents the vision of the hero of the Night Chant at the Lake of Whirling Waters. There he saw a gigantic cross made of spruce logs floating on the water. The gods were sitting on the arms of the cross and it was whirling in a sunwise direction; the entire figure made a huge sunwise swastika. In the Night Chant myths this figure is associated with secrets of fertility and healing which were later imparted to the hero.

The sand painting, about ten feet in diameter, is made on the floor of the hogan. A bowl of water sprinkled with charcoal is placed in the center to symbolize the holy lake. Extending in the four cardinal directions are the whirling logs in the shape of a cross, and on the logs sit eight gods, four male and four female, one pair on each log. Four larger gods standing outside the log circle seem to be whirling the logs around with their wands. Talking God is to the east with his white mask, his eagle plume of twelve feathers, and his squirrel-skin pouch. Calling God is to the west with his black dress, blue mask, and wand of charcoal. Two humpbacked gods to the north and south dressed as mountain sheep commemorate the first meeting of the Dreamer (the hero of the Night Chant) with the gods. They have blue masks and imitation sheep horns, and their packs are full of seeds. Between the cardinal directions are the four holy plants: white corn, beans, squash, and tobacco. Around the whole is the Rainbow Guardian, with an opening to the east.

The patient enters and sits on the painting, on the western limb of the whirling-log cross. When he is seated the gods enter with a whoop, and dip their sprinklers into the medicinal infusion contained in a gourd cup. Then they sprinkle the painting and the patient. The rites of the sand painting are then performed as previously described.

During the sixth day the beggar gods—two of the medicine man's helpers dressed as god-impersonators—are sent out to visit other camps; they must return before nightfall. When they get to the neighboring camp, they dance around uttering their cries and holding out a fawnskin bag to receive donations; gifts are usually food or tobacco. In the evening there are songs accompanied by the basket drum and the rattle. Outside the ceremonial hogan a rehearsal for the great dances of the last night is taking place. Also, visitors and relatives begin to gather for the final night ceremony.

THE SEVENTH AND EIGHTH DAYS

The process of identifying the patient with the gods goes on at an increased rate. Each day an elaborate sand painting is made and the rites performed. A painting is made on the seventh day showing the dance of the last night, as performed by the gods in the original ceremony. On the eighth day there is a painting of the gods of the Night Chant arranged around a central cornstalk, but other paintings may also be used.

Impersonators of many gods appear, offering succor to the patient and uttering their peculiar cries. The rites of initiation may be repeated and the last night dances are rehearsed.

THE NINTH DAY AND NIGHT

The ninth day is usually spent preparing the patient and the performers for the final all-night ceremony. Masks and ke-thawns are prepared and the dancing ground is made ready. The public performance of the last night begins with the most important ceremony of all, the dance of the Atsálei, or First Dancers. This is performed by Talking God and four male dancers identified with thunderbirds. They wear moccasins, long blue stockings, a short kilt or loincloth of red, a silver-studded belt from which a fox skin hangs, numerous rich necklaces borrowed for the occasion, and, most important, the plumed blue mask of the Yei gods with its collar of spruce. Each carries in his left hand a wand of spruce twigs and in his right a gourd rattle.

The patient and the medicine man come out of the hogan. The patient sprinkles corn meal on the dancers, then faces east with the medicine man. They intone a sacred prayer of invocation. All this time the dancers are swaying from side to side. There is perfect silence on the part of everyone present as the medicine man begins the evocation of the dark male thunderbird.

> In Tsegihi [White House],
> In the house made of the dawn,
> In the house made of the evening light,
> In the house made of the dark cloud,
> In the house made of the he-rain,
> In the house made of the dark mist,
> In the house made of the she-rain,

In the house made of pollen,
In the house made of grasshoppers,
Where the dark mists curtain the doorway
The path to which is on the rainbow,
Where the zigzag lightning stands high on top,
Where the he-rain stands high on top, . . .

First he describes the home of the god in order to identify him, a common beginning to Navaho prayers. Then he asks the god to be present.

Oh Male God!
With your moccasins of dark cloud, come to us.
With your leggings of dark cloud, come to us.
With your shirt of dark cloud, come to us.
With your head-dress of dark cloud, come to us.
With your mind enveloped in dark cloud, come to us.
With the dark thunder above you, come to us soaring.
With the shaped cloud at your feet, come to us soaring.
With the far darkness made of the dark cloud over your
    head, come to us soaring.
With the far darkness made of the he-rain over your
    head, come to us soaring.
With the far darkness made of the dark mist over your
    head, come to us soaring.
With the far darkness made of the she-rain over your
    head, come to us soaring.
With the zigzag lightning flung out on high over your
    head, come to us soaring.
With the rainbow hanging high over your head, come to
    us soaring.
With the far darkness made of the dark cloud on the
    ends of your wings, come to us soaring.
With the far darkness made of the he-rain on the ends
    of your wings, come to us soaring.
With the far darkness made of the dark mist on the ends
    of your wings, come to us soaring.
With the far darkness made of the she-rain on the ends
    of your wings, come to us soaring.

With the zigzag lightning flung out on high on the ends
   of your wings, come to us soaring.
With the rainbow hanging high on the ends of your
   wings, come to us soaring.
With the near darkness made of the dark cloud, of the
   he-rain, of the dark mist, and of the she-rain, come
   to us.
With the darkness on the earth, come to us.

                                        (Matthews, 1902: 143)

After this invocation by the medicine man, and identification of the patient with the powers of the god, the desired
transformation to good health (stage four) is described:

> *Happily I recover.*
> *Happily my interior becomes cool.*
> *Happily my eyes regain their power.*
> *Happily my head becomes cool.*
> *Happily my limbs regain their power.*
> *Happily I hear again.*
> *Happily for me the spell is taken off.*
> *Happily I may walk.*
> *Impervious to pain, may I walk.*
> *Feeling light within, I walk.*
> *With lively feelings, I walk.*
>
>   (p. 144)

In answer to the outside prayers and dances invoking the
god, the singers within the lodge confirm that he has heard
and will come:

> *Above it thunders,*
> *His thoughts are directed to you,*
> *He rises toward you.*
> *Now to your house,*
> *He approaches for you.*
> *He arrives for you.*
> *He comes to the door,*
> *He enters for you.*

Behind the fireplace
He eats his special dish.
"Your body is strong,
Your body is holy now" he says.

(p. 153)

The First Song outside is followed by the beginning of the all-night dance. Teams of specially trained dancers take turns keeping the dance going until dawn. The team consists of Talking God, the clown Tonenili, and six male and six female dancers. The female dancers are represented by small men and youths, but sometimes women or transvestites take part. Their bodies are daubed with white earth; they wear silver-studded belts, pendant fox skins, showy kilts, long woolen stockings, garters, and moccasins. Each wears a blue mask which allows the hair to flow out behind. They carry rattles and wands, but they have no spruce collar and no eagle feathers.

They keep up their high, shrill song throughout the dance, and move with their peculiar shuffling motion in long lines together and apart, back and forth. The effect is strange and otherworldly, and it is meant to be. These are the gods, dancing for hope and good health for their people, but they are different, and their nonhuman movements in the flickering firelight mark them as supernatural, beyond mortal ken. The same dance is repeated all night, the usual number of sets being forty-eight, with each of four teams performing twelve times. This takes about ten hours, but all must end at dawn. Since these ceremonials are given in the winter, the nights are deadly cold, and the effect on the audience is a numbing hypnotic state, a condition best suited for "seeing" the gods.

But there is a clown! While the others are dancing, Tonenili imitates them and gets in their way, dances out of order and out of time. He starts too soon and gets tired before the dance is done. He loses his clothing, pretends to be hunting for a fox skin, and often tries to take up a collection to which no one contributes. He is the relief to the heavy demands of the performance. Without the clown, who is as human as the gods are nonhuman, the blessings would not flow.

Inside the ceremonial hogan the medicine man, the patient, and other singers keep to their work. Songs of sequence are sung in their proper order all night long. When the dances have ended outside, the Finishing Songs are sung:

> *From the pond in the white valley,*
> *The young man doubts it,*
> *The god takes up his sacrifices,*
> *With that he now heals.*
>
> *From the pools in the green meadow,*
> *The young woman doubts it,*
> *He takes up his sacrifice,*
> *With that he now heals.*
> *With that your kindred thank you.*
>
> (p. 153)

The ceremonial is over, but the patient must return to the ceremonial hogan to sleep for four nights (stage five: release). He must not sleep until sunset, he must not eat certain foods, and he must keep to himself for the remainder of that time.

CHAPTER FIVE

Fear of Possession

GENERAL HISTORY

In regard to symbolic healing it has been demonstrated in
recent ethnographic work (Kiev, 1964; Middleton, 1967;
Turner, 1970) that not only the theory of illness and the
method of curing it, but also the actual form and content of
the illness itself, depend upon the culture in which that
illness occurs. Therefore, in order to see the general cultural
pattern in Navaho disease and healing, we should look at
the flow of their cultural change during recent centuries.

Linguistic evidence suggests that the Navaho came into
North America on one of the last waves of migration across
the Aleutian land bridge from Siberia. The Athapaskan language, which the Navaho have in common with their Apache
cousins to the east, is also spoken in related dialects by
several smaller tribes in northeastern Mexico, northern California, the northern Pacific coast, and the Mackenzie sub-

arctic area of the Yukon (Driver, 1961). Driver speculates that there was a single Athapaskan language, existing in the Yukon about two or three thousand years ago, that was intelligible to each of the groups. From the Yukon small bands migrated southward, entering the Southwest about the fourteenth or fifteenth century. Although the various groups' languages remained similar, almost everything else changed. For example the Hupa, an Athapaskan-speaking group on the north Pacific coast, now share with people of that area an extreme desire for wealth and prestige while the Navaho, at the opposite pole, regard too much concentration of goods in one individual as highly suspicious.

Prior to their entry into the Southwest, the Navaho were small bands of nomadic people with a shamanistic religion that is still practiced by the original Athapaskan tribes in the subarctic. A similar type of religion in the form of the vision quest is also practiced by most of the tribes the Navahos probably contacted on their long journey southward. In the vision-quest religion, not only the shamans or medicine men but almost every male member of the tribe seek special ecstatic experiences in the form of visions or supernatural helpers (Lowie, 1954; Eliade, 1964). The Apaches, not so influenced by the Pueblo tradition as the Navaho, still preserve much of the older ways, and their medicine men are closer to the shamanistic type.

The first evidence of the Navaho in the Southwest is found in the Four Corners country, the so-called Gobernador district (Schaafsma, 1966). The earliest Navaho remains are from the sixteenth century, and consist of black shards of cooking pottery and beams from a fork-stick hogan. This phase of Navaho culture, dating from about 1560 to 1696, is called the Dinetah phase. At that time the Navaho migrated into the San Juan Valley and its tributaries from the plains of the northern Rio Grande (Hester, 1962). It is noteworthy that no rock painting has been associated with this period.

In 1696 a revolt against the Spanish caused many of the Pueblo people to flee north in an attempt to free themselves from Spanish oppression. They lived in close association with the Navaho during the Gobernador phase from 1696 to 1775. "In the space of a few years the Navahos adopted the Puebloan styles of architecture, manufacturing techniques, and religious paraphernalia, plus many elements of non-material culture such as clans, matrilineal descent, matrilocal residence, the origin myth, and ritual" (Hester, 1962: 91). The change, when it came, was rapid and definitive. Farming became important, and evidence of corn, beans, squash, chili, cotton, pumpkins, watermelon, and gourds has been found. Herds of sheep, goats, horses, and cattle were kept. The first religious rock paintings date from this period, and Schaafsma says of them: "It is likely that the Navaho inclination to portray religious subjects in graphic form at this time was inspired by the Puebloan traditional wall, altar and perhaps sand painting" (1966: 9–10).

Objects used in the Night Chant, Witch Chant, Mountain-top Chant, Enemy Way, and Antelope Corral Way have been found dating back to the eighteenth century, indicating that the Navaho religion was already well on its way to the flowering complexity of the nineteenth. Many of the gods painted on the rocks from that time are like the figures in the sand paintings of today, and certain figures can be identified: Child of the Water, Hunchback, Fringemouth, as well as shields which bear the symbol of the Warrior Twins. Two shields of this type were found at the juncture of the Pine and San Juan Rivers—the center of the Navaho world, where the two sacred rivers in the origin myth cross. These shield paintings reminiscent of the Plains Indians are the most characteristic features of this early period, along with star paintings on cave roofs, and stylized versions of corn. There then follows a long gap in the archaeological record from 1775, when rock painting ceased, until about 1880, when the first sand paintings were recorded by Anglo observers.

For centuries the Navaho have lived, geographically and socially, at the point of conflict between two layers of cultural association. The older layer—characterized by individualism, the vision quest, and a free nomadic life—is gradually being overshadowed and suppressed by Pueblo values in which the individual is absorbed into the community, the vision quest is rejected in favor of organized religion, and members live in settled villages.

In recent times another powerful influence has come into play: the surrounding culture of the United States, which favors not only settled communities and organized religion, but also individualism and personal destiny. The pressure of this influence is enormous, and the Navahos are changing with all possible speed. With their capacity to borrow and assimilate, they may in the end become the only Indian group to survive with a living culture still intact and linked to the Indian past.

THE CULTURAL VARIABLE

Kiev in his introduction to studies in primitive psychiatry discussed the importance of the cultural approach. This approach had been put forward as early as 1938 by Hallowell, based on his theory that learned responses predominate over innate behavior patterns. Such learned responses include the effects of traditional concepts, beliefs, and institutions which provide affective experiences for the individual. In this way culture becomes the primary frame of reference for all emotional responses, defining the degree to which they are expressed and the form they will take (1964: 24).

In any discussion of neurotic manifestations, whether in preliterate or literate societies, attention must be paid to the cultural or subcultural variables. Among well-known psychologists only Fromm (1955), Erikson (1950), and Horney

(1937) have given culture the prominent position it deserves. While family and interpersonal experience from birth are what give neurosis its "degree of presence" in an individual, culture gives it form and social context. The family and the individual are immersed in culture as a fish in the ocean. Decades of anthropology have shown that culture is in the bone; objectivity is an illusion when it comes to viewing one culture from the standpoint of another.

Behind the cultural variable stand certain psychological properties—the ability of the human mind to dissociate and compartmentalize—leading to the many faces of neurosis. If we postulate that the human mind has a basic need to remain integrated and in harmonious relation with its parts, we must also realize that this can be done only with the readiness to tolerate much pain and conflict. To avoid the "legitimate pain," as Jung called it—the pain of being alive in a conflicted world—the psyche has the automatic ability to dissociate one part of itself from another and even remain unconscious of its sacrifice. If the pain gets too great it can be shut off or amputated, but feelings go with it.

Pierre Janet, in his studies of hysteria, was the first to write extensively about dissociation. It is prominent in hysteria, but it is also a part of obsessive compulsion and other neurotic manifestations. Freud showed vividly and conclusively how these split-off (repressed) parts did not disappear, but returned in a repetitious compulsive way to force unwanted images, ideas, and behaviors upon the mind. Jung (1960) demonstrated how these split-off parts could organize themselves into a small symbolic pattern of their own, which he called a "feeling-toned complex." These complexes may be represented by anthropomorphic or theriomorphic symbols; they are centers of energy which may temporarily invade ego consciousness and take control.

According to Jung, "The existence of complexes throws serious doubt on the naive assumption of the unity of consciousness, which is equated with 'psyche,' and on the supremacy of will" (1960: 96). He linked complexes to the phenomena of dream symbology: "Dream psychology shows us plainly as could be wished how complexes appear and personify form when there is no inhibiting consciousness to suppress them" (p. 97). They are *splinter psyches*. He also put his finger on the core of neurotic dissociation: "One of the commonest causes is *moral conflict* which ultimately derives from the apparent impossibility of affirming the whole of one's nature." If this goes far enough and the energy in the complex is strong enough, then "unconsciousness helps the complex to assimilate even the ego, the result being a momentary and unconscious alternation of personality known as 'identification with the complex'" (p. 98). Depending on the degree of severity, such a state would be described in modern psychiatric diagnostic terms as anxiety panic, conversion hysteria, fugue and amnesic states, or even multiple personalities and psychosis.

Patients often attribute these experiences to forces outside themselves, and indeed they do come from outside the conscious ego. For naive persons the mind is entirely "outside," in a projected identity with surrounding natural and social forces. These split-off or unwanted psychic fragments are felt as intrusions: object intrusion, spirit intrusion, the malicious effects of witchcraft, or punishment imposed by supernaturals for the breach of taboo. It is frequently a form of intrusive *possession* from outside which overwhelms the integrity of the individual and causes mental illness.

In order to see how the "moral factor" enters into the formation of culturally determined neurotic patterns, it is necessary to investigate the focus of moral conflict within the culture as a whole. This was understood by an early investigator of the pathology and treatment of hysteria (an eminently fertile field) as early as 1853. In a book called *On the Pathology and Treatment of Hysteria,* Robert Carter, a perceptive general physician, made the following observation:

It is reasonable to expect that an emotion, which is strongly felt by great numbers of people, but whose natural manifestations are constantly repressed in compliance with the usages of society, *will be the one whose morbid effects are most frequently witnessed.* This anticipation is abundantly borne out by facts; the sexual passion in women being that which most accurately fulfills the prescribed conditions, and whose injurious influence upon the organism is most common and familiar. Next after it in power, may be placed emotions of a permanent character, which are usually concealed, because disgraceful or unamiable, as hatred or envy; after them others equally permanent, such as grief or care, but which, not being discreditable, are not so liable to be repressed.

(quoted in Veith, 1965: 201)

This was written of European society in the mid-nineteenth century. It could be modified to fit any other modern or preliterate society, though the focus of the moral conflicts would be different.

In any culture, as Geertz points out, there is an implicit ethos: "A people's ethos is the tone, character, and quality of their life, its moral and aesthetic style and mood; it is the underlying attitude toward themselves and their world that life reflects" (1973: 127). But each culture is different, each culture has a tendency of its own and heads in a different direction. Each is a different experiment in interaction of human life and nature. To quote Geertz once more: "Elaborate initiation rites, as among the Australians; complex philosophical tales, as among the Maori; dramatic shamanistic exhibitions, as among the Eskimo; cruel human sacrifice rites, as among the Aztecs; obsessive curing ceremonies, as among the Navaho; large communal feasts, as among various Polynesian groups—all these patterns and many more seem to one people or another to sum up most powerfully what it knows about living" (p. 132).

This list of cultures also reveals that in its particular specialty culture sometimes goes too far. Like many individuals, it seems to be headed in a certain direction and does not know when to stop. Cultural manifestations often become excessive in a particular quality. In the beginning that quality may have been a source of cultural richness—a boon to survival and a catalyst to growth. But as it expands it may become a burden to the members of the culture, a stultifying tradition, and finally a destructive influence. From any balanced viewpoint, if there is such, culture can create bad as well as good.

There will always be some in the culture who cannot meet the demands it places on its members. They will break down and need a suitable cure. In middle European society of the late nineteenth century, for instance, sexual restrictiveness was too great. There was a veritable epidemic of hysterical neurosis, and from the work of Charcot, Janet, and Freud a workable cure was evolved. If any cultural tendency goes too far and too many people are psychologically incapacitated by it, a major cultural shift is in the offing. We are then left with the idea of neurosis as a *cultural sign* indicating an excess. Culture does not have an unlimited license; it must reckon with the psyche. It must stay within certain bounds or it becomes a sick culture. If a remedy is not found, it will die.

POSSESSIVE STATES

What excessive quality is at the focal point of Navaho culture, creating the fear and ambivalence that necessitates such extensive curing ceremonies? In order to grasp this question, let me summarize an important study done by the psychologists Kaplan and Johnson on the form of psychiatric illness among the Navaho (1964). In examining over six

hundred cases they found four distinct patterns of psychopathology. One was schizophrenia, which seems to claim a
small percentage of all cultures. The other three—of which
two are neurotic and the third more in the nature of a character disorder—are directly relevant to our question. They are
moth craziness, ghost sickness, and crazy violence.

Moth craziness, or Iícháa, was the main type of Navaho
mental illness (ibid., p. 210). It includes such symptoms as
nervousness, fits of uncontrolled behavior, convulsions, rage,
and violence. Idiopathic epilepsy was sometimes confused
with these cases, but most were clearly hysterical. The chief
symptoms can be described as "fits and spells." This disorder
is associated with incest, and is connected with the myth of
Moth Way (see pp. 76–77).

The second type of illness, ghost sickness, is thought to be
closely associated with evil power and witches (ibid., p. 212).
The symptoms include weakness, bad dreams, feelings of
danger, confusion, and futility, loss of appetite, suffocation,
fainting, dizziness, and generalized anxiety. One observer, William Morgan, saw periods of great fear and anxiety emanating
from a feeling of helplessness caused by the eruption of unconscious impulses, over which the individual had no control. There were delusions, nightmares, and hallucinations.
The person feels that something evil, a ghost perhaps, is
persecuting him from outside. He is not responsible for his
behavior. One of my informants described the case of a
woman with swollen feet and internal pain whom he could
not cure, until she confessed that she had held the head of a
dying woman on her lap long after she had died, which might
have caused the sickness.

The third syndrome, crazy violence, is associated with
drunkenness (acute and chronic alcoholism) (ibid., p. 216).
No one who has been on the reservation for long can fail to
notice the epidemic proportions of severe alcoholism, yet this
syndrome has often been neglected. Kaplan and Johnson con-
tend that it is another type of possession. Often violent fits

of rage are released, and brutal murders and suicides are associated with this behavior. As opposed to the hysterical patients who do not take responsibility for their actions, these persons supposedly know they are being violent and anti-social, but do not care. Since this illness occurs most often in males, as in other Indian tribes it may be associated with the loss of prestige of male activity among the Navahos. They can no longer engage in their traditional occupations of hunting and warfare; only the religious ceremonialism remains in their sphere of activity. If Navaho men in the future can again find a sense of pride and accomplishment in their work, then the crazy violence may abate.

All these forms of illness have at their core the phenomenon of dissociation, leading to possession and socially undesirable behavior. Kaplan and Johnson conclude that it is a state of possession, though vaguely and subtly stated, that forms the core of the Navaho concept of mental illness (p. 206). I think this is in agreement with the historical trend of Navaho cultural adaptation manifested in several important ways: (1) excessive fear of the dead and their ghosts; (2) the development of elaborate ceremonies with strict regulation based on knowledge alone; (3) the avoidance of psychic possession and the vision quest; (4) the reluctant acceptance of the peyote religion by many of the traditional medicine men.

FEAR OF THE DEAD AND THEIR GHOSTS

The objects most feared by the Navaho are those connected with the possibility of psychic possession. The most striking of these is fear of the dead—fear not of death or afterlife, but of the dead body and the ghost connected with it. There is little ceremony for the dead: they are gotten rid of as quickly and cautiously as possible.

Kluckhohn (1962: 141) noted that every part of the funeral ritual is intended to prevent or dissuade the dead person from returning to threaten his relatives. Even dead animals, except those killed for food, are dangerous to look upon. To bury the dead requires such elaborate precautions that it is a great relief to the Navaho if a white person undertakes this responsibility (p. 138). This fear is traced to ghosts who may "chase people, jump upon them, tug their clothes or throw dirt upon them. Their actions are not only frightening in themselves but also are omens of disaster to come. When a Navaho thinks he has seen a ghost or where one has appeared in his dreams, he is sure that he or a relative will die unless the proper ceremonial treatment is successfully applied" (p. 139).

All this is in accordance with what Natani Tso said to me: "In the beginning when Navahos emerged from the first worlds to the present, the first deaths occurred. The dead one went down below. The people sprinkled ashes so that was taboo from now on. The person became an evil one or ghost." Asked if people who died became ghosts, he said, "Yes, they become ghosts. We heard about ghosts. They travel around, people get chased. That's why Evil Way is performed, to do away with evil spirits."

Juan Sandoval, who knew the Evil Branch of Ghost Way, described the old customs surrounding burial: "Years ago there was no cemetery. They buried the body in caves or dug a hole and buried it. Now they have boxes. First the body was cleaned and dressed. Two people do this who wish to do the burying. They fix the body and everybody else goes to another hogan. These two wear only moccasins and loincloths and are covered with ashes. There are no songs. You just don't talk, eat, or wash until the body is buried. Even the kids aren't allowed outside at this time. A pregnant woman mustn't look at the body. When they bury the body they shouldn't leave tracks around the spot. Tracks should be erased. Sweat shouldn't drop on the burial place, or blood from a scratch or wound. You shouldn't talk. If they do something wrong at the burial, then this thing will come back on them and make them sick, so they ask for my sing."

I have heard that in the past the hogan where the person died had to be torn down, and the family moved to another place. This fear also explains why the Navaho, almost alone among Indian tribes, would not join the Ghost Dance Religion of the 1890s: they wanted no part of a movement to communicate with the dead who were treated as cultural guardians. In many cultures the living look to ghosts or ancestors—those who have gone before into death—for guidance and spiritual protection, and toward them feel both fear and reverence. But the Navaho show mostly fear. The good part of the dead person has gone into nature; only the bad part remains to plague his survivors. Usually malicious, it causes ghost sickness and other serious misfortunes. My impression is that behind all the avoidance is a secret wish to be *possessed*, to enter into communion with the dead and have ecstatic visions. But this wish is strongly prohibited by the culture.

CEREMONIAL RESTRICTION

The chants themselves are hedged in by the strictest regulations. Prayers and songs must be word perfect; sand paintings must be exactly reproduced. The medicine man must have a cool head, a sure hand, and the concentration of a surgeon. There is little room for spontaneity. The whole chant system is quite remarkable for its intricately meshing symbolic parts. But there is another side to this: the obligation to guard against all the taboos and undergo extensive ceremonials may be financially and emotionally exhausting.

The chant system itself is built around a core of powerful symbolic agents that can both infect and cure. They are (to

name a few): hail, water, lightning, thunder, st
moths, butterflies, snakes, darkness, deer, corn, eagl
arrows, flint, mountains, and ghosts. Even the name
have magic power. The particular animals have a lon
ciation with shamanistic journeys and vision quests.
cause infection and disease, but only when they are approached or handled improperly. One informant said he had
performed Wind Way for a man and woman who had seen
a snake crawl across the doorway while they were eating.
The man had thrown a stick, hitting the snake, and blood
had spattered on the family. He also performed the Shooting
Chant for a man who had been herding sheep near Ponderosa
Springs, when lightning struck a pine tree and killed five
sheep; the lightning fumes had been inhaled by the man,
who became sick.

The powerful agents must be approached *properly*. This is
done in the chants. Besides the chant heroes, the animals and
powers of nature appear in the sand paintings as Wind
People, Thunder People, Lightning People, Snake People, Coyote People, etc. The patient is brought into contact with them
again, ritually and reverently, and because of the proper procedure they are now enjoined to cure.

AVOIDANCE OF STATES OF POSSESSION

One might speculate that the Navaho medicine men emulate
the importance and individuality of the northern shamans,
while repressing the shamans' susceptibility to trance possession and dramatic, ecstatic behavior. The Navaho use symbols instead.

In the cultures of the Plains Indians there are self-inflicted
punishments, painful sacrifices, difficult vows, and extreme
tortures designed to move the supernatural beings to pity.
The Navaho have freed themselves from all this. They do not

want the vision, the possession by the spirit, the vow, the immolation and pity. When a Plains Indian is visited by powerful supernaturals, he is forced to obey their dictates. Among the Sioux, for instance, an animal will occur in a dream and give the dreamer a special song efficacious in healing certain kinds of illness. From then on he has no choice: he must use that song to heal.

One Sioux medicine man dreamed that a buffalo came to take him on a journey to the lodge of the Buffalo People, where he was given a song and the power to heal (Densmore, 1943). In the Navaho myths almost the same thing happens to the chant heroes, but not to the medicine men. The Navaho who undertakes to become a medicine man does so freely, without having to wait upon visions or vows, and he may withdraw whenever he wishes. Furthermore the rites of diagnosing, which are trancelike in nature, are kept separate from the chant ceremonies proper. Sometimes the medicine men do their own diagnosing, but it is always separate from the ceremonial itself, and diagnosticians do not enjoy the high regard accorded the medicine men.

Also, while the Navaho do pay attention to dreams (as we have seen), they do not use the dreams in a direct way as for instance do the Yuman, who live just to the west along the Colorado River. Among the Yuman, an old medicine man who visited the spirit land in his dreams was said to have so much power that neither heat nor cold could hurt him; he cured with songs that the spirits had given him and his father (Densmore, 1965). But with the Navaho, dreams are only omens or signs of good or bad fortune. They do not usually cure, nor do they confer power and prestige; knowledge alone does that. Any altered states of consciousness are devalued by the Navaho and given a peripheral place in their ceremonies. They are very cautious about the use of dreams, trancelike states, and visions.

THE PEYOTE RELIGION

Within the boundaries of Navaho country the traditional Navaho religion has three competitors. They are the Christian religions (mainly Catholic and Mormon), modern medicine, and the peyote religion. The Navaho religion and these rivals do not always compete; sometimes they co-operate, though warily. The first two are definitely foreign (non-Indian), but have achieved a large measure of success and seem respected by most of the medicine men. To be sure, sometimes this respect is tempered with the insistence that the traditional Navaho way has a place beside them.

Regarding peyote, however, the medicine men I interviewed denied any relationship between it and the traditional curing ceremonies. Denet Tsosi said: "I don't understand it [the use of peyote] at all. I have no interest in it, so I don't bother to inquire about it. Quite a number of years ago, when I first came into this area, a group got together at Wheatfield. I didn't know about it until it was all over. I was a councilman at the time. When I went into Window Rock, I was called in by the police chief. He said: 'I heard you had a peyote meeting near your place. What do you know about it?' I told him I didn't know anything about it. If I'd been more curious at the time, I might have looked into it, but I didn't. I haven't been concerned with it since. It is a cactus plant used by some people in Mexico. It came over to Oklahoma and Texas and then to other Indian groups like the Utes and Taos Pueblo. It splits people up. It will do that to your people, too, if they use it."

When asked whether peyote interferes with chant practice, Denet Tsosi said: "When I learned my chants, they were the only thing being used by the Navaho. There was no such thing as peyote. The chants were the only thing used for illness. A fellow at Fort Defiance, a strong peyote user, comes to me when he wants a Navaho ceremony. One time he said to me, 'My friend, if you add peyote to your treatment, it would make it stronger.' I told him he comes to me when he wants a ceremonial, because he thinks it does some good. I don't want to mix the two. I am suspicious of these peyote users. Maybe they will slip some of their medicine into my pouch. I told him that if he still had faith in the chants, he should do them and drop peyote. If he didn't have faith, then he should drop the chants and go to peyote."

Another chanter, Natani Tso, said: "Many of these members of the Native American Church come to see me. They head up here when they need help. They need chant treatment like the others. There is no connection between the two."

To understand why this attitude is as strong as it is, one must know something of the peyote religion. It has been described fully by Aberle (1966) and La Barre (1938). There is no official dogma or priesthood within the movement; though Christian to some extent, it is really a pan-Indian religion. Originally it came from Mexico, but it spread extensively among Indian tribes within the United States. Recently it has gained a foothold on the Navaho reservation as a separate alternative to the traditional Navaho religion. Since the core of its sacrament is the use of peyote, which contains the psychedelic substance mescaline and comes from a small cactus found in the Southwest and Mexico, it has met strong opposition from conservative Indians and non-Indians alike. In some areas of the reservation I have been told that medicine men have a more friendly, or at least tolerant, attitude toward peyote.

The peyote ritual has many things in common with the traditional Navaho religion. Each meeting has a sponsor who calls the meeting for a specific purpose—usually to cure, but sometimes to give thanks or a special blessing. This sponsor corresponds to the patient in traditional Navaho ceremonials, who is the center of the gathering. Like the chant ceremonies, the peyote meeting takes place in a hogan, lasts all night, and involves many traditional songs and ritual drumming.

Participants move about the hogan clockwise. The whole ceremony is under the guidance of one man, called the Road-man, who is responsible for it. There is a great deal of traditional symbolism: an altar with the primary symbol, Chief Peyote; a firebird of glowing coals; symbolic foods such as corn, fruit, and meat; and powerful special ceremonies called the Midnight and Morning Water Calls. There is also a life way called the Peyote Path, symbolic of harmony and loving brotherhood, which can be compared with the traditional Pollen Path (Laney, 1972).

Even so, the difference between the peyote and Navaho religions is crucial. The peyote ceremony involves direct experience and spontaneous expression of religious emotion, while the traditional Navaho religion relies instead on symbol, knowledge, and ritual. Yet I was favorably impressed with the therapeutic value of the peyote ritual in providing an outlet for the repressed emotion of the Navaho people, especially the men, in an atmosphere of warmth, brotherhood, and faith. This is a task that perhaps the traditional religion was not fully prepared to meet.

CONCLUSION

All the considerations put forth in this chapter show fear of spirit possession to be one of the strongest influences in the formation of Navaho religion and other facets of Navaho culture. The traditional Navaho attitude toward visionary dreams and direct mystical experience is not openly hostile, but gently discouraging. Fear of possession is connected with the excessive fear of ghosts and the dead; with the strict taboos around burial practices; with the possessive forms of psychoneurotic illness described by Kaplan and Johnson; and with the ambivalence shown toward the use of peyote by the traditional medicine men.

The other side of the picture—the counterweight to fear of possession—is the Navaho reliance on reason and knowledge in regulating their moral and ethical behavior, and in building their extensive healing system. In a study of the Navaho moral code, Ladd (1957) characterized them as rational, prudent, and practical. When faced with a problem, they believe in talking it over, examining all sides, and arriving at a reasonable solution. By itself, appeal to authority or tradition is not a sufficient guide. The solution must be prudent, offering the greatest good to the welfare of the individual and the group, and it must be practical. The Navaho are primarily oriented toward what works. Their discussions center on what has worked in the past and what may be expected to work in the future.

These traits are closely connected with their idea of universal order. The world is filled with natural forces that operate according to well-defined laws governed by supernatural beings. Through detailed knowledge, the whole system of healing seeks to control the forces causing disharmony and disease. Thus that system is essentially rational, though based on premises different from scientific ones.

It is important to the Navaho that control and clarity of consciousness counterbalance the unconscious desire to "let go" and be carried out of oneself. Love of self-control has never allowed the Navaho to sacrifice these values for ecstatic visions. Nor do they have a place for sin as we conceive it. Reichard explains: "The code tells a Navaho what he should or should not do, what the punishment is—not for the transgression, but for the correction of error. . . . The nearest Navaho approach to the concept of sin is 'being out of order, lacking control,' a definition that involves rationalization, not salving a bad conscience; confession of error, not a feeling of guilt" (1950: 125). The laws regulating the universe, including the ceremonies of healing, were laid down in the beginning when the first beings emerged from the underworld. They have governed life ever since.

CHAPTER SIX

Return
to the Origins

Eliade has said of the origin myth: "As the exemplary model for all 'creation,' the cosmogonic myth can help the patient to make a 'new beginning' of his life. The *return to origins* gives the hope of rebirth. Now all the medical rituals we have been examining aim at a return to origins. We get the impression that for archaic societies life cannot be *repaired*, it it can only be *re-created* by a return to sources. And the 'source of sources' is the prodigious outpouring of energy, life, and fecundity that occurred at the Creation of the World" (1968: 30).

Thus the presentation of the origin myth in song, prayer, and sand painting is not only for the purposes of remembrance and education, but to allow the patient to identify with those symbolic forces which once created the world, and by entering into them to re-create himself in a state of health and wholeness. The healing myth is part of the cosmogonic myth and can be separated only partially and analytically from the greater myth of which it is an integral part. The origin myth of the Navaho stands at the very center of the entire complex, and all the chant myths branch out from it. Thus the return to origins is the first principle of symbolic healing. To understand this return in the Navaho context, we must gain some idea of the original cosmogonic myth from which the system of Navaho healing emerges.

THE ORIGIN MYTH

Several origin myths have been recorded from Navaho medicine men. The three most reliable and authentic are the ones I shall refer to here. The earliest was recorded by Washington Matthews (1897). The second is the emergence myth according to the Hanelthnayhe or Upward Reaching Way, recorded by Berard Haile (1908) and rewritten by Mary Wheelwright (1949). The third was given to Mary Wheelwright by Hosteen Klah (1942). All these myths have certain differences, but there is an overriding unity. We shall follow the main lines of progression and relate these to the healing process and its effect on the patient.

The strongest trend in the Navaho origin myths is the emergence out of darkness and chaos into light and order. The myth culminates in three significant events which together provide a foundation for Navaho culture: the growth and maturation of Changing Woman, the great Earth Goddess; the birth of her two sons, Monster Slayer and Child of the Waters, who begin the cycle of heroic myths that give rise to the chants; and the sons' journey to their Sun-Father to receive from him the power to rid the world of monstrous evils and make it ready for Navaho civilization. Let us examine how these events are depicted in the Upward Reaching Way, the story of the ascent of the primordial Navaho beings from the four underworlds below to the present world.

This particular type of origin myth, describing how man came out of a series of underworlds inside the earth, is common among the Indians of the Southwest, and the Navaho most probably borrowed it from the similar myths of the Pueblos. The Pueblo myths tell of a layered universe and a Creator—bisexual among the Zuñi, or feminine among the Keres—who made the first people in the lowest womb. The Sun-Father created two sons who went down and led the people up to the present world. These hero sons also killed monsters and made the earth habitable for men. In those days everyone understood one another: animals, plants, trees, and stones could talk, and the gods came in person rather than as masked dancers (Parsons, 1939; Underhill, 1965).

In the Navaho myth there is no mention of the original creation by Sun-Father or of aid coming from above. The first world is black (in Matthews's version, red)—a dismal and barren place. There are no mountains, no stones, no plant life, and no light, though several latent chthonic powers lie ready to set in motion the upward climb of the original beings. This world corresponds to what Erich Neumann called the matriarchal realm in which ego consciousness is at an infantile level and the maternal side is predominant. He said: "Anything big and embracing which contains, surrounds, enwraps, shelters, preserves, and nourishes anything small belongs to the primordial matriarchal realm" (1954: 14).

The original beings, the first forms of life, are present in the form of insects, which are neutral or free of evil. There is also Black God, the Navaho Fire God, who represents control of fire and fire-making, and who came into being with the earth. He is a dark masculine force deep within the Mother. Slow-moving and phlegmatic, and sometimes thought of as aged, he is also brave, and calm in the face of danger. Offerings to him must be exactly right. According to the Wheelwright version, he is a jealous and angry god, who began burning the lowest world and forcing the other beings to move to the world above.

First Man and First Woman were also in the lowest world. They were said to be transformed from two primordial ears of corn. In the myth they seem to be generally helpful in the progressive ascension, but there is about them a strong suggestion of evil and witchcraft. There also in the lowest world was Salt Woman—possibly the first earth form of Changing Woman. Said to be the companion of Changing Woman before there were people on the earth, she is stubborn and practical, but inclined to be helpful to man, though not tenderhearted. In some variants of the myth Begochidi and Coyote were already there.

Because of Fire God's anger (Klah version) or uncontrolled adulterous impulses (Matthews version), or because the lower world was not fit to live in (Haile version), the primordial beings made their way up to the second world.

In the second world, which is red (Haile) or blue (other versions), the beings were received as honored guests by the Swallow People, but they again entered into adulterous relations with the women, especially the wife of Swallow Chief, and were finally asked to move on (Matthews). First Man engaged in a powerful struggle with the Feline People, who were tricksters, and finally overcame them with his magic power (Haile).

In the second world Begochidi made a pair of twins, male and female, and he was pleased. Then he gave the Fire God permission to kill them, and made of their bodies the symbolic figures called Ethkay-nah-ashi, mysterious transmitters of life. He breathed into the male figure and there was a great sound: the cotton he had planted in four directions rose up and became clouds. As he breathed into the female figure, the four holy plants grew up under the clouds. So vegetation was created and the people were happy. But the Fire God threatened to burn the waters again, so they all moved up to the Third World (Klah and Wheelwright, 1942).

In the Third World, which is yellow, the beings encountered the wicked Snake People, and First Man put yellow and red streaks in the east, representing disease. The original beings had to make First Man a gift of a perfect shell disc, and then he removed the obstacles. In this world the people accused First Man of being evil, and he said: "It is true, my grandchildren, I am filled with evil, yet there is a time to employ it and another to withhold it" (Haile).

Then Begochidi created the rivers: a female river running from west to east turning south, and a male river running from north to south, crossing the female river and turning west. These rivers made a gigantic swastika shape whose intersection was called the Place of Crossing Waters. Begochidi breathed through the dead substance of the Ethkay-nah-ashi and gave life to water animals, monsters, lightning, cyclones, birds, trees, and all creation. He made new men and women, and all creation understood one language. He put the hermaphrodite in charge (Klah and Wheelwright, 1942).

In this moving upward through the lower worlds, Coyote's energy and First Man's cunning, though sometimes evil, were indispensable. The constant upward movement was necessary either because the lower worlds were barren, unsuitable, and full of dangerous animal people (Haile); or because the beings themselves were evil, and quick to offend their animal friends with adulterous actions (Matthews); or because the Fire God was angry at some slight and drove them upward by fire (Klah).

As the fourth world—the blue or white world—was reached, the primordial union was finally broken. When the beings entered this world it was said they were still evil, but the four mountains were placed in the four directions and were given their color and all their attributes. The land began to assume its form and contour. What once had been static, barren, and unconscious was now raised to the level of light and consciousness.

The hogan was established by First Man as a miniature cosmos with its opening toward the east, its fork posts representing deities, and all the powers of the universe ranged in their appointed places on the north and south side around the center, which was also the center of the world. Male and female genitalia were made and the first segregation of the sexes was begun. In this Coyote played an important part. This is where he said: "No one of you seems to be able to guess what these things are. I roam about and have little sense, but I have guessed all of them. You must all pay great attention to this ceremony since it concerns you all, for this is the Creation of Birth" (Haile, 1949: 14).

Throughout, the control of sexual impulses had been particularly difficult. Finally, because of some supposed wrongdoing on the part of the women, the men decided to separate from them. This carried the drama one step further than the separation of earth and sky, and symbolized the eternal separation of maleness and femaleness, hitherto joined in unconscious incest. Having the dominant role in this separation, the men fared better. They hunted, planted, and established the proper way things should be done; the first ceremonies came into being. Meanwhile the women became lax, dissolute, and degenerate.

But the sexual urge could not be controlled by either side. In an early version of the origin myth Badger wanted to copulate with them, but he had a penis crooked like a hook. It made them crazy with desire. They masturbated with a corncob, or tried to swim the river to get to the men. Some died crazed with desire (Stephen, 1930: 98, taken from a myth collected in 1885). The men worked harder, but were unable to control their sexuality. They used an antelope's liver with a hole in it to perform masturbation. Some who copulated with a deer were struck down by lightning as punishment. Others who copulated with an antelope doe or a mountain sheep were killed by a rattlesnake or a bear. Finally the men called the women back, and after considerable ceremonial purification established normal relations (*ibid.*, p. 99). Though necessary, the separation could not go too far!

The people were still in an evil (uncontrolled) state, the Navaho descriptions of which bring to mind the Biblical accounts of sexual license and promiscuity preceding the Flood. The flood came for the Navaho, too. Again it was Coyote—some say with the help of Spider Woman—who stole a baby with long black hair from the Water Monster at the place of floating water. Coyote kept the baby hidden under his blanket for four days, until the theft was finally discovered and the baby returned, but not before a great noise arose in the east and traveled around. Begochidi knew it was a storm and sent out messengers for news. A crow went to the east and found a black storm coming; a magpie went to the south and reported a blue storm on its way; to the west, a hummingbird told of a yellow storm; to the north a dove sighted a white storm. Then the people, animals, and all created things gathered plants and put them in a great reed. Finally they made the reed grow, and Locust was the first to burrow through the crust of mud and water into the present world (Klah and Wheelwright, 1942).

Since no one else would venture up first, Begochidi went himself. He found an island in the middle of the water. He went to a white cloud in the east and found Talking God. Then he went to a blue cloud in the south and found Bringer of Seeds. He found Calling God on a yellow cloud to the west, and another Bringer of Seeds to the north. They all rejoiced (Klah and Wheelwright, 1942). In this world everything was properly placed. The Sun and Moon were fixed. Dawn, darkness, winds, the stars, and the seasons all began to function in their proper order. The male genitalia remained in the sky, and the female genitalia on earth. The separation of the sexes was at last achieved, and the womb of the mother successfully transcended.

Sheila Moon says in her study of the origin myth: "But a final unifying spiritual principle is yet to come. In the beginning the warm, dark earth (Mother-night-nature) held all the creatures in her womb. That state is no more. . . . For when consciousness becomes a goal, unconscious totality must be renounced, lost, and the undifferentiated unity falls apart. This unity must be again bound up and comforted, but in another way and by another sort of female principle. There is needed a less time-bound Eros life and relationship begotten by the spirit. Changing Woman is born at this moment, with Darkness as her mother and Dawn as her father" (1970: 175).

Thus time, space, and consciousness are established out of darkness and chaos. The origin-myth cycle ends and the Blessing Way cycle begins at this point. The mother womb no longer surrounds and suffocates, but has been transformed into "the spiritual-psychic aspect of the feminine, the image contained in the idea, presiding over the making of man against the monsters. As such she goes beyond nature, beyond the lunar cyclic rhythms of primitive existence; this is indicated by Changing Woman's disavowal of First Man and First Woman as parents" (*ibid.,* p. 178). She becomes mother of the twin culture heroes, filled with maternal solicitude and yet willing to set her children free to return to their Sun-Father. She is the grand symbol of periodic rejuvenation in the life of earth and man. At the core of the Navaho mystery, she represents a final wisdom accessible only to those who are steeped in the meaning of these powerful symbols. "She is the mother in a transforming and releasing fashion. She is the divine and the eternal *within* the substance and the material" (p. 179).

SONGS OF CREATION

The structure of symbolic healing can be further understood in a cycle of songs assembled by Hosteen Klah to outline the creation myth. In his original creation chant there were 568 songs illustrating this structure. I will give some examples from these songs, which were collected by Dr. Harry Hoijer

(1929). The songs are more intense and immediate than the myths. The myth is only the narrative background for the processes—purification, evocation, identification, and transformation—that occur in the songs, prayers, and rites.

Purification is illustrated by a song that is sung in the sweat house. This song expresses the idea that everything has been put in its place and is therefore in its original, pure form.

> *The earth has been laid down; the earth has been laid*
>   *down;*
> *The earth has been laid down; it has been made.*
>
> *The earth spirit has been laid down,*
> *Its top is clothed with all the growing things,*
> *It has been laid down;*
> *The sacred words have been laid down;*
> *The earth has been laid down, it has been made.*
>
> *The sky has been set up; the sky has been set up;*
> *The sky has been set up; it has been made.*
>
> *The black sky has been set up,*
> *Its top is clothed with all the heavenly bodies,*
> *It has been set up;*
> *The sacred words have been set up;*
> *The sky has been set up; it has been made.*
>   (Sweat House Song number 8, first part)

The song goes on to describe the same laying down of mountains, waters, water spirits, clouds, and fog.

The songs having to do with evocation are best represented by the Tobacco Song. Among the American Indians smoking tobacco has always been a ritual action that by its thin blue smoke represented communication with the spirit world. The Tobacco Song describes the preparation of an offering for the gods.

> *I prepare it for him, I prepare it for him;*
> *I, I am he who steps around with soft stuffs,*
> *I prepare it for him;*

By means of a white shell pipe, I prepare it for him;
By means of wide leaves, I prepare it for him.
By means of a plant, I prepare it for him;
As he smokes, as he blows out the smoke, a multitude of
    people
Come wearing soft stuffs, they come in to me;
As they come in with me, they go out with me;
Though many come in, no one is harmed; I prepare it for
    him;
I, I am Sahanahray Bekay Hozhon, I prepare it for him.
(Tobacco Song number 3, first part)

The Navaho words in the last line are untranslatable holy
words, but they mean something like ultimate beauty and
peace (see Chapter Nine, p. 224).

The culmination of the song rites, like that of the prayer
and sand-painting rites, is the identification of the patient,
the medicine man, and the audience with one of the powerful deities. This process is illustrated by a last example which
identifies the singer with the earth spirit who is Changing
Woman, although she is not mentioned by name. Here is the
song in its complete form:

It is lovely indeed, it is lovely indeed, it is lovely indeed,
    it is lovely indeed, it is lovely indeed.
I, I am the spirit within the earth;
    it is lovely indeed, it is lovely indeed,
    it is lovely indeed, it is lovely indeed,
The feet of the earth are my feet;
    it is lovely indeed [repeat three times]
The legs of the earth are my legs;
    it is lovely indeed [repeat three times]
The bodily strength of the earth is my bodily strength;
    it is lovely indeed [repeat three times]
The thoughts of the earth are my thoughts;
    it is lovely indeed [repeat three times]
The voice of the earth is my voice;
    it is lovely indeed [repeat three times]
The feather of the earth is my feather;

it is lovely indeed [repeat three times]
All that belongs to the earth belongs to me;
  it is lovely indeed [repeat three times]
All that surrounds the earth surrounds me;
  it is lovely indeed [repeat three times]
I, I am the sacred words of the earth;
  it is lovely indeed [repeat eight times].

(Song of the Earth Spirit, number 12)

Here the earth spirit no longer exists apart from man. She is part of his essence, as he is part of hers. The healing transformation occurs through the loveliness of her image.

THE SAND PAINTINGS

The sand paintings of Blessing Way center around fertility, Changing Woman, and man's emergence into the present world. Corn and Corn People, Pollen Boy and Corn Beetle Girl are found in many of the paintings. Images of Changing Woman are found in no other sand paintings except those of Blessing Way. In one called Wide Cornfield she is shown as a maiden all in white with long black hair, standing between and touching two tall corn plants. In others she is shown in association with Corn Beetle and Pollen Boy. In several paintings the Place of Emergence is shown as a large circle at the center, with the sacred mountains, sacred plants, clouds, animals, and birds arranged around it. The patient is placed in the midst of this world, surrounded by symbols of growth, fertility, and immense creative power (Wyman, 1970: 65–102).

One of the sand paintings made for Blessing Way is a vivid abstract design representing man's journey through life (P1#4). The main figure is a large white rectangle representing the present world. At the bottom, the footsteps of man are shown coming from the underworld along a red and blue path, the path of the uninitiated. First, he must pass through the gateway formed by two Holy People, the Ethkay-nah-ashi, meaning "Those who go together." They are said to be the gods through whom the spirit of man is transmitted into substance. As man is created between their outstretched arms, the path becomes yellow. It has been blessed and has become the Pollen Path (see Chapter Nine).

In this sand painting the path next traverses the present world in the form of a corn plant passing through the center of the painting from top to bottom. The stalk is contained in a white field bordered in yellow—the holy field of ritual ceremony that is man's life. The footsteps follow this path up-ward, encountering first the female rainbow arching on the right side of the cornstalk, and then its complementary oppo-site, the jagged male lightning on the left. On both sides of the plant in the white field are the figures of Dontso, the Big Fly. As a spiritual messenger he tells the chant heroes what to do and what to avoid, when to obey and when to rebel. Finally the path emerges at the top and proceeds past the fig-ure of the Bluebird, the symbol of new beginnings and spiritual joy.

THE BLESSING WAY CYCLE

The principle of return to the origin is illustrated most fully in the Blessing Way cycle. Blessing Way began on the rim of the Place of Emergence and includes all the important events which occurred afterward, including the placing of the inner forms in all things, building the first hogan, and giving the first no-sleep ceremony. It includes Changing Wom-an's birth and her miraculously rapid maturation to puberty. Her puberty ceremony became a prototype for every adoles-cent girl on the occasion of the first menses.

Not long after her maturation, Changing Woman was impregnated by the Sun and gave birth to the Warrior Twins, Monster Slayer and Child of the Water. They inaugurate a new cycle (discussed in Chapter Eight) in which they journey to their Sun-Father to obtain from him the power to rid the earth of monsters. Changing Woman is also credited with bestowing corn and both domestic and game animals on mankind. In one myth it is said that the ancestors of the Navaho themselves were created from little balls of her skin.

Later on, when the gods were moving farther away from mankind, she was persuaded by her warrior sons to move to an island off the western shore (some locate it off California). She was very reluctant to go and afraid she would be lonely, but she was promised a most beautiful and luxurious house equal to Sun's house in the east. She was offered power over all rain and vegetation, eternal youth, and custody of the "road of perfection" (sa'ah naagháí bik'eh hózhóón). Still, all this did not move her until war was threatened. The last to go was Child of the Water, her favorite. She had hoped that he would stay with her, but when he said he wanted to go with his brother, she consented. The myth says: "As her baby went out of sight in the darkness, though she had sent the others away quickly without indulging in regrets, Changing Woman wept" (Reichard, 1950: 418).

Part of the Blessing Way myth is a clan origin myth which details the inception of the Navaho clans; then the myth closes with the story of the abduction of two special children, their journey to Changing Woman's home in the west where they are taught Blessing Way, and their return home to bring the ceremony to the people. The children later depart in the manner of the chant heroes to live with the supernaturals, but the Navaho keep the ceremony as a precious heritage.

Blessing Way is not concerned with the healing of a specific disease, but with the establishment of peace and harmony. Nothing connected with evil, witchcraft, sorcery, or imperfection is allowed to enter the main body of Blessing

Way. Blessing Way does touch on the healing of mental disturbances which upset a person's harmonious balance. Wyman says of it:

> Blessing Way practice embraces birth and adolescence, the home or hogan, weddings, maintenance and acquisition of properties, protection against accident, forewarning in dream and imagery, an endeavor to prolong life as long as possible. No other ceremonial in the Navaho system offers the native assistance in every walk of life as Blessing Way does. It knows a solution for disturbing dreams and fancies. In social affairs it strengthens leaders. In religious affairs it adjusts mistakes and errors. It provides a powerful medicine to acquire the comforts of life. It makes the goal in life—old age—a possibility.
>
> (1970: 8)

According to the medicine men themselves, Blessing Way is also the main stem from which all the other chantways derive. In a study of Navaho pottery David Brugge found evidence that Blessing Way assumed its present form about the middle of the eighteenth century as "the core of a reassertion of the Athapaskan way of life" (1963: 22–25). So from the pottery there is evidence that Blessing Way is at least that old, and maybe older. The Navaho themselves trace it back to the first ceremony performed at the rim of the Place of Emergence.

The performance of Blessing Way occupies the better part of two days. It is often given without sand paintings or prayer sticks. No medicines are used and medicine songs are absent. The preparations begin on the afternoon of the first day, during which all necessary provisions are brought. Usually a group of people, including relatives of the patient and friends of the medicine man, attend the performance; the patient must provide enough food for all. At one ceremony the patient brought a live sheep, which when butchered provided mutton for the duration of the ceremony. The patient was also required to present to the medicine man a special ceremonial basket, several different kinds of print material or sateen, and three yards of pure white material. These materials were folded together to form the "altar" on which the medicine man laid out the contents of his medicine bundle.

At the beginning of the ceremony the medicine man usually washes his hair in yucca suds, puts on his finest jewelry, and lays out the contents of his Blessing Way medicine bundle. The most important item in this bundle is the mountain-soil bundle, which contains bits of soil from the four sacred mountains that mark the boundaries of the Navaho land. In fact, it is the only piece of religious property absolutely necessary for the performance of Blessing Way. Each portion of the sacred soil is supposed to be wrapped in an unwounded buckskin, and a recognition jewel is tied to the bottom of each bag. Pollen and sometimes other properties are added and the whole is wrapped in the buckskin, with a white shell bead on the outside to mark the position of the east bundle. Once the bundle has been closed it is not disturbed, and it is guarded carefully as an heirloom of the singer and his family or clan.

The medicine bundle I saw also contained a flint crystal, a bag of pollen with an organite stone to keep it "alive," two pieces of wood from lightning-struck trees, and two talking prayer sticks, male and female. A turquoise bead indicated the male stick and a white shell bead, the female. A feather attached to the bundle ensured its liveliness and energy. The patient held the mountain-soil bundle and the two talking prayer sticks when the important prayers were being given.

But the true power of the Blessing Way ceremony lies not in its ritual behavior, but in the songs and prayers which identify the patient with the inner forms of the very earth itself. The Navaho believe that all natural things in themselves are devoid of life except for an inner form which is personified in human shape. This inner form gives life to all things.

*The patient in a Blessing Way ceremony is purified
with suds from yucca root*

In the first ceremony at the Place of Emergence, First Man created what is thought to be the earth's form and the inner forms of all things. These became the Holy People. "When he had covered them four times as described, a young man and woman first arose from there. Absolutely without their equals in beauty, both had long hair reaching to their thighs. . . . To fix your gaze on them was impossible, the glare from them was surprisingly bright. 'This is the only time that any of you have seen them, from now on none of you will see them again. Although they are right around you, even though they are taking care of your means of living to the end of your days around you, none of you will ever see them again,' he told them. . . . First Man announced, 'All these things (that exist) will have inner forms,' but added nothing more" (Wyman, 1970: 112).

These two persons created by First Man are usually referred to as Long-Life Boy and Happiness Girl. These names hardly convey their numinous power. Together they symbolize duration and continuance of happy conditions from the past into the present and future. They represent thought and speech, the supreme achievements of human life through which, especially in prayer, one can make contact with the supernatural world. They are the inner forms of the earth and as such represent the esoteric goal of Blessing Way. Because they bring together male and female, winter and summer, thought and speech, duration and contentment, they are prime examples of the reconciling and transforming symbol. They can hardly be visualized because of the light they radiate, but if they are understood in their hidden meanings, which one must meditate to appreciate, then the conditions they symbolize become inner reality (*ibid.*, pp. 29–30).

At the very beginning Blessing Way is concerned with the creation of the hogan in which the ceremony is to take place. The actual ceremony begins with a blessing of the four main posts of the hogan, and with the singing of the hogan songs, which conclude with a prayer given by the medicine man

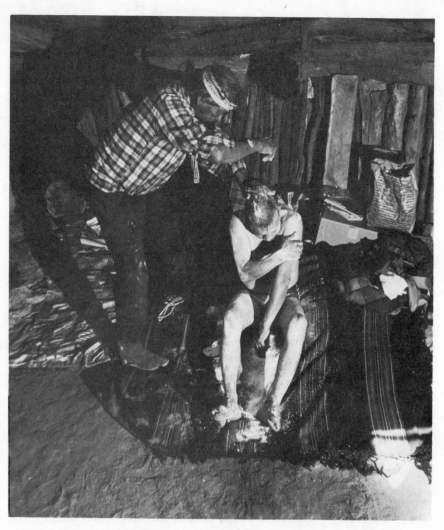

Medicine man administers ritual bath to Blessing Way patient

while the patient holds the mountain-soil bundle. The Hogan Songs dedicate the hogan anew to its religious purpose. They describe the setting up and blessing of the original hogan. The support pole to the east is dedicated to Earth Woman, the one to the south is dedicated to Mountain Woman, and the poles to the west and north to Water Woman and Corn Woman. The ensuing prayers and songs pay increased attention to the identification of the patient with the inner forms of the earth, the mountains, Changing Woman, Talking God, and other deities.

Here is one example of such a prayer to Earth's inner form:

It is surprising, surprising . . . yi ye!
It is the very inner form of earth that continues to move
*   with me,*
that has arisen with me,
that is standing with me,
that indeed remains stationary with me.
Now it is the inner form of long life,
now of happiness that continues to move with me,
that has arisen with me,
that is standing with me,
that indeed remains stationary with me.
Surprising, surprising.

                                        (Wyman, 1970: 136)

The process of identification is described in great detail with every subtle nuance. If followed with concentration, this process brings the symbol to life and gives it the power to heal.

Songs describe how Changing Woman was found on the summit of Gobernador Knob by Talking God and First Man. Here is an excerpt from one of the song series:

Now on the summit of Gobernador Knob
he found her, he found her, ni yo o.
Talking God found her,
he found Changing Woman, ni yo o.
Now dark cloud, male rain, rainbow and collected wa-
*   ters lay*

there when he found her.
Cornbeetle's frequent call with its pretty voice
lay there when he found her.
As long-life-happiness he found her.
Before her it was blessed,
behind her it was blessed,
when he found her, he found her, ni yo o.

(ibid., pp. 141–42)

After the songs describing Changing Woman's maturation and first and second puberty ceremonies, there are many songs describing Talking God's part as a mentor and teacher. This section is called Blessing Way's Blessing Part, and it is said to be the main set of songs.

When Changing Woman departed for her home in the west, she left without giving instructions for the performance of Blessing Way. Thus two children of Rock Crystal Talking God had to be carried to her house and instructed. They were picked up in a cornfield, and before entering her home they were subjected to a purifying bath, because of the human smell that clung to them.

On the second day of Blessing Way a mound, called the corn-soil mound, is placed in the middle of the hogan. On this mound, which is marked with a white cross in corn meal, the yucca suds are prepared which the medicine man uses in a purifying ritual to cleanse the patient in the same way as the two children. The suds are applied to the patient from the feet upward to the head. Afterward the same application is made with corn meal. Through this ritual the patient is identified with the corn deities and with the two children who were abducted and taught by Changing Woman. All during the ceremonial baths the medicine man sings songs linking the patient with the inner forms of corn and pollen.

The ceremony of the last night consists of singing continuously from about ten or eleven o'clock to dawn. The number of songs will vary with the length of the night. Many different sequences may be used, but the evening will always begin with the Hogan Songs and end with the Dawn Songs. Other sequences may include Talking God Songs, Songs of the Inner Forms of the Mountains, Songs of the Earth, Songs about the Origins of Changing Woman, Songs of Talking God's Hogan, Blessing Way's Blessing Part, Songs of the Corn Beetle, etc.

Here is a last example of one of the Dawn Songs:

> *'e ye . . . there is a thrill in its call for me, it calls to me.*
> *Crystal Boy I am as it calls to me.*
> *To the summit of Blanca Peak it calls for me,*
> *Now it is your Talking God Boy who calls for me, ni yo o.*
> *He has a small bluebird for a headplume as he calls to me.*
> *At its tip a cornbeetle swings with it as it calls to me, ni yo o.*
> *I step along in pollen as it calls to me, ni yo o.*
> *A rainbow dark in color encircles me as it calls to me, ni yo o.*
> *With it various fabrics encircle me as it calls to me.*
> *With the pollen of this, keeping it invisible, it encircles me as it calls to me.*
> *Now I am long life, now happiness as it calls to me.*
> *Before me it is blessed as it calls to me, behind me it is blessed as it calls to me, there is a thrill in its call to me, ni yo o.*

(ibid., p. 160)

At the first hint of dawn the patient goes outside the hogan, faces east, and breathes in the dawn four times.

Even with such a brief description of this profound and beautiful ceremony, one can see that it is an orderly but mystical penetration into the mysteries of fertility and healing. The patient is steeped in the origins and mythological history of the Blessing Way chant. The images are built up detail by detail, in slow and painstaking repetition. The patient is closely and repeatedly linked with the inner forms of Earth, Changing Woman, Corn, Talking God, and other deities. The beauty and power of each sacred personage is patiently explored, and the emotional effect is repeatedly emphasized by expressions of surprise and delight. The songs, myth, rites, and prayers are welded together intimately and intensively, so as to produce in the patient the great concentration necessary to unite psychically with these Radiant Powers that can give release from pain and sorrow, bestow strength and vitality, and point the way to a long and joyous experience of life.

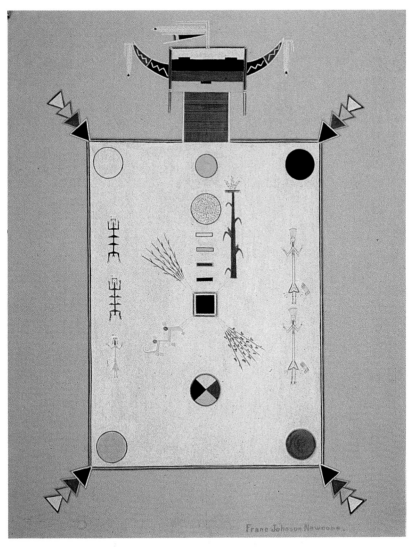

White Spirit Land sand painting from Blessing Way.
(The Wheelwright Museum of the American Indian, Santa Fe, New Mexico)

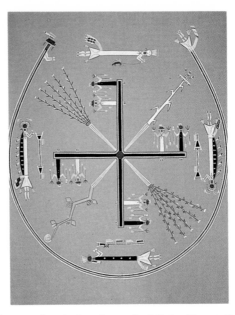

Whirling Log sand painting from the Night Chant. *See pp. 86-87.*
(The Wheelwright Museum of the American Indian, Santa Fe, New Mexico)

Emergence sand painting from Blessing Way.
(The Wheelwright Museum of the American Indian, Santa Fe, New Mexico)

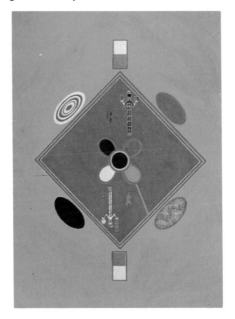

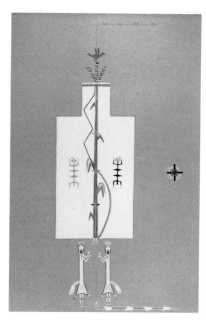

White Earth sand painting from Blessing Way. *See pp. 121-122.*
(The Wheelwright Museum of the American Indian, Santa Fe, New Mexico)

Endless Snake sand painting from the Beauty Chant. *See p. 217.*
(The Wheelwright Museum of the American Indian, Santa Fe, New Mexico)

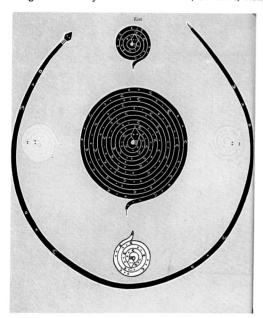

Holy People and Buffalo sand painting from the Male Shooting Chant. *See pp. 220-221.*
(The Wheelwright Museum of the American Indian, Santa Fe, New Mexico)

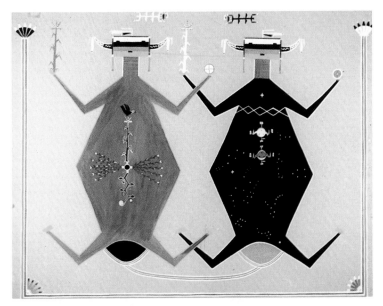

Mother Earth and Father Sky sand painting from the Male Shooting Chant. *See p. 206.*
(*The Wheelwright Museum of the American Indian, Santa Fe, New Mexico*)

First Night Dancers sand painting from the Night Chant. *See pp. 87-88.*
(*The Wheelwright Museum of the American Indian, Santa Fe, New Mexico*)

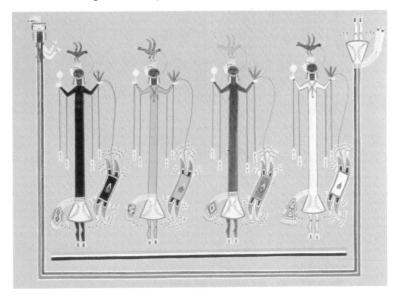

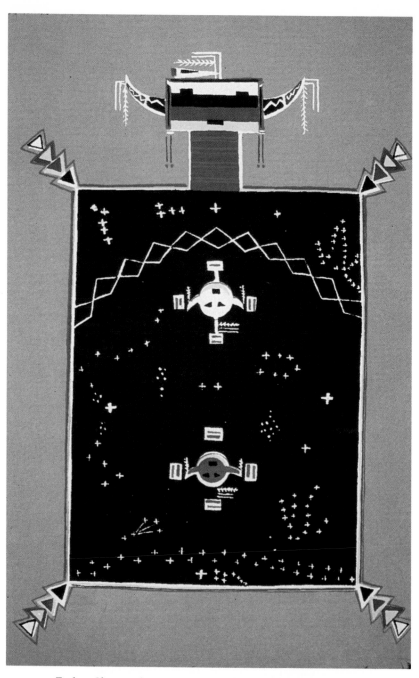

Father Sky sand painting from Blessing Way. *See p. 206.*
(The Wheelwright Museum of the American Indian, Santa Fe, New Mexico)

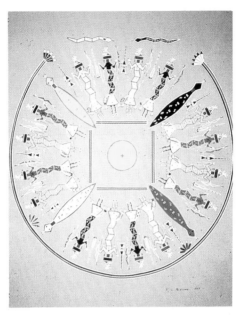

Snake People sand painting from the Male Shooting Chant. *See p. 217.*
(The Wheelwright Museum of the American Indian, Santa Fe, New Mexico)

Night Sky sand painting from the Hail Chant. *See p. 214.*
(The Wheelwright Museum of the American Indian, Santa Fe, New Mexico)

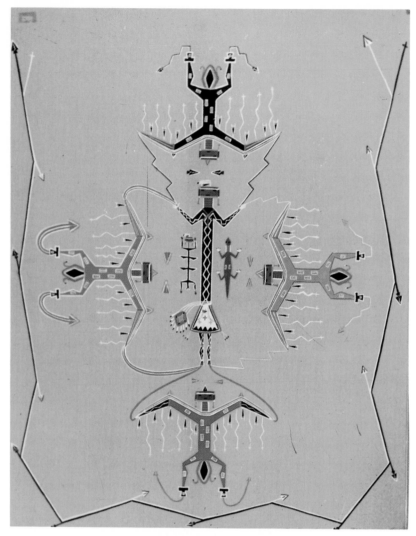

Holy Man and Thunderbirds sand painting from the Male Shooting Chant. *See p. 218.*
(*The Wheelwright Museum of the American Indian, Santa Fe, New Mexico*)

CHAPTER SEVEN

The Ritual Control of Evil

Shortly before his death Kluckhohn wrote: "While a comprehensive interpretation of any myth or of mythologies must rest upon the way in which themes are combined . . . nevertheless the mere recurrence of certain motifs in varied areas separated geographically and historically tells us something about the human psyche. It suggests that the interaction of a certain kind of biological apparatus in a certain kind of physical world with some inevitables of the human condition (the helplessness of infants, two parents of different sex, etc.) bring about some regularities in the formation of imaginative productions, of powerful images" (1960: 48).

Evil, in the form of hatred or animosity, is one of those inevitables. If it were to go unchecked, it would destroy the social fabric of culture. So there are always effective symbolic methods for isolating and controlling it. In the same article quoted above Kluckhohn noted that, of all cultural phenomena, the themes of witchcraft are the most wide-spread. According to a large-scale survey of ethnographic data, even certain details recur: (1) the presence of weird animals who move about at night with miraculous speed, gathering in witches' sabbaths to work evil; (2) the notion that illness, emaciation, and eventual death can result from their magic, or from the introduction of certain poisonous substances into the victim's body; and (3) some connection between witchcraft and incest.

These elements are found so regularly that Clements (1932) postulated that they were part of an original Paleo-lithic cultural complex which persisted and became diffused throughout the world. Even so, the complex varies greatly in degree and configuration, depending on the ethos of the par-ticular culture into which it must be integrated. It can be an obsession in one culture and a mere trace in another. The witchcraft that played such a prominent part in European history and persisted until modern days is a related phenom-enon. Though still connected with the ancient forms, it has branches which recognize the use of witchcraft for good as well as evil.

In his classical study of Navaho witchcraft, Kluckhohn (1967) found no hard evidence that Navaho witches actually exist, but there are extensive reports of their activities and most Navahos believe in them. First Man and First Woman were the first to practice a prototype of witchcraft in the pre-emergence period; they were the founders of Witchery Way. Witches are believed to grind the flesh of corpses, preferably children, into a pollenlike powder, which they drop into the hogan of their intended victims. Dramatic symptoms of ill-ness, including black and swollen tongue, fainting, and syn-cope, should follow, and the victim is thought to waste away and die. Witches, both men and women, are associated with the dead and with incest. Part of the initiation into Witchery Way is said to be the killing of a sibling or near relative. Greed and envy motivate the witch; he is said to obtain valuable articles by grave robbing. He can move about at night and appear in the form of various animals: wolves, coyotes, bears, owls, foxes, or crows. Witches may gather at meetings which an informant described as "just like a bad sing" (Kluckhohn, 1967: 25–30).

Kluckhohn called a second category of Navaho witchcraft sorcery, a possible branch of Witchery Way. The sorcerer is not as active or dramatic as the witch. He works his malevolence from a distance by means of special charms or spells, using bits of the intended victim's bodily secretions or personal possessions, which he buries in a grave or under a lightning-struck tree. The sorcerer recites his spells and waits for the victim to die. The spell may be chanted as a prayer, sung, or spoken as a formula, and there may even be special evil-wishing sand paintings. It is said that the sorcerer makes doll-like images of the person he intends to kill and tortures these effigies. Richard Van Falkenberg found a small image made from pinewood in a cave near Lukachukai, with a turquoise bead punched into its heart. Not only people but animals, grain crops, and other personal property may be bewitched. Apparently it is thought that special winds and some animals, notably dogs, can also perform sorcery. By the use of the secret sorcery the weak, the dependent, or the old may threaten those who become too strong or arrogant (Kelly, Lang, and Walters, 1972).

The third category, which he called wizardry, Kluckhohn thought to be of more recent origin. The wizard projects an object into his intended victim, causing injury and illness. As possible objects used by wizards informants mentioned ashes from a ghost-haunted hogan, beads that belonged to the victim, bits of bone or teeth from a corpse, grains of sand from a red anthill, pieces of yucca, porcupine quills, olivella shells, deer hair, wildcat's whiskers, or fragments of rocks burned for a sweat bath. The objects are shot into the victim's body—a practice referred to as "bean shooting." As in witchcraft and sorcery, the killing of a sibling or other close relative seems to be necessary for initiation into wizardry (Kluckhohn, 1967: 34–35).

The fourth category of witchcraft is Prostitution Way. Kluckhohn thought this was a combination of several activities, one of which was the use of certain plants including datura and poison ivy as "love magic," or to ensure success in gambling, hunting, or trading. Kluckhohn called this "frenzy witchcraft." The intended victim is secretly given one of the plants in food or cigarettes, or possibly by kissing (unkindest cut of all!). Practitioners of "frenzy witchcraft" do not engage in the more nefarious practices of the other groups.

Prostitution Way may also refer to a chant used to cure victims of "frenzy witchcraft." It has never been described, but it was said to be good not only for victims of "frenzy witchcraft" but also for lewd women. It was closely linked with Coyote Way and Moth Way, and may have used datura in its rites. There may have been prayer sticks and small sand paintings. This chant is probably now extinct (ibid., pp. 36–42).

Gall medicine is a specific antidote for witchcraft. The gall of eagle, bear, mountain lion, and skunk are most frequently used, but wolf, badger, deer, and sheep are mentioned. Another antidote is ground corn, which Navahos may carry when they feel themselves to be in dangerous areas (ibid., p. 47). Ceremonial knowledge and equipment are certain protection against witchcraft. Strong chanters who are in possession of ceremonial knowledge feel themselves most immune from witches. However, chanters are often suspected of being witches themselves. Prayer ceremonials, especially the prayers of liberation, are great cures for witchcraft. Evil Way chants may be used (pp. 50–51). Sometimes it is said that curing an illness caused by witchcraft is possible only if a confession is forced from the witch, or better still if the witch dies. In former times accused witches were often executed in the belief that this was the only way to cure the victim. But a confession was sometimes accepted and the witch exiled.

All this provides a highly dramatic way of handling excess hostility. Kluckhohn says: "The existence of this belief in Navaho culture permits the socially tolerated expression of direct and displaced aggression. It channels the expression of aggression. . . . But my thesis is not that given the amount and kind of aggression which exists in Navaho society witchcraft belief *must* exist. My thesis is only that given these conditions some forms of release must exist. When other forms are inadequate, and when the witchcraft patterns were historically available, witchcraft belief is a highly adjustive way of releasing not only generalized tension but also those tensions specific to Navaho social structure" (1967: 106). But of course many innocent men and women were tortured and killed because they were suspected of witchcraft not only in Europe and Salem, but also among the American Indians in times past. That was the price paid for this way of releasing social tension.

THE EVIL-CHASING PRAYERS

The social displacement of excess anger and aggression into the symbolic mode of witchcraft gives it reality and vitality. It becomes a real carrier of evil and must be neutralized by another symbolic system, the chantways, which in symbolic terms can attract good and exorcise evil.

Contrary to Christian dogma, with its strict division of holy personages into good and bad, Navaho religion recognizes intermediate deities of every shade. Certain personages such as Changing Woman are nearly all good, and others like White Thunder are nearly always destructive. Coyote, the embodiment of mischief, often supplies the energy and the deep wisdom of including the negative side as a necessary ingredient in creation. This is illustrated by his insisting that death be included in mortal life, whereas the other supernaturals were in favor of *letting* men live forever. Coyote also injects disorder and meaninglessness into what might be too tight and orderly.

Although Navaho religion seeks mainly to integrate all things within a framework of cosmic harmony, there is always a residue, called *tcindi,* which cannot be included in that harmony and must be rejected. *Tcindi* is associated with sorcery and witchcraft; its rejection is accomplished by the evil-chasing prayers. By the exact wording of the prayer text and by carefully controlled symbolic devices, the evil power is brought under control and bent to the will of the medicine man. In one type of prayer the evil is banished beyond all earthly boundaries and the witch destroyed. In another type the evil is concentrated in a limited space and there disarmed by the blessings of the medicine man. In both cases the medicine man identifies with the patient in his confrontation with evil, and in almost all the prayers handles the evil so closely that he nearly identifies with it himself. In certain of the prayers he does finally identify himself with it, thus risking all the effects of evil upon himself in order to banish it from the patient. The risk seems more apparent than real, but in the context of a ceremonial system where evil *is* evil, it is a serious matter.

The first prayer we shall consider was given by Natani Tso in August 1969 at his ceremonial hogan near Rock Point. He had just finished a sand painting of four Star People, each carrying a large arrow in one hand and a large bow in the other. The color variations in the sand painting, repeated in the prayer, were like variations on a musical theme which repeats the same configuration many times with a slightly different elaboration. The first warrior was made of dark blue outlined in white, and the second of light blue outlined in yellow; the third was mostly of yellow outlined in dark blue, and the fourth of white outlined in dark blue, completing the theme. The bolder, more masculine colors were always complemented by the softer, more feminine hues. By the symbolic process of multiplication and color complementation, all four warriors formed a whole in which the stronger and more masculine qualities contrasted with the gentler and more feminine ones. The fact that they were dressed in flint armor and carried formidable weapons in their hands made their power strikingly apparent.

The prayer begins with the evocation of lightning and snake, both sky powers like the stars, to protect the patient.

On earth, coming from the points of big black snake's feet,
Black flint, together with lightning, stands as a shield to protect me;
Coming from the point of big black snake's knee,
Black flint, together with lightning, stands as a shield for me;
Coming from the points of big black snake's body,
Black flint, together with lightning, stands as a shield for me;
Coming from the points of big black snake's hand,
Black flint, together with lightning, stands as a shield for me;
Coming from the points of big black snake's shoulder,
Black flint, together with lightning, stands as a shield for me;
Coming from the points of big black snake's lips,
Black flint, together with lightning, stands as a shield for me;
Coming from the points of big black snake's head,
Black flint, together with lightning, stands as a shield for me;
Black flint, with your five-fingered shield moving around,
With this keep fear away from me,
Keep the fearful thing away from me,
Hold it and stop it!
Black flint, the power you possess in your medicine pouch
At the point where the black snakes meet and cross,

Put up a protective shield in front of me.
After that, I'll be safe behind it.
Then I'll be safe.
Behind this the fearful thing will not reach me or get me.
The fearful thing did not reach me.
The fear missed me.
I am the one saved from the fearful thing behind it.
All of us are saved from the fearful thing behind it.
Each one of us is saved from the fearful thing behind it.
The fear missed us!
The fear missed us!
We're saved!
We're saved!
I am glad!
I am glad!
Pah!

The first invocation is to the earth, where the patient is and where the ensuing drama takes place. The color of the snake is very carefully given; in this part of the prayer it is black, and associated with flint armor and lightning. In other parts of the prayer other colors and materials are used, but this part is the darkest and strongest. The next three parts become lighter and gentler as the theme is carried out.

The power is always thought of as concentrated in the tips or points of the body of the deity. From these points the power radiates out of the deity to the patient. The five-finger shield refers to a movement of the hands going alternately in front of the body and then in back, forming a kind of protecting all-around shield. Behind this shield the patient can retreat.

In the last part of the section just cited, it is stated emphatically that the fearful witch power has missed the patient and left him safe and well. The final "pah" is a ritual blowing away of all fear and evil from the vicinity of the patient.

The second part of the prayer repeats the same pattern, using different colors and materials. It begins:

On the earth coming from the points of big blue snake's
feet,

Blue flint, together with lightning, stand as a shield to protect me;
Coming from the points of big blue snake's knee,
Blue flint, together with lightning, stand as a shield for me.

The same refrain is repeated for the points of big blue snake's body, hands, shoulders, lips, and head. The third and fourth segments repeat the same formula, changing the color of the snake to yellow and white respectively. These parts are gentler than the first part with its blackness and lightning, but there is the same general content and the same conclusion.

The next section of the prayer invokes all parts of the snake warrior's body for the patient's benefit. It is also divided into four parts, each with its characteristic color. It begins as follows:

Black snake, the power you possess in your feet,
That is what we'll use:
The power you possess in your legs,
That is what we'll use;
The power you possess in your body,
That is what we'll use;
The power you possess in your brain,
That is what we'll use;
The power you possess in your mind,
That is what we'll use;

The power is then evoked and described for black snake's cap, bow, arrow, and knife, and used to stop the evil power, hold it behind the shield, and save the patient.

This same stanza is repeated for the various parts of blue snake's body, mind, and weapons, then yellow snake's and finally white snake's. It ends with the evil-chasing formula.

From the bottom of the east
The power of the evil thing has turned away from me;
From the bottom of the north
The power of the evil thing has caused him to fall toward the north.

A blood mark was left pointing north.
His head points north,
His eyebrows, eyes, hair, mouth, navel, urine stream,
  hip, knee and feet point north.

The evil power of the witch has been turned back against himself and he has fallen toward the north, which is thought to be black and the source of evil. He is taken to the ends of the earth and then out beyond into "outer space." There the evil power goes inside him and kills him.

In speaking of Navaho prayer, Reichard said: "Exorcism therefore is undertaken either from a limited space, the circle of confusion, outward toward limitless space or from unbounded space to a controlled circle of protection" (1944b: 16). This prayer is an example of the first technique, the "space" referred to being not scientific outer space, but a mythological place beyond the confines of the known sacred country. After the evil being is expelled and destroyed, a line is drawn ritually so that he cannot return (evidently he is not quite dead). The line, as might be expected, is drawn in multiples of four.

Away he went behind the first muddy red river,
Away he went behind the second muddy red river,
Away he went behind the third muddy red river,
Away he went behind the fourth muddy red river.

Away he went behind the first red rock,
Away he went behind the second red rock,
Away he went behind the third red rock,
Away he went behind the fourth red rock.

This is repeated for four red sticks and four dark nights. Red is the color of poison, evil, and danger. Illustrated in this part of the prayer are the symbolic devices of multiplication, using supplemental images, incremental repetition, and completeness. The prayer continues to describe the destruction of the evil thing.

Also in the witch's hogan,
The entrance of his hogan,
The area surrounding his hogan,
The paths to his hogan,
The corner of his hogan,
The fireplace corner of his hogan,
The back part of his hogan,
The witch's power (turned against him) makes his brain
  small.
His tears start flowing.
He bows down.
He can't think anymore,
He doesn't look up with his witchcraft.
He doesn't talk.

The evil thing is then exorcised to the land of the "people who don't move." Behind the magical lines of protection, the evil thing has been completely and mercilessly destroyed. Such punishment must give pause to one who has been tempted to use witchcraft.

Finally, everything must be put back in place and restored to harmony.

The earth goes back in front of him.
Outer space goes back in front of him.
The sunflowers go back in front of him.
The red sky blocks him out.
The mountains are back in place.
The rocks are back in place,
The trees are back in place,
The vegetation all grows back in place,
Everything is beautiful again.
The fear missed me.
The fear missed me.
We are all saved!
We are all saved!
Blessings on me.
Blessings on me.
I am glad!

I am glad!
I am glad!
I am glad!

The fourfold repetition signals the end of the prayer, but after a brief thought Natani Tso added another part, a blessing prayer which contains no mention of an "evil thing."

IDENTIFICATION WITH EVIL

Another prayer, in which the medicine man goes even further in not only confronting evil but identifying with it, was recorded by Gladys Reichard (1944b: 59–93). It is from the Male Shooting Chant, Evil Branch. The chanter deliberately invokes the evil, symbolically takes it upon himself, and then dismisses it. (Natani Tso did not go that far.) This is one of the most solemn and dangerous moments in all the chant ceremonies, for a mistake here is thought to have the most serious consequences for both patient and medicine man. The full prayer is 399 lines long and full of incremental repetition which adds to its power—but not to its readability. Here is an excerpt:

Just as you are the one whom crowds of evil move away
    from,
So may crowds of evil move away from me.
Just as you are the one dreaded by evil,
So may I be dreaded by evil.
Just as you are the one who warns off evil by winking,
So may I warn off evil.
Invisible to the weapons of evil sorcery may I go about.
Just as you are the one avoided by weakness,
May weakness leave me on account of it.
Just as you are the one whom weakness merely grazes,
May weakness merely graze me.

Just as you are the one who has become like evil,
So may I become like evil.
(lines 201–13)

The identification is now complete, and strength of purpose is invoked.

Just as you are the one who stands (firm) because of it,
So may I stand firm because of it.
Just as you are the one who gets well on account of it,
So may I get well because of it.
(lines 214–17)

Having conquered evil, the medicine man now disperses it.

Surely this day the power of every kind of evil
To a point above has gone
Opposite has gone
To a point inside has gone.
It is normal again.
It is normal again.
Surely this day well may I go about
Invisible to evil power of any kind may I go about.
(lines 226–33)

This part of the prayer then concludes in benediction and a restatement of the desired healthy condition.

Natural Boy I have become again, I say.
With safety before me may I go about,
With safety behind me may I go about.
(lines 236–38)

Natural Boy I have become again.
These things I have become.
These things I have become.
It has become beautiful again.
It has become beautiful again.
(lines 241–45)

EVIL-CHASING CEREMONIES

Enemy Way is an important evil-chasing ceremonial, and was probably once a war chant. It differs from the usual pattern in that there may be more than one patient, and more than one medicine man directing it. It is given in the summer, and is used to combat infections from outsiders. It was used, for instance, when young Navahos were drafted into the army. It is a three-day ritual beginning at the patient's hogan and moving to a new location on each successive day. The new location is about a day's horseback ride away. The time in between the events is spent in gambling, telling stories, and giving presents (Reichard, 1934: 233–43). The most important symbol of the ceremony is a trophy, representing the ghost of the enemy, which is attacked and ceremonially killed. In the old days this was an enemy scalp, but now it may be only a piece of hair or skin from a non-Navaho.

Blackening is usually a feature of this chant. A black salve is applied to the patient, especially on the chin and scalp, and the audience also apply it to their faces. White tallow is rubbed over the patient's body and he is painted with soot. More red salve is applied to his face, and his body is spotted with white to represent stars. This is done, it is said, because Monster Slayer blackened himself so evils would fear him. The stars and the blackening also protect earth people from evil by making them invisible, especially at night when evil is most likely to be abroad (Reichard, 1950: 627–28).

On the third day the Black Dancers appear. They perform a mud dance in which they sometimes seize the patient, throw him into the air, and stretch him face down in a mud hole. This looses the hold on him of the evil spirits. (I suspect we would say it knocks the devil out of him.) After the patient is dealt with, other spectators may be similarly caught and given a mud bath for their evil spirits.

On the evening of this ceremonial a dance is held, popularly called the Squaw Dance. It features eligible young women who invite young men to join them in a round dance. At the end of several rounds the man must produce a token payment to the girl for the privilege of dancing with her. This lasts all night with much teasing. The ceremony of this kind at which I was present was indeed a good-natured, relaxed affair. Everyone danced and sang for hours. In addition, everyone got very drunk, and joking and horseplay were the order of the day. The ghosts were definitely vanquished.

The Big Star Chant, another evil-chasing ceremonial, contains many features typical of symbolic purification. It is a five-day chant given at any time of the year. Natani Tso described the approximate daily order of the rituals.

On the first evening and every one thereafter, an unraveling or *wohltrahd* rite is performed in which wool strings are tied around bunches of herbs. As these are pressed against the patient's body they are untied, thus freeing the patient from his illness. On the first morning a fire is lit by means of the ancient fire-drilling method; this fire must be kept lit throughout. The procedure after that is much the same for each day.

First a sweat and emetic ceremony is held, and then the *tse-panse* or hoop rite. In this ceremony the patient approaches the ceremonial hogan from each of the four directions along a specially prepared ritual path. On the first day the patient approaches from the east. He wears cinctures and a bear-claw bracelet, and has a prayer plume in his hair. He holds a prayer stick while the medicine man accompanies him along the path with prayers and songs. He steps over four small mounds symbolizing the sacred mountains, and passes through five transforming hoops. The first hoop, made of soft oak, is black; the second of coyote bush is blue; the third of hard oak is yellow; the fourth of cedar is white; the fifth is red rosewood. The patient has a white cotton garment over his head, and as he steps through the first hoop the garment is lowered to his chin. As he passes through each succeeding hoop the garment is lowered a little more, until after the red hoop it is discarded, symbolizing the shedding of an old skin and rebirth.

After that a spruce-dress rite is held, in which a long string of yucca fiber with spruce branches fastened to it is tied around the patient's body. A mask of spruce is put over his face, and holy plants are tied to the top of his head. The garment is then cut away with a stone knife, freeing the patient again from evil entanglement.

In the late afternoons a sand painting is made, usually of Big Star Man or Star People. The patient sits on it at a certain time of the night, when the moon and stars are in the correct position. Then the medicine man prays, and shoots arrows over him with a miniature bow and arrow to frighten ghosts away. On the last night the patient's body is blackened, and he sits on the sand painting all night until the singing is finished at dawn.

THE MYTH OF BIG STAR

The meaning of these rituals can be better understood if I include here a part of the myth of the Big Star Chant given me by Natani Tso in 1969. This is a shortened version of the myth, but it agrees in most of its details with the myth given to Mary Wheelwright by Yuinth-nezi in 1933 (McAllester, 1956: 3–55). Like dreams, myths have many levels of interpretation, but this myth emphasizes the conflict between man's hero nature, with its thirst for spiritual attainment, and his coyote nature (shadow), with its lust and indolence. The hidden identity between the two is revealed later in the myth, which relates the story of the hero Badger, who ascends to the sky, procures the powers of the Big Star ceremonial, and brings them back for the benefit of his people.

The Badger was the one who started this chant. Coyote came to Badger and said, "Come on, let's go to the top

of those cliffs. There are some eagles up there." Coyote
was interested in the wife of Badger and hoped to play
a trick on Badger. Coyote persuaded him to climb up the
cliff while he stayed down below. When Badger got to the
top he saw no eagle's nests, only grasshoppers.

Coyote plays upon Badger's greed to inveigle him into this
dangerous climb, which results in an almost fatal inflation.
Thus it is not spiritual aspiration which starts the hero on his
spiritual journey.

While Badger was on the top, Coyote blew on the butte
from each of the four directions. It started rising up into
the air until it reached almost to the sky and then
stopped. Badger had to stay up there four nights. There
was nothing to eat and drink. I don't know what he did.

Coyote exaggerates the inflation. He wants to get rid of the
hero in order to have illicit sexual relations with his wife,
but at the same time this inflation puts the hero within striking distance of his spiritual goal.

Four racer snakes saw Badger from the sky. These racer
snakes were Divine Beings. They were like sentries to
the upper world. The Divine Beings told the racer snakes
to get Badger and bring him up. So they went to the cliff,
crisscrossed themselves and carried Badger up to the
sky. At that time Badger was a person, just as Coyote
and the racer snakes were persons too. The racer snakes
were like watchmen for the upper world.

The Snake People are intimately associated with the Star
People in the upper world. These sky-traveling snakes may
represent a variant of the North American thunderbird or
the winged serpent of Mexican mythology. Their affinity to
the sky is attributed partly to their zigzag resemblance to
lightning. Here the snakes are under ritual control, and ac-
complish the first steps in the hero's journey upward from his
inflated position.

When he got into the upper world Badger saw that the beings there were living together in a community. They gave him some deer meat and he told them all about himself, the story of his life. The Star People then gave him secret knowledge that concerns dead people. Badger stayed up there for four years learning different branches of the Big Star Way until he knew it all perfectly. Then he was told to return home, taking his knowledge back to his people.

This part of the myth is greatly abbreviated by Natani Tso, either because he did not know the rest of it or because he was withholding it due to its sacred nature.

According to other versions, there were in the upper world two concentric circles of houses with a house in each of the four directions. The inner circle contained the houses of the Bird People, and the outer circle the houses of the greater powers, the Star People. The Star People were friendly to Badger and gave him many friendly warnings which, one by one, he disregarded. However, by disregarding these warnings he was able to gain the powers which enabled him to learn the Big Star Chant. They told him, for instance, not to go near the place where the hole leading down to the earth was located. He went there anyway because he longed to see the earth. Suddenly the rock wren placed a rock on top of him and pinned him down. The Star People missed him and found him under the rock, but it was too heavy for them to move. They finally captured the rock wren and refused to let him go until he lifted the rock. He agreed to do it, but on condition that the hero learn three songs from him to use in the ceremony.

It seems probable that rock wren and the other small earth-bound creatures—bees, wasps, and left-handed winds— represent powers which bind the hero to the earth. These small but persistent beings distract him from his spiritual quest and must be dealt with. Therefore he helped the eagles to defeat the Bee People, and the Hawk People to defeat the

Wasps; he made peace between the Hawks and the Wren People, and helped the Eagles defeat the Left-handed Winds. After these victories the Star People regarded him as a hero in his own right, and began to teach him the ceremonial procedures for the Big Star Chant.

The racer snakes crisscrossed again and set him down where his home had been. Then they disappeared back into the sky. It had been four years since he left and his home was abandoned. He found the poker behind the door, and the poker spoke to him and told him that Coyote had come and taken his family away toward the east. He went east and found another old shack, and found out from poker that his family and Coyote had lived there a year and then moved east again. The same thing happened four times.

While the hero was away on his spiritual mission, his Coyote side was left at home to function as husband and father.

When he came to the fourth hut he found his wife and children in a pitiful state. He called to his children but they didn't even recognize him because he had been gone four years. He gave them deer meat that had come from the Divine Beings. Then he heard Coyote howling outside, and he saw that he was returning with an old flea bag of rabbits. Coyote called Badger's children beggars, and commanded them to come out and meet him as they were supposed to do. Then he came into the doorway and saw that they were with their father.

Once more the hero and Coyote meet face to face. But this time the hero has been transformed and has his own spiritual center, which leaves Coyote at a distinct disadvantage.

When he came into the hut he saw Badger had a nice piece of deer meat, much better than the skinny rabbit he had caught. He said, "Cousin, give me a piece of that." Badger then gave him a piece, but he put a small star from the sky world wrapped inside, and Coyote ate it. All of a sudden Coyote just took off around the house. You could hear his footsteps as he ran, and suddenly they just stopped. Coyote just keeled over because of the piece of star inside him. Badger went out and saw that Coyote was dead. The star burned in his throat. Then he went back and saw that his wife was sick because of her stay with Coyote. So he performed Evil Way (Big Star) over her and she recovered. That is the place Evil Way was started.

The hero principle triumphs and the trickster is done in by his own greed, which cannot stand up against the spiritual substance from the Star People. His plans are foiled, but he lives to scheme another day.

Meanwhile a little inchworm came and dragged the dead Coyote away toward the north. That's the reason Evil Way prayers always go toward the north. To help his wife get back her strength, Badger went to gather some herbs and berries. As he was out looking, Coyote's skin suddenly came upon him. It was Coyote back again and he still wanted that woman.

Where lust is concerned, Coyote never stops. But in this part of the myth the hidden identity is revealed: the hero is Coyote, and even though he had undergone spiritual ordeals successfully, his original trickster nature is never far away.

His eyes couldn't see anything because the skin was over them. While he was crawling around he came in contact with four kinds of bushes. He spent the night at each one and later these bushes were the ones used to make the hoops of the hoop ceremony. Finally a bayonet yucca made holes in his skin. After four nights in the bushes, Badger asked Big Fly to go to Holy Boy and tell him what had happened. He asked that two of the Star People should visit him. They came and held a special healing ceremony with five big hoops, one for each direction. As he crawled through the last hoop Coyote's skin was removed from him. That's why the patient in these ceremonies wears a white cloth and sheds it as he passes through the last hoop. That's the way Big Star Way, Evil Branch, got started. The Stars performed this particular ceremony which helped him get rid of that Coyote skin. That's the way the prayers go from the beginning to the last day. This ceremony is for people who are wounded or injured in part of their body. It is also for throat trouble or for burning in the throat, as when Coyote swallowed the star. Also it is for people who have lost their eyesight, as when Coyote's skin covered Badger's eyes. Also it is for a person who is sickly and thin as Badger's wife, because she had been with Coyote so long. Coyote is very bad. He is always scheming. I don't know where he gets those things. He was interested only in sex with Badger Man's wife. That's the way Big Star Chant got started. It really concerns Evil Way. That's as far as I learned it.

Through his struggles with his own coyote nature, the hero is forced to undertake a journey to a higher plane, and there, by his defiance of their warnings, he creates in himself a new order. After he has won these powers he must still undergo transformation on earth. He must establish a new relationship with his wife, who later on becomes a medicine woman in her own right. As in nearly all the myths, after the hero has taught his newly won ceremonial knowledge to his family, he can no longer stay on earth. He must return to the Divine Beings with whom he has become too intimate. He has become something of a savior who sacrifices his earthly life for the good of his people.

In a commentary on the Big Star myth, McAllester says: "The Star People announce that there must always be three kinds of people, Snake Men, Coyote Men, and Star Men, and that only trouble would come from the crossing of these classes. Here the three kinds of vital forces are clearly stated and one realizes that this, after all, is the meaning of the entire myth. The Snake is the awakening, the Coyote is man's animality and the Star is man's spirituality" (1956: 86).

COYOTE

As Natani Tso notes at the end of his myth, Coyote is the embodiment of the trickster principle. Paul Radin (1956) presents evidence that the trickster cycle is one of the oldest and most persistent myth cycles among the American Indians. The most ancient attributes of the trickster are that he is excessively greedy, full of lust, and a wanderer. He has no particular aim in life except to cause trouble, yet it was he who stole fire from the Black God and brought it to First Man and First Woman. He was able to control the sun and the vital processes of creation, and he presided over the inauguration of genital sexuality and childbirth. He stole Water Monster's baby and brought on the flood, but he is also connected with fertility and a certain kind of practical wisdom. In the chant myths Coyote has an openly antagonistic attitude toward the chant heroes, but secretly his opposition often spurs them on in their spiritual quest. The hero finds meaning, but Coyote has the vitality to give that meaning substance.

One more interesting manifestation of Coyote, his relationship to death, is revealed in a story told by Natani Tso.

In the beginning when Navahos emerged from the first worlds to the present one, the first death occurred. . . . The dead one went down below. The people sprinkled ashes so that was taboo from then on, because then the person would become a spirit or a ghost. Asked, "What happens to Navahos when they die?" he said: "The spirit goes back to the first death, down there, where it is connected with the emergence from the first worlds. At that time First Death said, 'I'll be down here, you come down here. Come back to me.' The body is partly skeleton, and decomposes, but there is a spirit which goes back to First Death."

When asked, "Is First Death a person?" he said: "First Death was a woman. From that time on, instead of continuous living there was death. It was decreed there should be death. The reason for that was that birth would also be continuous. Then people will die of old age, and First Death is waiting down below. 'Don't be afraid, come down with me,' she says. She's the chief of the dead, the queen."

When asked, "Does Coyote play any part in this?" he said: "Yes, when everything was all settled, he jumped up. He said that if a person was walking along and died suddenly that he would make a meal of him. After First Death gets her part, I'll get what I want, which is the best. I'll be between death and life. That part is mine. I'll eat the flesh that lies between death and continuous life."

Coyote is one of the most enigmatic figures in North American mythology, yet as the trickster he has his counterparts everywhere. Among the Winnebagos he is Wakdjunkaga, the Tricky One. On the northwest coast he is Raven, who is also associated with creation, has an insatiable appetite, and gets what he wants by forceful guile. Among the Oglala Sioux he is Spider, whose father was the Rock. In the Far East he is represented by his cousin, the fox, who causes mental derangement, seduces young men and women, and bewitches people so that they lose their memory and fall into his power. He has been compared to Loki in Germanic mythology, Maui in Polynesian mythology, and Hermes in the Greek, but he is more raw, more erotic, more frankly ambiguous than any of them. He is difficult for the rational intellect to grasp, but he enchants the imagination. Once his cunning, lascivious image is seen by the inner eye, it haunts the mind. It is easy to recognize one's own face in him, peering out of the darkness, resentful of the light, hating the hero for his deed of glory, yet attracted to him for his brightness. He is the animal who, in his painful passàge through the many-wombed earth, has become partially divine.

In his comments on the trickster myth, Jung says: "If at the end of the trickster myth the savior is hinted at, this comforting premonition or hope means that some calamity or other has happened and been consciously understood. . . . In the history of the collective, as in the history of the individual, everything depends on the development of consciousness. This gradually brings liberation from imprisonment in unconsciousness and is therefore a bringer of light as well as of healing" (1959: 271). Coyote is a partner in that liberation: he forces the hero to be conscious. One would not exist without the other. They are the great symbolic antagonists of world mythology, each opposing and undoing the other. Yet in their reconciliation lies the hope of mankind for vitality and wholeness.

CHAPTER EIGHT

Death and Rebirth: Process of Renewal

Death and rebirth are the mythological symbol for a psychological event: loss of conscious control, and submission to an influx of symbolic material from the unconscious. This is always felt to be a great sacrifice, a dying to one's old self. Of all the basic healing processes, this is the one most closely allied to maturation and growth. Personality growth is usually thought of as cumulative, a gradual expansion through time as ego consciousness gains experience and wisdom. But often it turns out to be only a pursuit of illusory ideals. Then there is cessation of growth, stultifying depression, or, more ominously, severe physical illness. At that point no halfway measures will do; a thoroughgoing transformation is necessary for the individual's survival. Like the sun, the ego must prepare itself for a plunge into the darkness of the unconscious underworld, there to experience rejuvenation.

The symbolic process of death and rebirth is found wherever there is a life crisis necessitating rites of transformation, rechanneling psychic energy from old patterns to more functional new ones. Healing rites are one form of these transformations, rites of passage another. Among the latter are the familiar initiation ceremonies of tribal cultures, with their elaborate ordeals and rituals designed to bring adolescents into full tribal membership. It includes also initiations into special cults, mystery religions, and secret societies. Even the symbols associated with burial customs depict death as a preparation for rebirth.

The initiations and curing rites of Siberian shamans, for example, show the familiar death-rebirth symbolism also found in Navaho myths and prayers. The shamans experienced these symbolic events in ecstatic trance and felt them to be real. Among the Tungus the prospective shaman was said to be pierced with arrows until he lost consciousness or was dead. Then his ancestors cut off his flesh, drew out his bones, and counted them. He became a shaman only if they were all accounted for. Among the Buriat, another Siberian tribe, the initiate was reportedly tortured by having his body cut up with a knife, and his flesh cooked.

Eliade sums up these scenarios as follows: "First, torture at the hands of the demons or spirits, who play the role of masters of initiation; second, ritual death, experienced by the patient as a descent to hell, or ascent to heaven; third, resurrection to a new mode of being—the mode of 'consecrated man,' that is, a man who could personally communicate with Gods, demons or spirits" (1958: 91). When the shaman has demonstrated his power to suffer death and be revitalized in his own person, he is in a position to perform this act for the suffering patient. He may himself undergo in a trance the supernatural journey necessary to cure the patient, as among the Siberians, or he may accompany the patient on a symbolic journey created by the images, myths, and prayers.

Among the Navaho myths, the nearest equivalent to these shamanistic scenarios is the healing procedure of Gila Monster, who symbolizes the healing power of the medicine man. This is described in the Flint Way myth, which is here abstracted from an original translation by Berard Haile (1943a). This part, similar to the myth of the Hail Chant, begins after the hero has been "shattered beyond recognition" by White Thunder as punishment for the seduction of his wife. The hero's family and friends seek out Gila Monster as the only one able to restore him.

Big Fly, who acts as doorguard for Gila Monster, informs them that Gila Monster knows what to do. Offerings are made to Gila Monster four times, with an extra bundle added on each trial. To the family's sorrow, these offerings are ignored until Big Fly gives instructions for their proper preparation and presentation. Although suspecting who has told the secret of his sacrifice, Gila Monster accepts and smokes tobacco from the offering. However, despite being urged to hurry, he takes his time in coming to the ceremonial gathering. The hero's family weeps in sorrow and apprehension that he cannot restore their son.

Gila Monster's procedure is to have himself cut up first and then restored as an example of his power to restore the patient. After his parts have been scattered and then reassembled, Wind blows through them to restore breath, Sun shines on them to restore winking, and finally Gila Monster's Two Agate Pouches step over the assemblage ritually and he revives.

Having amply demonstrated his power by having himself dismembered and restored, Gila Monster, like the Siberian shamans, is now ready to do likewise for his patient.

The hero's parts are collected and replaced. His blood is gathered by ants, his nerves replaced by spiders, his eyes and ears by Sun, his body and hair by Moon and Darkness People, his face by Dawn People, his mind by Talking God and Pollen Boy and his "traveling means" by Cornbeetle Girl. Then Thunder's participation is nec-

essary, and after receiving his proper offerings he creates a lightning storm similar to the one that originally
destroyed the hero. This time the hero comes back to
life. Finally Sun restores the hero's tears and replaces
his eye nerves. The Wind People cause his nerves to
move and he is carried home on a stretcher prepared by
Spider and Bird People. Healing songs are sung throughout these rites.

In a later part of the myth even the spectators are torn to
bits by dancing birds, but Gila Monster is able to restore
them in a mass healing ceremony. Then he calls for a rain of
flint that destroys the destructive birds, and the ceremony is
concluded.

THE HERO'S QUEST

The highest expression of death-rebirth symbolism is the
transforming symbol of the hero or savior, who is the longed-
for integration of the human and the divine. All heroes are
different; they are products of the culture from which they
spring, and they bear the characteristics and idiosyncrasies
of that culture. But their stories have a common underlying
unity, reflecting everyman's experience of himself in the inner
reality of his psychic life, where he receives the call to adventure, and journeys into the darkness to do battle and win
some great treasure which he brings back for the benefit of all.
　The culture hero is exemplary for the culture he represents,
but not normative. This is clearer if one reflects on the familiar myths of Christianity. Christ is the ideal figure, the
hero-savior, but he does not represent the average man, but
rather the inner man. The Navaho hero, too, represents a
paradigm for his culture, but not the daily life of the ordinary
Navaho.
　Each chant has its own hero or heroes—two of them have

heroines—and the adventures of each are slightly different. The prototypes for all are the Warrior Twins, Monster Slayer and Child of the Water (or Child-Born-of-Water). They go in search of their Sun-Father to obtain from him the power to rid the earth of monsters and establish the Navaho culture. There are several versions of this myth; the one I use was collected by Maud Oakes (1943) from the medicine man Jeff King.

This myth is nearly universal in the scope of its symbolism. It can easily be read as an archetypal journey to the center or source, represented by the sun, to obtain the power and blessing to confront the demons that haunt the inner psychic world of man. The myth is here abstracted:

> Changing Woman lived by herself in a hogan, but she was lonely. One day she wandered off and sat in the sun and fell asleep. When she awoke she felt as if someone had been with her. In two days she gave birth to a baby boy. She dug a hole beside the fire and hid him there. Then she wanted to wash herself so she stood under water dripping from a ledge. Two days later she gave birth to another boy. She raised them together and protected them from the giants and monsters who wanted to harm them. They grew exceedingly fast and when they were twelve years old they were ready for their great adventure. They set out to seek their father.

Most chantway heroes are born of ordinary parents, but the parentage of the Warrior Twins is extraordinary. Their mother, the earth goddess Changing Woman, is impregnated with light and water by the Sun-Father. The twins are raised amid humble and perilous conditions, and must return to their father for their birthright.

> On their journey they had to pass many difficult obstacles. The first was Sand Dune Boy, who reached out and pulled people under the sand. They stood on waterspouts and prayed to the monster. Not having been treated this way before, he let them pass.

Next they came to an old woman carrying a bundle. She was Old Age Woman. She was surprised to see them where earth people never came, and she advised them not to walk on her path. They ignored her, did it anyway, and quickly became old and decrepit. She returned and took pity on them, so she sang and rubbed their bodies until they became young and strong again.

To seek their father they must renounce the path of mortality. This is brought about by an act of disobedience. With the help of the old woman who keeps that path, they are reconstituted in a new dimension.

Next they met Spider Woman, who lived in a small house in the ground. It looked too small, but they were able to enter easily. (They are no longer subject to the laws of size and space.) She gave them food which replenished itself magically, and placed in it a piece of turquoise for the elder and white shell for the younger. After they had swallowed these, she gave them a live eagle feather, saying: "Whatever you do, don't show it; hide it next to your heart. It will help you and protect you when you are in trouble. Don't tell your father the Sun that I have given it to you, for I stole it from him."

As Old Age Woman is the symbol of physical mortality, Spider Woman is the symbol of fate. Spider Woman gave the Navahos the gift of weaving (patterns made in space and time). Her home is on a tall, inaccessible spire in the middle of Canyon de Chelly. She is friendly, but not to be taken for granted. She gave the twins a live eagle feather, a gift stolen from the Sun-Father, without which they could not survive the coming ordeals. It is a symbol of the indestructible spirit. It can be trusted because it is the immortal component, and always seeks the right path.

After leaving Spider Woman they came to the dangerous Cutting Reeds, who promised at first to let them pass, but then started to cut them to pieces. Undaunted, they stood on their feathers and skimmed right through.

Next they slipped through the Rocks-that-clap-together and narrowly avoided the Cat Tail People who stab people to death. With the help of their spiritual advisor Little Wind, Rainbow Man who could transport them over any obstacle, and their feathers, they gained safe passage.

Here is the gateway to the other world, the Rocks-that-clap-together, of which Coomaraswamy has written: "Whoever would transfer from this to the other world, or return, must do so through the undimensioned and timeless 'interval' that divides related but contrary forces, between which, if one is to pass at all, it must be 'instantly' " (1947: 486). There must be no hesitation or fear at this point, or the journey is over before it is begun.

Then they came to a body of water so vast it went into the sky and became one with it. The twins were helpless, but they trusted their feathers and let themselves be carried across. They said, "We shall know where we are going when we get there."

Once past this gateway the twins are confronted with the vast, trackless ocean of the other (inner) world. They are at a loss, but the spirit feather knows the way.

They crossed the great water and came to Sun's house guarded by four bears, four big snakes, four big winds and four thunders. There they met Sun's daughter, who was called Turquoise Girl as well as White Shell Girl and Grandchild of Darkness (names also given to their mother, Changing Woman). She questioned them and they told her who they were. She knew the danger that awaited them and tried to hide them in clouds rolled up above the doorway. Each of them still had the feather next to his heart. Sun came home in a bad humor and complained that he had seen strangers enter the house. He pulled down all the clouds until he found them.

The danger was great. Sun did not believe their claim, so he devised painful ordeals to test them. First he put them in a sweat house so hot that the stones inside cracked and flew apart. Sun's daughter took pity on them and dug holes in the ground. When the house heated up and the rocks flew, they were safe deep down in the holes. Sun was astonished to find them unharmed.

Next Sun tried to feed them poisoned mush, but they were warned by their friend the inchworm, and ate only that part the inchworm told them was safe. Sun began to believe that maybe they were his children.

The last ordeal was worst of all. Sun led them into a room where there were four poles, black, blue, yellow and white, covered with sharp flint knives. He took the older brother to the top of the black pole and told him to lie face down. He pushed him off right over the knives; older brother held tightly to his feather, just missed the blades, and landed safely on his feet. The same thing happened to younger brother. Sun, still not quite convinced, pushed them each a second time off the other two poles. When they landed safely from these too, he acknowledged them as his sons.

The twins encounter the Terrible Father who has no mercy or kindness in him. He wants to kill them, and in the most agonizing ways he can devise. The death and rebirth theme is expressed in the total acquiescence of the twins to the father's will. They offer no resistance; they do not even protest or complain. They are completely passive and trustful of their eventual salvation. And their trust is justified, for they are saved by hidden aspects of the father himself: the care of his daughter, and the feather given by Spider Woman. His terrible aggressive nature is frustrated (or tempered) by his softer feminine side. The whole scenario is an initiation whose outcome is predestined. It is part of the twins' necessary experience; they must submit to the father in the face of almost certain death, risking everything on the strength of a secret promise.

In a different version of the story the twins must undergo another ordeal by freezing coldness, but their friend Otter comes up to cover them and keep them warm (Reichard, 1939: 39).

All these ordeals by heat, cold, and dismemberment are typical shamanistic experiences in initiation and healing.

> Now the Sun Father turned his beneficent side and offered them the choice of all his rich domain contained in four great rooms open to the four directions. The twins saw it all, but asked only for the medicine and weapons to kill the marauding monsters. Sun was sorry —the monsters were his sons also—but he reluctantly agreed to help. His daughter molded their bodies with special magic until they were strong and beautiful, and she called them her brothers. Sun gave them flint armor, black for the older brother, blue for the younger. He put an image of a man four inches long into their mouths, and called them by their warrior names, Monster Slayer and Child-born-of-water. They were ready to descend and Sun took them to the skyhole for a test of their knowledge of the geographical features below. When they showed their abilities with the usual help of Little Wind, he said: "I will give you my wisdom before you go down. You must always use it and hand it down, so that my wisdom will always be on the earth." Sun gave them each a feather different than the one Spider Woman had given them, and they descended. They landed on Mount Taylor at dawn, and put on their armor. Sun gave them their weapons of lightning arrows and spears, and they were ready for combat.

With these weapons and Sun's help, the heroes killed Big Monster, symbol of man's undisciplined lustful appetites, and made way for the new Navaho culture.

They killed many lesser monsters as well, including (in other versions) Horned Monster, Rock Monster Eagle, Eye Killers, Tracking Bear, Traveling Stone, Rock Swallows, and Overwhelming Vagina. They also wanted to kill Sleep, Hunger, Poverty, and Old Age, but were persuaded that these were necessary correctives for the hubris of mankind. In the end they were sick and emaciated from so much fighting and killing, and the present War Ceremony was sung over them four times before they recovered.

THE STRICKEN TWINS

As a counterpoint to the myth of the Warrior Twins there is another myth, part of the Night Chant, called the myth of the Stricken Twins (Matthews, 1902: 216–65). In this myth the daughter of a poor family living near Canyon de Chelly was taken in secret marriage by Talking God—a much less powerful deity than the Sun, and closer to humanity. She was afraid to tell her family at first, but when she gave birth to twin boys they accepted them and thought perhaps they were kin to the gods. Like the Warrior Twins, they left home at an early age to search for their father, but they did not have the same success. They were caught in a rockfall, and though they escaped with their lives, the older brother was blinded and the younger one lamed.

Because they were now a great burden on their family, they were turned out and forced to wander around in their pitiable condition, asking the gods for help. Though they were rejected many times because they did not have a suitable offering, Talking God secretly protected them and endorsed their plea. He hinted to the gods that these children might be their kin. Only when they had been tested—though not nearly so severely as the Warrior Twins—and recognized as the children of Talking God, did the gods relent and agree to hold a curing ceremony. Unfortunately, while the ceremony was in progress the twins cried out in joy at the hope of being cured, breaking a stringent taboo against talking in the sweat house. The ceremony suddenly ceased, and the gods departed, leaving the twins as they were.

The description of the twins' departure to wander up and

down once again in their maimed condition is one of the most poignant moments in the myth literature. Here is Matthews's translation:

So the poor blind boy told his brother to mount again on his back. They walked in sadness down the canyon and mourned for what they had done. They now knew not what way to go nor what trail to take; they had no purpose; they wept as they walked along and as they wept they began to sing. At first they sang only meaningless syllables; but after a while they found words to sing. They cried to music and turned their thoughts to song. The Holy Ones stood grouped behind them and, hearing the song, said one to another: "Why do they sing?" "I wonder what they are singing about?" and they sent the father of the children to bring them back. When Talking God overtook them he said "Come back, the Yei wish to see you again and speak to you." The blind boy replied "I shall not go back. They have told us, in anger, to be gone. They are only making fools out of us." But the cripple urged: "Let us return once more and find out what they wish to say." When they returned someone asked them: "What were you singing as you went along?" They answered: "We were not singing. We were crying." "And why did you cry" "We cried because you bade us to go away and we knew no longer where to go." The Yei still persisted: "What kind of song did you sing? We surely heard words of a song," and the boys said: "We were not singing, we were crying." When the Yei asked this question for the fourth time the cripple spoke: "We began to cry, and then we sang; we turned our cry into a song. We never knew the song before. My blind brother made it up as we went along, and this is what we sang:

"From the white plain where stands the water,
From there we come.
Bereft of eyes, one bears another.
From there we come.

Bereft of limbs, one bears another.
　　　From there we come.
Where healing herbs grow by the waters,
　　　From there we come.
With these your eyes you shall recover.
　　　From there we come.
With these your limbs you shall recover.
　　　From there we come.
From meadows green where ponds are scattered,
　　　From there we come.
Bereft of limb, one bears another,
　　　From there we come.
Bereft of eyes, one bears another,
　　　From there we come.
By ponds where healing herbs are growing,
　　　From there we come.
With these your limbs you shall recover.
　　　From there we come.
With these your eyes you shall recover.
　　　From there we come."
　　　　　　　　　(Matthews, 1902: 244–45)

The gods, upon hearing this song, determined never again to turn away their own children, so the twins were instructed by the gods how to use their cleverness to gain the necessary offerings. Then the curing ceremony was begun, and they were restored to full health. The daughter of Calling God shaped them to make them as beautiful as her brothers.

In this myth we have an indication how the songs of the chantways, or at least some of them, originated in a heartfelt longing for health and wholeness. The feeling, when it is strong enough, finds expression in song, and the song cannot help but move the gods and compel them to do what is desired. The Warrior Twins strike a bold, dominant theme and bring a larger boon to mankind; but the Stricken Twins, echoing the same mythic pattern, transpose it to another key —a gentler, softer tone that is closer to ordinary humanity. They mollify the gods not by bravery or endurance or even clever trickery, but by the longing of their hearts expressed in song. The gods cannot refuse.

THE CHANTWAY HEROES

The Warrior Twins are definitely of supernatural origin, and the myth of their encounter with the Sun-Father seems to be of more ancient lineage than the myths of the other chantways. The other chantway heroes usually start out quite human, and only after their adventures and ordeals among supernaturals do they become godlike. Each one has a different temperament and his own tale to tell, although certain well-known themes keep recurring. To my mind, the most outstanding and moving are the myths of Rain Boy (Hail Chant), Younger Brother (Big Star Chant), the Dreamer or Visionary (Night Chant), He-Who-Teaches-Himself (Plume or Feather Chant), and Beggar Boy (Bead Chant).

The Dreamer of the Night Chant (Matthews, 1902) was quiet and gentle. He was beloved of the gods and his ordeals were not too severe. His family scoffed at him because he was impractical and disinterested in hunting. But soon they noticed that his predictions usually came true, and they began to take another attitude toward him. But it was too late! One day while following his more vigorous brothers on a hunting trip, he came face to face with the Yei Gods, who appeared as mountain sheep. He tried to shoot them with his arrows at first, but when he found that his arm could not pull the bow, he realized who they were. They began to speak to him in a kindly way, and with only a little persuasion he agreed to accompany them.

They took him to a beautiful Night Chant ceremony (also called Yeibechai) being given for the daughter of Calling God. Talking God was supposed to watch over the hero, but he became so interested in the dancing that he did not see

Changing Coyote spirit the Dreamer away. Finally the gods missed the boy and with great alarm began to look for him everywhere. Somebody remembered seeing him go off with Coyote, and by means of magically pointing prayer sticks they took up pursuit. Coyote had taken the Dreamer up to the sky from Mount Taylor, past many dangerous places. There were four rows of hot sweat houses, four spinning tops which distract and confuse people, four distaffs which distort people's bodies, and monsters who chop travelers to bits. Because they knew the correct ceremonial names, Coyote and the Dreamer were able to pass these dangers unharmed. Their pursuers were able to do likewise, and with the final help of the high god, Begochidi, the Dreamer was rescued and told to go back and learn the chant fully and effectively.

After a brief visit with his family, Dreamer was taken on many journeys for power and saw many beautiful ceremonies. The greatest of these was held at the White House in Canyon de Chelly and many of the gods, including Fire God himself, attended. After that ceremony the gods decreed that the White House should stay there forever as it was for this first ceremony; it is still there.

Finally the Dreamer went back to his family and taught the entire ceremony to his younger brother, which took six years. One day he told his brother he would have to leave, though he would watch over them and be present at every ceremony. The Dreamer rose into the air and passed through a great stone bluff nearby, which opened like a door to receive him, and was seen no more among men.

The Dreamer in this myth does nothing to incur his fate, but accepts it passively, as he does his abduction by Coyote. He is entirely trustful and willing. There is only a moment of danger when he is traveling with Coyote, but that seems to pass without incident. The death-rebirth theme appears in its most subdued form.

The hero of Plume Way, He-Who-Teaches-Himself, is very different (Matthews, 1897 and 1902). He is more aggressive and rebellious than the Dreamer, and the danger he encounters is greater and requires more risk and effort on his part. He is aided by the gods, but he is not their favorite, as was the Dreamer. He has to strive and suffer to win his own way.

In the beginning He-Who-Teaches-Himself was addicted to gambling and lost much of his family's property. His brothers threatened to kill him, and drove him away from home to live in poverty and disgrace with his grandmother and niece. Restless and dissatisfied, he decided to embark on his own adventure. For this purpose, he began to hollow out a log, inside which he hoped to journey down the San Juan River. The gods noticed him and tried to dissuade him because of the great danger, but he was adamant. Finally they helped him to hollow out the log with lightning and to install windows of rock crystal and cushions of cloud. His pet turkey could not bear to leave him, so she followed him down the river. The gods hid seeds for his new garden in the turkey's feathers.

The next part of the myth contains all the elements of a night sea journey: containment in a small vessel, submergence in water, great danger from monsters and other enemies, rescue through supernatural aid, and final deliverance to a new land. As he floated down the river in his log, the hero was first captured by the Pueblo People, but they were driven off by a storm. Then he was pulled under to Water Monster's house. Water Monster would not release him until Fire God came down and threatened to burn the water, at which point he became afraid and relented. Finally after other ordeals the hero emerged into a huge whirlpool said to be located near the source of the San Juan River. (This part of the myth is also found in the Night Chant.) The log spun in wider and wider circles, then came to rest on the shore of the new land. When the log was unsealed the hero stepped forth and took on a new name, He-Who-Floats. He had conquered the terrors of the underworld.

In the new land he was greeted by his pet turkey, who comforted him and from under her wing produced seeds of squash, corn, melon, and tobacco. The seeds were planted and the garden grew in an amazingly short time. The hero soon became restless and went out exploring. He followed a light he saw in the night, and at a neighboring hogan he found a young girl sewing buckskin. He was ashamed to enter in his poor clothes, so he took them off and entered clad only in a breechcloth. He was surprised when the father of the girl greeted him warmly as his son-in-law. But the father turned out to be extremely treacherous and tried to feed the hero poisoned tobacco. Because of previous warnings the hero was able to turn the tables on the old man, and fed him tobacco so strong that it caused him to swoon. In return for restoring the old man, he demanded the girl's hand in marriage.

He took the girl to see his farm, and taught her how to prepare and cook corn. She was greatly pleased. In return the daughter and the old man showed him their game farm, which could be reached only by going underground through magical doors. There, rooms opening out into the four directions contained vast herds of deer, antelope, mountain sheep, and elk. Later the hero divulged his secret name to his wife, and learned the secret name of his father-in-law, which was Deer Raiser.

Until recently, besides kinship names and Anglicized names, the Navaho had another secret name or "war name" which carried power with it and was seldom divulged (Kluckhohn and Leighton, 1962: 114–15). Someone who knew another's secret name had power over him. The secret name and character of Deer Raiser is strongly reminiscent of the animal owners of North American mythologies, who kept large herds in a secret reserve, releasing them only when they were satisfied that the hunters showed proper respect for the lives of the animals.

The crops that the hero raised, as well as the turkey, were indigenous to the Southwest long before the Navaho came.

They were part of the old Anasazi-Pueblo culture, which pre-dated the Navaho by centuries. The myth refers to contact and conflict between the agricultural way of life of the south, represented by the hero, and the older hunting ways of the north, represented by Deer Raiser. Among the Navaho the agricultural way achieved dominance because of the gradual disappearance of big game animals from the reservation lands.

As the myth continues, the old man Deer Raiser proved to be a powerful witch, not easily subdued. He practiced incest with his daughter and was enraged when the hero took her away from him. He poisoned the hero's food, but each time the hero was warned and refused the poisoned part. Then Deer Raiser lured the hero into a box canyon where his pet bears could attack and kill him. The hero slyly stayed near the entrance and ambushed the bears as they came in. The old man was moved to sorrow over the death of his pets. After several similar acts of treachery, the hero finally confronted the old man and accused him of evil ways. After being sorely defeated so many times by superior wisdom and power, the old man confessed to his witchcraft and asked to be cured. The hero held the first performance of Plume Way over him and reformed the witch.

Later the hero journeyed back to his old home to teach his new ceremony to his people, but stayed no longer than was necessary for the teaching. When it was thoroughly learned by a member of his family, he departed for the new home and wife awaiting him by the Lake of Whirling Logs.

THE NAVAHO HEROINES

The position of women in Navaho culture is important in several ways. For one thing, they own most of the property. For another, lineage is reckoned through the mother: a Navaho *belongs* to his mother's clan, and is said to be merely "born for" his father's. Furthermore, the women have a strong and decisive voice in family affairs and are responsible for much of the work, including crop raising, care of the animals, weaving (a major source of income), and household chores.

With this background, it is no surprise that there are heroines whose role is just as adventurous and dangerous as their male counterparts. They also play an important part in the origin of the great curing ceremonies. The foremost of these are two sisters, Glíshpah and Bispáli, whose story begins in the myth of Enemy Way (Haile, 1938b). Part of this myth tells how the Navaho warriors carried out a strong and sustained attack on Taos Pueblo, with the intention of capturing two sacred scalps as trophies. The brave warriors who won the scalps were to be rewarded with these two lovely maidens in marriage. When the battle was over, to everyone's consternation it was found that two ugly and disreputable old men had won the scalps. This was not acceptable, so various suitor tests were proposed in which the girls would be given to the one who shot farthest or most accurately. To the shame of the other contestants, the two old men won every time by an easy margin. Still, the warriors were reluctant to award them the prize.

After dancing in the evening, the girls were tired and went to find a drink of fresh water. They smelled the odor of sweet tobacco coming from the place where the two old men were camped. Following the smoke, to their surprise they found two handsome young suitors with fine clothes, beautiful jewelry, and well-made weapons. They asked for some of the sweet-smelling tobacco, and when they inhaled it their senses became so clouded that they were easily persuaded to spend the night. The older sister, Bispáli, went to Bear Man, and the younger, Glíshpah, to the Snake Man.

When the girls awoke in the morning, instead of the handsome young lovers they found ugly old men again. They were disgusted, but a growling bear on one side and a rattling snake on the other prevented them from leaving. Their kin were furious when they found out what had happened. They sentenced the girls to be whipped to death. Glíshpah and Bispáli could not go back now, so they fled into the wilderness pursued by their two ugly suitors. The old men were able to follow their flight by means of magic smoke. Soon the girls realized that if they were to escape they would have to separate. They took leave of each other with many tears, not knowing if they would ever meet again. The elder went west and became the heroine of Mountaintop Way; the younger went east and originated Beauty Way.

THE BEAR MAIDEN

Bispáli fled to the mountains, where she was cared for in a cave by supernatural protectors. She remained there for a long time and gave birth to a bear-girl baby who had fur on her limbs, breasts, and back of her ears, but a white human face. Then she started on a journey for power, during which she met many holy personages and learned from them the ceremonies of Mountaintop Way. Her bear husband tried to claim her but she was protected by her guardians, who returned her to her own people but kept her daughter with them. She was welcomed back by her family and later married and had a son, who was also brought up by bears. The myth then leads into his adventures and those of Dsilyí Néyani, the male hero of Mountaintop Way (Spencer, 1957: 126–33).

It is clear from the myth, as well as from other elements of the Mountaintop Way, that the older sister is identified closely with bears and bear power. The figure of the bear mother is familiar in Indian mythology, especially on the northwest coast. There is a marvelous sculpture of the Haida

Indians showing the bear mother in agony, suckling two bear children whose teeth tear at her breasts. Thus, according to the myths, the woman's way of taming wild power is through marriage to the beast and the maternal care of its young— quite different from the hero's way of battle and triumph.

Sometimes the Navaho think of bears as humans in disguise, especially because of the way in which they suckle their young. Bears are sometimes referred to as the ancestors of the Navaho. They are said to carry powerful medicine and are associated with the mountains, healing herbs, and fire. Their power is so great that the Navaho regard them with fear; they are rarely hunted and never eaten. They are part of the special guardians of Sun's house, and in the Shooting Chant an impersonator of Bear suddenly enters and rushes at the patient, causing a trancelike shock that is part of the cure (an early form of shock therapy).

The negative or evil side of bear power is associated with Changing Bear Maiden, who is the dark counterpart of the chant heroine. She is also called Bear Goddess or, because of the many deer-hoof pendants she wears, Maiden-Whose-Clothes-Rattle. She is Coyote's wife.

In the beginning Changing Bear Maiden was virtuous and beautiful. She kept house for her twelve brothers, and whenever a suitor came she set certain difficult tests for him to pass, before he could claim her in marriage. Coyote decided to try, and because his life force was hidden in the tip of his nose and the tip of his tail, he was almost indestructible. Her brothers were angry and tried to kill him, but could not. As one of her suitor tests, he killed Brown Giant and brought the scalp back to her. In another test she crushed him three times with stones, then the fourth time ground him to bits. Each time he revitalized himself, though the last time took longer. When he did finally succeed, she had to accept him as her husband. From that time on she sided with him against her brothers and was evil.

Coyote taught her the ways of witchcraft, and like him she

was able to hide her vital force outside her body. As a test, Coyote killed her four times; each time she restored herself. She could turn into a great she-bear whenever she wished. Seeing these terrible things, all her brothers fled, but she followed them and killed them one by one, except for the youngest, who hid in a hole deep in the ground. The gods were helping him, but Bear Woman hunted him and found his hiding place with magic. She coaxed him till finally he emerged. Intending to kill him, she offered to take care of him and comb his hair. As he sat to have his hair combed, he was warned by Wind to watch her shadow. He saw her snout get longer and longer, and just as she was ready to bite off his head, he jumped up and rushed to attack her vital force, whose hiding place had been revealed to him.

Because his power for good was now stronger than her evil power, he was able to find that vital force and destroy her. He held a ceremony over her to revive her (death and rebirth symbolism are used here to transform an evil person), and then turned her into an ordinary she-bear. Forever after she would roam the mountain forests, wary of men, yet using her powers for the benefit of the people. Meanwhile, he had thrown her nipples up into the pine tree, where they became piñon nuts for the people to eat in time of need.

SNAKE WOMAN

The myth of the younger sister, who originated Beauty Way, is a more complete and unified version of the Navaho heroine's journey for power, and it differs only in matters of emphasis from the typical hero's journey. The version presented here is a condensed abstract from a myth recorded by Haile (1932) and published in Oakes and Wyman (1957).

After parting from her older sister, Glíshpah continued her flight through thunder and rain. Her lower clothes had been torn away and she held a bundle of mountain rice over her crotch. As she knelt to drink she heard the voice of a beautiful young man warning her that this was no place for earth people. She told him her story, and he took her to a land beneath the earth where there were gardens and beautiful hogans. It was, after all, the home of her husband's people, the Snake People.

As in Plume Way, here the journey is downward, and concerns snakes, which are closely connected with fertility and medicine power. Except for her seduction by Snake Man, the heroine has trials imposed upon her through no fault of her own. But now, like the heroes, she begins to ignore instructions.

When she went to sleep on the first night her hosts warned her not to relight the fire because they were ugly in shape and didn't want to be seen. She did it anyway and found herself surrounded by big, terrifying snakes. She sought to escape, but could find no way out. She had to stay where she was until dawn. The next day her hosts complained that she had stepped on their backs during the night and caused them pain.

Here is a strong beauty-and-the-beast element. In the beginning the heroine hoped to unite with a handsome young man, but instead finds herself surrounded and held captive by frightening and ugly snakes. This she must (and does) endure, and through them gains her benefits and powers.

One day the heroine prepared a meal of beans and corn, but the portions she used increased magically until they filled the whole hogan. Her hosts admonished her; she should have known that only two corn kernels and two beans were enough. On another occasion she opened two water jugs against which she had been duly warned. Storms of dust, hail and rain were let loose. It was only with great difficulty that the Snake People were able to return to their hogan and correct the situation. They put up with her patiently.

This describes a goddess's apprenticeship. Snake Woman has great, latent fertility powers which she does not yet know how to use and control. She can make increase of food and control the rain but, like the sorcerer's apprentice, she does not yet know how to shut it off.

The heroine was forbidden by her hosts to go to the east, south and north, but of course she went anyway. On the first day she wandered to the east and was rolled up in a ball of squash. She had to be extricated with flint knives. On the second day she wandered south and ran into Toad Man by a pool of water. He was a witch and shot mudballs into her, laming her in all joints. Big Snake Man fortunately had greater power and removed the darts and shot them back at Toad Man who became lame and crooked himself. The third day she wandered north and the worst happened. She was utterly crushed by a rock fall brought about by rock wrens. She was restored only after great efforts were made to assemble all her parts (similar to the efforts made for the hero of the Bead Chant). At the end Wind breathed life back into her body.

Symbolic death-rebirth means leaving the sphere of ordinary earthly life and entering supernatural domains to return, if successful, full of power. As in other myths, here there is literal dismemberment and annihilation, from which the hero or heroine must be rescued by the joint efforts of many supernatural powers. In the final and most severe of her catastrophes Snake Woman took the danger upon herself, saying that she had always previously returned safely, so why should this be an exception. She is beginning to know and trust her powers.

The heroine spent four years learning Beauty Way from her snake husband, whom she once hated and feared. He also performed the first ceremony over her. Because of this they could not live as man and wife. Then she journeyed home to impart her precious knowledge to her people. She met her sister on the way who was now the teacher of Mountain Top Way. They embraced warmly and wept with joy. At first they feared to enter their old home, but they plucked up their courage and went in. At first they were not recognized, but then they were warmly welcomed. Both sisters taught their ceremonies to the youngest brother, and when the teaching was complete with nothing withheld, they departed. The older sister went to the Bear People, and the younger to the Snake People where she was in charge of clouds, rain, mist and vegetation for the benefit of earth people.

The heroine is now quite at home with her husband, and the ugliness and horror seem to have faded away. In a second version of the myth they live together happily, and she is allowed to return home only when she promises to come back to live with him. At the end of her apprenticeship, she is fully invested with all her power, and is truly a goddess of fertility and healing. The sand paintings of her ceremony are associated with many kinds of snakes, and her cure is good for snake infection, which manifests itself as sore joints, sore throat, stomach trouble, kidney and bladder trouble, skin disease or sores, swollen joints, and mental confusion or loss of consciousness (Oakes and Wyman, 1957: 17–18).

THE MYTH PATTERN

It is interesting to compare the Navaho myths with the general pattern of hero myths. Joseph Campbell has extracted from these myths a condensed key which he called the monomyth.

> The mythological hero, setting forth from his common-day hut or castle is lured, carried away, or else voluntarily proceeds to the threshold of adventure. There he encounters a shadow presence that guards the passage.

The hero may defeat or conciliate this power and go alive into the kingdom of the dark (brother-battle, dragon-battle, offering, charm) or be slain by the opponent and descend into death (dismemberment, crucifixion). Beyond the threshold, then, the hero journeys through a world of unfamiliar yet strangely intimate forces, some of which severely threaten him (test), some of which give magical aid (helpers). When he arrives at the nadir of the mythological round, he undergoes a supreme ordeal and gains his reward. The triumph may be represented as the hero's sexual union with the goddess-mother of the world (sacred marriage), his recognition by the father-creator (father atonement), his own divinization (apotheosis) or again —if the powers have remained unfriendly to him—the theft of the boon he came to gain (bride-theft, firetheft); intrinsically it is an expansion of consciousness and therewith of being (illumination, transfiguration, freedom). The final work is that of the return. If the powers have blessed the hero, he now sets forth under their protection (emissary); if not, he flees and is pursued (transformation flight, obstacle flight). At the return threshold the transcendental powers must remain behind; the hero re-emerges from the kingdom of dread (return, resurrection). The boon that he brings restores the world (elixir).

(1949: 245)

In the Navaho variant of this world myth, the hero or heroine generally comes from a humble family. He may be driven out because of his irresponsible behavior (Hail Way, Beauty Way, Mountaintop Way), ridiculed for his visions (Night Way), or tricked into the journey by Coyote (Big Star Way). He may wander off in search of adventure (Plume Way, Navaho Wind Way), or be captured by enemies like the Pueblos or Utes and forced to flee (Bead Way, Mountaintop Way). He may be seduced first by the wife of one of the powerful supernaturals like White Thunder (Hail Way, Flint Way) and thus encounter immediate danger, or he may be

favored by the gods from the beginning and depart peacefully
with their help (Night Way, Plume Way). If he goes to the
sky world, he may be carried across the boundary by the gods
in the form of winged snakes (Bead Way, Big Star Way),
mountain sheep (Night Way), or powerful birds (Shooting
Way). Or he may descend to an underworld in a hollow log
(Night Way, Plume Way), or he may fall in a lake (Coyote
Way, Shooting Way). He is then tested, subjected to ordeals,
and taught the sacred healing ceremony. He is always in danger, and sometimes is completely destroyed and then restored
by the supernaturals (Hail Way, Big Star Way, Beauty Way,
Navaho Wind Way, Bead Way, Flint Way).

Through trials and ordeals leading to the death-rebirth experience, the hero or heroine becomes stronger and more confident. Although at first he may stumble on the adventure or
be seduced or tricked into it, later he is strong enough to
choose it by himself and defy warnings given by the supernaturals themselves. He may then have enough power to help
the supernaturals in their struggles with their enemies. As a
result of their success and the powerful teachings of their
mentors, the chant heroes are granted a three-fold boon:
sexual conquest and marriage, the secrets of agriculture, and
knowledge of the chantways.

First, there may be a sexual conquest in which the hero
wins a wife from a jealous protector. In Prostitution Way
this is the main theme:

> The hero was a poor beggar who lived with his grand-
> mother near the Hopi villages. They were barely able
> to eke out a living, and finally, because the boy de-
> stroyed some sacred prayersticks, they were chased
> away by the Hopis. But the boy was favored by the gods.
> In this case they did not give him a curing ceremony to
> take back to his people, but love and hunting magic for
> his own use. With this magic he was able to lure Hopi
> women into the woods and seduce them one by one.
> Even the grandmother benefited from the magic and se-

duced the young men from the village in the same way. Together they took care of all the young people in the village, none of whom were hard to persuade. Finally the boy seduced even the sacred non-sunlight struck virgins, won their father's consent and took several to wife. He went right on with his seductions, using the women he conquered carelessly, sometimes rejecting them and causing their deaths. But unlike Don Juan he was never punished for his philandering.

(Kluckhohn, 1967: 158–74, abstracted)

He-Who-Teaches-Himself (Plume Way) won his bride from her evil witch-father, and used his power to make good his conquest in spite of many challenges. The hero of Coyote Way married coyote woman at each of the four houses he visited in the four directions. Beggar Boy (Bead Way) married Eagle Girl, when he stayed in Eagle's house to learn the Bead Ceremony.

The hero's marriage was not always so fortunate. The hero of Navaho Wind Way was warned not to visit a Female Shooting Way ceremony, but of course did so anyway and allowed himself to be won in a contest by a seemingly beautiful maiden. She took him home and put him to sleep with magic; when he awoke next day he saw only an ugly old crone lying next to him, in a dilapidated hogan with strips of human flesh hanging about as food. Her name was Woman-Who-Dries-You-Up. He tried to escape, but she lived on a high mesa from which there was no descent. When he ran away, she came hobbling after him until he was exhausted. Two turtledove maidens appeared and said tauntingly to him: "Isn't it true that you used to value yourself very much? It's quite clear now that you are only an ordinary person." They chided him but they gave him food and drink, and showed him how to get down from the mesa with the help of Big Snake. In this way he escaped (Spencer, 1957: 179–80).

With the exception of the Wind Way myth above, the heroes' marriages to Coyote People, Snake People, Buffalo People, Eagle People, etc., seem secondary to the acquisition of power. In the case of the heroines, marriage to supernatural men is central to the myth and forms a strong bond, making them true kin to the Holy People and binding them to the supernatural world in a particularly intimate way.

The second boon that some of the heroes acquire is the knowledge of agriculture, to replace an older hunting economy. In Plume Way, for instance, the hero's pet turkey shook out from under her wings seeds put there by the gods, and helped the hero plant a magical garden of beans, corn, squash, melons, and tobacco with great success. Later he taught this new knowledge to his wife and her people (Spencer, 1957: 170). The hero of Coyote Way obtained the secret of planting and raising corn from the Coyote People in his sojourn in the underworld (McAllester, 1956: 102–4).

The third boon that the Navaho hero or heroine brought back was the ritual and ceremonial knowledge of the chantways, which forms the core of the entire culture. The teaching took a long time because every detail had to be memorized, and because the sand paintings, though reproduced on sacred scrolls at first, were always destroyed in that form and committed to memory instead. When the hero had learned everything, he was allowed and even encouraged to return to his family on earth, to impart his sacred knowledge to them. On the way home he often met Owl, who gave him final instructions and special incense to use. He was usually well received at home, even though there may have been much enmity at the time of his departure. There was immediate recognition of his transformation and his new powers.

The teaching of the ceremony took many years. Often his youngest brother, who appeared sleepy and lazy, learned the ceremony faster and better than anyone. In Hail Way the hero took his sister into the sky world, where he divided his duties with her. In any case, after the ceremony had been taught to a younger brother or other relative, the hero felt a longing to return to the supernatural world. Too sacred now to remain on earth, he was taken wholly and harmoniously into the great balance of nature as one of its powers—invisible, but always present and well disposed toward his people.

PRAYER OF LIBERATION

The myths provide the background for the death-rebirth symbolism, but they do not touch the patient directly. In the prayers the patient is an active participant and the symbolism comes alive. The medicine man intones the prayer, which is often about an hour long, and the patient repeats it line for line. One of the most famous of these prayers, and one that describes the death-rebirth symbolism in vivid images, was given to Washington Matthews (1888) by an old singer. The singer, who was over seventy, vouched for the antiquity of the prayer and considered it the most powerful one in his repertoire. It could not be repeated twice on the same day, and no part could be given outside the context of the whole. The singer intoned the prayer to counteract the bad effects of recounting the origin myth to an outsider, as he had just done for Matthews. It is probably taken from the Night Chant.

The first part, the invocation, describes the arrival of the potent Warrior Twins, Monster Slayer and Child of the Water, in answer to the need of the suffering patient and the call of the medicine man. One comes from the east (Jemez Mountain) and one from the west (San Francisco Mountain). They meet at the center in the Navaho country (Carrizo Mountain), and from there proceed to the Place of Emergence. Actual geographical places are mentioned in the beginning of the prayer. With subtle technique these are blended with mythological places until by gradual increments, and without any perceptible break in stride, the patient is led from the familiar country of his native soil to the mythical land of the prayer's main action.

In the original text most of the stanzas begin with the phrase "Again on this side thereof," which is omitted here.

1. *From the summit of Jemez Mountain, Monster Slayer comes for my sake.*
   From the summit of San Francisco Peak, Child-born-of-water comes for my sake.

2. *From the top of Black Mountain, Monster Slayer comes for my sake.*
   From the White Ridges, Child-born-of-water comes for my sake.

3. *From the summit of Carrizo Mountain, Monster Slayer comes for my sake.*
   From the summit of Carrizo Mountain, Child-born-of-water comes for my sake.

4. *At the Place of Emergence, Monster Slayer arrives for my sake.*
   At the Place of Emergence, Child-born-of-water arrives for my sake.
   Although Smooth Winds guard the door,
   Monster Slayer with his black wand opens the way for me.
   He arrives for my sake.
   Behind him Child-born-of-water with his blue wand opens the way for me.
   For my sake he arrives with him.

The Place of Emergence leads into the mythic landscape, where the Warrior Twins with their wands of power begin their descent into the underworld to recover a soul body of the patient lying helpless there. Each step in the descent is repeated four times, forming a sequence of color change. The colors give a directional tone to the prayer, which has its visual counterpart in the sand paintings. The cloud levels, which are encountered first, show a sequence of gradually softening colors: black, blue, yellow, white.

5. *Through the first room made of the black cloud,*
   Monster Slayer with his black wand opens a way
   for me.
   He arrives for my sake.
   Behind him Child-born-of-water with his blue wand
   opens a way for me.
   For my sake he arrives with him.

6. *Through the second room made of the blue cloud,*
   Monster Slayer with his black wand opens a way
   for me.
   He arrives for my sake.
   Behind him Child-born-of-water with his blue wand
   opens a way for me.
   For my sake he arrives with him.

7. *Through the third room made of the yellow cloud,*
   Monster Slayer with his black wand opens a way
   for me.
   He arrives for my sake.
   Behind him Child-born-of-water with his blue wand
   opens a way for me.
   For my sake he arrives with him.

8. *Through the fourth room made of the white cloud,*
   Monster Slayer with his black wand opens a way
   for me.
   He arrives for my sake.
   Behind him Child-born-of-water with his blue wand
   opens the way for me.
   For my sake he arrives with him.

The prayer is cast in the words of the patient, and establishes an intimate relationship between the heroes and himself. Child of the Water always follows his brother Monster Slayer and they form a complementary pair. Their wands are emblems of the power given them by the Sun-Father. Child of the Water's blue wand is slightly less powerful than his brother's black one, because he is the gentler of the two. In their further descent the twins enter the four layers of mist, which have exactly the same color sequence as the clouds and are described in the same way. After the "fourth room of the white mist," they come to a place of descent from one world to another.

13. *Through the Red Rivers Crossing One Another,*
    Monster Slayer with his black wand opens a way
    for me.
    He arrives for my sake.
    Behind him Child-born-of-water with his blue wand
    opens a way for me.
    For my sake he arrives with him.

The introduction of the color red means that it is a place of evil and danger. In addition to the color and place symbolism, animals now appear, guarding the various levels that the heroes must traverse to reach the patient. They are powerful animals—bear, snake, coyote, and hawk—but they cannot stop the Warrior Twins with their wands of power.

14. *Through the first room made of the black mountain,*
    Although the Red Bear guards the door,
    Monster Slayer with his black wand opens a way
    for me.
    He arrives for my sake.
    Behind him Child-born-of-water with his blue wand
    opens a way for me.
    For my sake he arrives with him.

15. *Through the second room made of the blue moun-*
    tain,
    Although the Great Red Snake guards the door,
    Monster Slayer with his black wand opens a way
    for me.
    He arrives for my sake.

Behind him Child-born-of-water with his blue wand
opens a way for me.
For my sake he arrives with him.

And so on through the third room of the yellow mountain
and the fourth room of the white mountain guarded by Red
Coyote and Red Hawk respectively.

They arrive in the land of the dead, which is sometimes
said to be ruled by a woman whom the Warrior Twins must
overcome in order to free the patient from her grasp. The
implication is that some part of the sick patient, perhaps a
soul body, is already in the land of death, while another part
—his physical body—lies helpless on the floor of his hogan
on earth. I have allowed the repetitions to remain here to
show how gradually and dramatically the scene is laid for the
crucial encounter.

18. *Again in the entrance of the red-floored lodge,*
    The house of Woman Chieftain
    Monster Slayer with his black wand opens a way
    for me.
    He arrives for my sake.
    Behind him Child-born-of-water with his blue wand
    opens a way for me.
    For my sake he arrives with him.

19. *At the edge of the lodge,*
    Monster Slayer with his black wand opens a way
    for me.
    He arrives for my sake.
    Behind him Child-born-of-water with his blue wand
    opens a way for me.
    For my sake they arrive together.

20. *Beside the fireplace of the lodge,*
    Monster Slayer with his black wand opens a way
    for me.
    He arrives for my sake.

Behind him Child-born-of-water with his blue wand
opens a way for me.
For my sake they arrive together.

21. In the middle of the lodge,
Monster Slayer with his black wand opens a way
for me.
He arrives for my sake.
Behind him Child-born-of-water with his blue wand
opens a way for me.
For my sake they arrive together.

The incremental repetition serves to rivet the patient's attention on the action of the prayer, and leads him step by step along the symbolic way.

22. In the back of the lodge,
Monster Slayer with his black wand opens a way
for me.
Behind him Child-born-of-water with his blue wand
opens a way for me to
Where my feet are lying,
Where my limbs are lying,
Where my body is lying,
Where my mind is lying,
Where the dust of my feet is lying,
Where my saliva is lying,
Where my hair is lying.

The last three mentioned parts—dust, saliva, and hair—might refer to body parts often used in witchcraft. The Warrior Twins use three implements of power to rescue the patient: their colored wands, their great stone knife, and their sacred talking prayer stick. All these properties, used by god-impersonators, appear in the Night Chant.

23. Monster Slayer places his great stone knife
And his talking prayerstick in my hand. With them
He turns me around sunwise until I face him.

"Woman Chieftain! My grandson is now restored to me.
Seek not to find him.
Say not a word.
Now we start back with my grandson.
He is restored to me."

The crucial ordeal is over. The Warrior Twins have overcome death for the sake of the patient (whom they call their grandson), and the steps to the familiar world are now retraced.

24. *Again in the middle of the lodge,*
    Monster Slayer with his black wand opens a way for me.
    He goes out returning before me.
    I go out returning behind him.
    Behind me Child-born-of-water with his blue wand opens a way for me.
    He goes out returning behind me.
    They go out returning with me.

This stanza is repeated for different parts of the lodge, and then the three of them again encounter the mountains with the animal guards. They arrive and traverse the Place Where the Red Rivers Cross, and continue through the rooms of the mists and the clouds. Finally they arrive at the Place of Emergence.

40. *Again at the Place of Emergence,*
    Although Smooth Wind guards the door,
    Monster Slayer with his black wand opens a way for me.
    He climbs up returning before me.
    I climb up returning behind him.
    Behind me Child-born-of-water with his blue wand opens a way for me.
    He climbs up returning behind me.
    They climb up returning with me.

As they near home the places have a familiar ring and local designations are used: they are no longer in supernatural territory. Consequently instead of Monster Slayer and Child of the Water, who are fierce warriors, Talking God and Calling God take over as guides on the last lap of the journey home. They are gentler gods, more concerned with the patient in his everyday, domestic environment.

45. *Again at the place where I can see the direction in which my hogan lies,*
Talking God with his white wand opens a way for me.
He goes out returning before me.
I go out returning behind him.
Behind me Calling God with his blue wand opens the way for me.
He goes out returning behind me.
They go out returning with me.

47. *Again in the middle of my broad fields,*
Beautiful with the white corn,
Beautiful with the yellow corn,
Beautiful with the round corn,
Beautiful with all kinds of corn,
Beautiful with the pollen of the corn,
Beautiful with grasshoppers,
Talking God with his white wand opens the way for me.
He returns upon it before me.
I return upon it behind him.
Behind me Calling God with his blue wand opens the way for me.
He returns upon it behind me,
They return upon it with me.

Similarly the patient is escorted by Talking God and Calling God to the entrance of his hogan, the edge of his hogan, beside the fireside of his hogan, through the middle of his hogan.

Then he can be returned to his earthly body, which has been lying on the floor in a pitiable condition. Then the world is restored in harmony around him.

52. *Again toward the back of my hogan,*
Talking God with his white wand opens a way
for me,
He sits down before me.
I sit down after him.
Behind me Calling God with his blue wand opens
the way for me.
He sits down after me.
They sit down after me.
They sit down with me on the floor of my hogan,
Where my feet are lying,
Where my limbs are lying,
Where my body is lying,
Where my mind is lying.
Where the dust of my feet is lying,
Where my saliva is lying,
Where my hair is lying.

The patient has returned to his feet, limbs, body, and mind, to the dust of his feet, to the saliva of his mouth, to his hair, all are restored for him. Then comes the formal ending, the benediction that completes the prayer.

55. *The world before me is restored in beauty.*
The world behind me is restored in beauty.
The world below me is restored in beauty.
The world above me is restored in beauty.
All things around me are restored in beauty.
My voice is restored in beauty.
It is finished in beauty.
It is finished in beauty.
It is finished in beauty.
It is finished in beauty.

CHAPTER NINE

Mandalas of Healing and the Pollen Path

One of the main functions symbolic healing shares with mythology in general is the construction of a symbolic world in which the individual can feel familiar, safe, and comfortable. Sometimes, as among the Navaho, this is done with mandalas. Eliade said of them: "The mandala is primarily an *imago mundi;* it represents the cosmos in miniature and, at the same time, the pantheon. Its construction is equivalent to a magical re-creation of the world. . . . The operation certainly has a therapeutic purpose. Made symbolically contemporary with the Creation of the World, the patient is immersed in the primordial fullness of life; he is penetrated by the gigantic forces that, *in illo tempore,* made the Creation possible" (1968: 25).

These images of world order are sometimes paintings (or sand paintings), in the form of a schematic diagram showing the balance of forces in the symbolic universe. The Tibetans

and the American Indians have developed this kind of mandalic form to a degree found nowhere else. They have not
only drawn the mandala in sand paintings, on war shields,
and in rock paintings, but also projected it out into space
and time.

Black Elk has described such a mandala as it looked to the
Oglala Sioux, although they saw it in the form of a medicine
wheel:

> Everything the Power of the World does is done in a
> circle. The sky is round, and I have heard that the earth
> is round like a ball, and so are all the stars. The wind, in
> its greatest power, whirls. Birds make their nests in cir-
> cles, for theirs is the same religion as ours. The sun
> comes forth and goes down in a circle. The moon does
> the same, and both are round. Even the seasons form a
> great circle in their changing, and always come back
> again to where they were. The life of man is a circle
> from childhood to childhood, and so it is in everything
> where power moves. Our tepees were round like the
> nests of birds, and these were always set in a circle, the
> nation's hoop, a nest of many nests, where the Great
> Spirit meant for us to hatch our children.
>
> (Black Elk, 1961: 198–200)

The Navaho symbolize this mandalic round on two levels.
The first, as among the Oglala Sioux, is associated with the
physical features of their ancient land and the annual round
of life. It imparts a symbolic meaning to every part of the
Old Land (Dinetah), and anchors the myths of origin and
the heroes' journeys firmly to physical reality. It puts everything in relation to one another: geography, the passage of
time, and the stages of man's life. Everything is contained,
ordered, harmonious. I refer to this as the macrocosmic mandala, to distinguish it from the second level of symbolism
found in the sand paintings, which mirror this world order
in microcosm.

THE MACROCOSMIC MANDALA

The main feature of the Navaho macrocosmic mandala is the four sacred mountains which delineate the borders of the Navaho territory and have a geographical reality, though at times a debatable one. These mountains provide a home for the gods. Furthermore, in keeping with the mandalic quality of the whole, each sacred mountain with its direction has a long list of symbolic attributes, of which color is one of the most prominent, as summarized in Table III (Reichard, 1950: 20).

Sis Najini is the mountain of the east. It has been variously identified as Blanca Peak in Colorado, Pelado Peak in New Mexico, and several others (Wyman, 1970: 18). It is usually represented as white, although this may vary for particular ceremonials. It is covered with white dawn and fastened to the earth by lightning. On its peak are the jewel symbols of white shell and a belt of dark clouds; spotted white corn is its plant, and the pigeon or dove its bird. Its voice is like thunder in Young Eagle's mouth, and it is moved by Spotted Wind. On it live Rock Crystal Boy and Girl, White Shell Boy and Girl, and Dawn Boy and Girl. It is known for white lightning, dark clouds, male rain, and white corn. Talking God is its deity. The inner form of this mountain is described in Blessing Way songs as a Beautiful One dressed all in white shell, gazing upon the singer and calling with a beautiful voice. Similar songs are sung for each of the other directional mountains and the inner form which gives them power.

Tso Dzil, the Tongue Mountain, is the sacred mountain of the south. Always identified with Mount Taylor, it is represented by the color blue, and is associated with midday and the heat of the sun. It is covered by blue sky and fastened to the earth by a great stone knife. On its peak are the jewel symbols of turquoise; blue corn is its plant and the bluebird its bird. It is moved by Blue Wind and on it live Turquoise Boy and Girl. It is known for dark mist, female rain, and wild

TABLE III

CREATION OF THE EARTH

Direction	Color	Mountain	Fastened by	Covered by	Jewel Symbol	Bird Symbol
east	white	sisnádjini˙	lightning	daylight dawn	whiteshell whiteshell with belt of dark cloud	pigeon white thunder
south	blue	Mt. Taylor	great stone knife	blue sky blue-horizon-light	turquoise	bluebird blue swal-lows
west	yellow	Mt. Humphreys	sunbeam	yellow cloud yellow eve-ning light	abalone	yellow warbler
north	black	dibéntsah	rainbow	darkness	jet various	blackbird cornbeetle
center		dzil˙ náxodili˙	sunbeam	mirage	various mirage soft goods	bluebird
center		'ak'i dahne˙st'â˙ni˙	mirage stone			grass-hopper
east of center		tc'ô˙l'í'í	rain-streamer	rainbow heat	various	

TABLE III (cont.)

CREATION OF THE EARTH

Vegetation Symbol	Sound Symbol	Part of Earth's Body	Peopled by	Moved by	Extra Gifts	Tutelary
spotted white corn	thunder in young eagle's mouth		Rock Crystal Boy Rock Crystal Girl Whiteshell Boy Whiteshell Girl Dawn Boy Dawn Girl	spotted wind	white lightning dark cloud male rain white corn	xa'ete'é ''óyan
blue corn			Boy-who-carries-one-turquoise Girl-who-carries-one-corn-kernel Turquoise Boy Turquoise Girl	blue wind	dark mist female rain wild animals	Black God
black yellow corn			White Corn Boy Yellow Corn Girl Evening Light Boy Abalone Girl	black wind (?)	dark cloud male rain yellow corn wild animals	Talking God
red, white, blue variegated corn	thunder four times		Pollen Boy Cornbeetle Girl Darkness Boy Darkness Girl	yellow wind	dark mist vegetation of all kinds animals of all kinds rare game	Monster Slayer
			Soft Goods Boy Soft Goods Girl		dark cloud male rain goods of all kinds pollen	Talking God
all kinds			Mirage Stone Boy Carnelian Girl		dark cloud male rain	
		heart	Jewels Boy Jewels Girl			

TABLE III (cont.)

CREATION OF THE EARTH

Direction	Color	Mountain	Fastened by	Covered by	Jewel Symbol	Bird Symbol
ridge running north and south		noxozili˙			flint	
'way over on west side'						
prairie						

Reprinted by permission from Gladys Reichard, *Navaho Religion: A Study of Symbolism*, Bollin-

animals. Black God is its tutelary deity. The inner form of this mountain is described as a Beautiful One dressed in turquoise.

Doko'o'slid is the Shining-on-Top Mountain of the west, always identified with Mount Humphreys in the San Francisco Peaks. It is represented by the color yellow, and is covered by yellow evening light and fastened to the earth by a sunbeam. On its peak are the jewel symbols of abalone; the yellow warbler is its bird and the yellow corn its plant. On it live White Corn Boy and Yellow Corn Girl, Evening Light Boy and Abalone Girl. It is known for dark clouds, male rain, yellow corn, and wild animals. Calling God is its associated deity. The inner form of this mountain is described as a Beautiful One dressed in abalone.

Dibe Ntsa is the sacred Big Sheep Mountain of the north. Its identity is uncertain; some say it is Hesperus Peak in Colorado. Represented by the color black, it is covered by darkness and fastened to the earth by a rainbow. On its peak are jewel symbols of jet; the blackbird is its bird and variegated corn its plant. On it live Pollen Boy and Corn Beetle Girl, Darkness Boy and Girl. It is known for dark mist, and

TABLE III (cont.)

CREATION OF THE EARTH

egeta- on ymbol	*Sound Symbol*	*Part of Earth's Body*	*People by*	*Moved by*	*Extra Gifts*	*Tutelary*
		skull				
		breast				
		pericardis and dia- phragm				

for all kinds of vegetation and animals, including rare game. Monster Slayer is its associated deity, and its inner form is described as dressed in jet.

These four mountains are not the only geographical landmarks. The reservation is dotted with many others that have strong mythological associations. The center of the reservation is usually thought of as Mountain-Around-Which-Moving-Was-Done, identified as either Huerfano Mesa or Gobernador Knob (Spruce Hill). This was the birthplace and early home of Changing Woman. Later she moved to an island off the Pacific coast. Her sons, the Warrior Twins, are thought to live on Navaho Mountain, while a tall, thin rock in Canyon de Chelly is the home of Spider Woman. There too are the famous White House ruins where the first great performance of the Night Chant was held. Even the monsters have their landmarks: a lava flow near McCarty's is associated with Big Monster's spilled blood, and Cliff Monster is said to have turned into Shiprock Mesa after he was killed by the Warrior Twins. The confluence of the Pine and San Juan Rivers is sometimes thought of as the place of the "crossing of the waters," and farther up the San Juan is the mythical location of the Lake of Whirling Logs. The Place of Emergence can no longer be found, but it is said to be somewhere in the Colorado Mountains. There are many more examples. The journeys of the heroes and heroines are replete with identifiable place names, and elaborate maps have been drawn to trace their paths over the mountains and canyons of the Navaho country (Oakes and Wyman, 1957: 36–37).

All this symbolism has a definite purpose: to link the mythic events to physical reality, just as the prayers do when they begin with familiar places and proceed to mythic ones. This allows the psyche to fix on well-known images such as familiar mountains, rivers, canyons, etc., and then gradually move beyond them into an inner mythic landscape.

Not only the geography but also the turning seasons of the year are part of the great round, which is not static but in constant rhythmic movement. In his creation myth Hosteen Klah said:

> They made the Sun of fire with a rainbow around it, and put the Turquoise Man into it as its spirit. They put the Fall and Winter in the West and North, and the Spring and Summer in the South and East; the month of October was claimed by Coyote, and is half summer and half winter and is called the Changing Month. Then all the spirits went to the places where they belonged, and they raised the Sun and Moon, Stars and Winds. The Fire God placed the North Star, and the other Gods placed other constellations, the women placing the Milky Way and other stars. . . . They put the forty-eight cyclones under the edges of the world in the four directions to hold it up, and sent other winds to hold up the sky and stars. Begochidi then took the Ethkay-nah-ashi, the mysterious transmitters of life, and motioned to all creation and it came to life and moved at different speeds.
>
> (Klah, 1942)

THE MICROCOSMIC MANDALA

The mythical drama of the Navaho is played out in a smaller but more intense form in the microcosm of the sand paintings. Eliade says of them: "The [Navaho] ceremony also includes executing complex sandpaintings, which symbolize the various stages of Creation and the mythical history of the gods, the ancestors and mankind. These drawings (which strangely resemble the Indo-Tibetan *mandala*) successively re-enact the events which took place in mythical times. As he hears the cosmogonic myth and then the origin myths recited and contemplates the sand paintings, the patient is projected out of profane time into the fullness of primordial time; he is carried 'back' to the origin of the World and is thus present at the cosmogony" (1968: 25–26).

It is indeed remarkable, as he notes, that a process with such similar characteristics should be carried out among the Tibetans. They make large four-sided designs in sand on the temple floor, just as the Navaho do in the hogan. These also are oriented to the four directions, and bring into relationship around the center of the mandala the powers ruling those directions. The Tibetan paintings are usually even more complex than the Navaho paintings and take a long time— sometimes weeks—to prepare. They are made for certain initiatory procedures, and are destroyed and remade each time the ceremony is given. These Tibetan mandalas are probably not used for healing, but both the Tibetan and Navaho mandalas are expected to bring about important transformations in the participants (Tucci, 1969).

The Navaho sand paintings are also similar to some of the pre-Columbian codices from Mexico. One of these analyzed by C. A. Burland (1950) was made on whitened hides, like some Navaho paintings. The orientation of the painting to the four directions; the sacred personages guarding the cardinal points; the appearance of four sacred plants; the use of color symbolism—all are reminiscent of the Navaho mandalas.

However, the main purpose of the Navaho sand paintings is not to orient the patient to the Navaho cosmos (macro or micro) or to commemorate its history. It is to identify him with the images of power that are represented in the paintings. As Reichard said: "By identification, a symbol that stands for a power is the power. Hence to understand the symbol with its various meanings is to comprehend the power and the techniques required to invoke it" (1950: 149). Every sand painting is a pattern of psychic energy. The painting focuses the power, and the medicine man transfers it to the patient through the physical medium of sand. The patient not only makes use of the power of the figures in the painting, he becomes that power.

What are the images found in these mandalic paintings? Most often they are supernatural personages who represent the forces of the natural world. In many cases the sand paintings consist mainly of four Holy People standing in a row. In others the figures may be multiplied many times— always in multiples of four—to represent augmented power. More often the Holy People are arranged in true mandalic (circular) form. An important reference point such as the Place of Emergence, a deep pool, a central fire, the home of the gods, or the main hero of the chant occupies the center of the painting. Around this central point the Holy Powers to be evoked are placed in the cardinal directions: north, east, south, and west. These Powers might be Wind People, Star People, Cactus People, Cyclone People, Buffalo People, Thunder Birds, or Snake People.

In the northeast, northwest, southeast, and southwest are secondary beings. Often these are the four sacred plants— corn, beans, tobacco, and squash—that originally came to the Navaho from the valleys of Mexico. Around the painting there is usually a protective figure such as the Rainbow Guardian. There is always an opening to the east, with two small guards stationed there to protect the entrance. These may be two snakes, bears, insects, or other small creatures. The sacred mountains, represented by circles in the traditional colors, are sometimes placed outside the main area bounding the painting in the four directions. In some paintings actual mounds of earth or upturned ceramic pots are used to represent mountains, and bowls filled with water become sacred lakes. There are numerous variations, and in any particular picture one or more of these typical features may be absent.

Sometimes the paintings commemorate an episode in the story of the chant hero, or the historic pilgrimage of the Navaho ancestors in their upward-reaching way. This is seen in the sand paintings of the flood (P1A#8) and Coyote stealing fire (P1A#10). The sand paintings of the Bead Chant and the Two-Who-Came-to-Their-Father illustrate the myth in a series of closely related pictures.

The simplest paintings are those which show a schematized ground plan for a ceremonial rite. They indicate by means of footprints and other devices where the patient should stand or sit, and where the men representing supernaturals will stand and move during the ritual. They may indicate a special altar or place where a certain ceremonial action is to be performed.

Another kind of sand painting shows an entire place or "land" symbolized in the form of a giant rectangle, oval, or diamond. In one Blessing Way painting (P1#12) the Earth Mother, probably synonymous with Changing Woman, is depicted with a large yellow oval body and a small rectangular head with blue-tipped horns. The blue Sun is contained between these horns and the white Moon is near her tail. Her face is streaked with white dawn, black night, blue midday light, and yellow evening glow. Her spine is a cornstalk; in her hands she carries all the seeds for food and medicinal plants found on the earth. In the great oval of her body the sacred mountains are placed to represent her organs: Jemez Mountain, her heart; Mount Taylor and La Plata Mountain, her liver; Huerfano Mesa, her kidney; and San Francisco Mountain, her bladder. She is surrounded by the blue ocean.

Earth Mother's counterpart is another Blessing Way painting of Father Sky (P1#15). It is a large black rectangle figuratively held up at each corner by four triangular cloud symbols. In this dark land are the blue-horned Sun and white-horned Moon. The Milky Way is scattered across the black sky among many constellations. To the east is Eastern Star; the Great Medicine Star is in the southeast corner; and the Twin Stars are near the center. Coyote Star is in the south, Lesser Medicine Star below it, and the Great Serpent Trail running from south to north. White mist is scattered over the painting.

One of the finest sand paintings is from the Male Shooting Chant (P4#4), showing Mother Earth and Father Sky side by side, joined at the top by a thin line of yellow pollen from head to head, and at the bottom by a rainbow path from tail to tail. Father Sky has a large black oval body, but his tail is the blue color of Mother Earth. Mother Earth has a large blue oval body, but her tail is the black color of Father Sky. As in the yin-yang symbol, each large division has in it a part of the other, symbolizing that they are not irrevocably separate.

SYMBOLISM OF COLOR, PLACEMENT, AND NUMBER

Color and placement are the organizing principles that bind the entire chantway system into one organic whole. Placement means the arrangement of the figures in the design of the sand painting. This is closely linked with the symbolism of numbers in the context of the Navaho chant system.

I have already indicated that each direction is symbolized by a particular color, but the symbolism of color is much more complex. Besides representing a direction, each color in the sand paintings is associated with a time of day, a season of the year, a stage of man's life, and one of the underworlds from which the original beings emerged. The most important of these symbolic colors are white, blue, yellow, and black.

White is usually the color of the east and dawn. It is also the color of spring, youth, and the upper world into which man ascended. White represents new beginnings and spiritual purity; it is the source of blessings for which man prays each morning as the sun rises. It has the feel of distance and coldness, and is the moon's color in the sand paintings. It is a powerful force for good, but can also work ill. The Spirit Land is always white, as are the Ethkay-nah-ashi, the mysterious transmitters of life. Talking God is usually dressed in white, and many of the gods have upraised arms that are white to indicate spiritual blessing. But there are destructive forces such as White Thunder and the Great White Serpent, who can do much harm and are hard to appease.

Blue is the color of the south, and of the fierce heat of midday. It stands for summer, for the middle years of man's life, and in most myths for the second of the underworlds into which man ascended out of darkness. It is a strong force for good, and symbolizes the burning heat of the sun that brings the life force to earth and makes things grow. No green is used in Navaho sand paintings, so blue stands for corn and all vegetation. Turquoise, the substance of Sun's blue mask, brings blessing and good fortune. The bluebird means spiritual happiness, and rain, warmth, and fertility are symbolized by blue. Despite all this good, there is still a negative side—a powerful Blue Star that is evil and causes misfortune, and a great Blue Snake that brings epidemics.

Yellow is the color of the west and evening twilight. It stands for the autumn and the ripe maturity of man's life, as well as the third of the underworlds through which man ascended. Its great virtue is that it is the color of pollen and the Pollen Path, which is the quintessence of spiritual goodness. It is almost never harmful, and always carries with it spiritual blessing and physical well-being. All yellow objects, such as jasper stone and yellow flowers, are thought to have healing properties. Yellow pollen is carried in special bags and sprinkled liberally as a sign of blessing and benediction during healing ceremonies. Yellow points to the essence of things and embodies a ripened wisdom. It is feminine, as compared with white; in the ceremonies yellow corn meal is given to women and white to men.

Black is the color of the north and of night, winter, man's old age, and death. It stands for the first and lowest of the underworlds; the Place of Emergence is usually colored black. Black is primarily a negative color associated with evil, the underworld, destruction, and witchcraft. Black Wind, Black Hail, and Black Lightning are all destructive entities. But there is a beneficent side. Black mountains set at the north, and sometimes at the east, are barriers to protect the Navaho from their enemies. Black clouds and black thunder, though fearful, bring rain and fertility.

Red is not a directional color, but it is used to symbolize fierce power, life force, danger, and poison. In some myths it stands for the lowest of the underworlds. Red at the tip of an arrow or on a snake's head in the sand paintings indicates poison and death. Red caps worn by warriors indicate the power to slay. The Red Ant Way chant, deriving from the origin myth, has several sand paintings in which red is a prominent color of the ant people, who are generally dangerous or poisonous. On the other hand, red can stand for the life force. When animals are drawn, they may contain a red life line running from the mouth to the heart. Used with blue, red is often the color of the Rainbow Guardian who surrounds and protects many of the sand paintings. Finally, it is the color of fire and warmth. A red cross in the center or on the periphery of a sand painting marks the position of the fire. There is a sand painting of the mountain goddesses dressed in four red pyramids of fire. Sand paintings depicting the fire dance ceremonial of the final night have a red cross in the center to symbolize the great fire around which the dances take place.

If color gives substance, placement gives form to the microcosm of the sand paintings. Sometimes only one great supernatural power is depicted in a sand painting, but this is infrequent and may imply the existence of a second painting which contains the other member of a pair. This is true of the separate paintings of the blue-masked Sun and the white-masked Moon, and of Mother Earth and Father Sky.

There are a few beings who have no twin and are depicted alone in the sand paintings. They are usually considered negative, such as the evil Black Star and the Great White Serpent. There is Whirling Wind, usually destructive, and Thunderbird, who is hard to approach. Besides these, some of the chant heroes are depicted alone, and Begochidi is thought of as a supernatural who has no twin.

But most of the major powers are represented as pairs. The Sun and the Moon are one such pair, and the Sun and Changing Woman another. Mother Earth and Father Sky, Changing Woman and White Shell Woman, Talking God and Calling God, Monster Slayer and Child of the Water, the Stricken Twins, Holy Man and Holy Boy, Holy Woman and Holy Girl, First Man and First Woman, and Corn Beetle Girl and Pollen Boy (symbols of regenerative power)—all are examples of this pairing, of which many more could be found.

There are two kinds of pairing: one of opposite pairs such as Mother Earth and Father Sky, and one of complementary pairs such as Monster Slayer and Child of the Water. Monster Slayer is more aggressive and his brother gentler and more human, but they are always thought of as twins. When these pairs are represented in sand paintings they may be placed side by side, but more often they are placed across from each other on the north-south or east-west axis of the painting.

These pairings lead naturally to a quarternity: four is the

ruling number of Navaho mythology. It is the number of stability and balance, of orientation in this world and the upper and lower ones, and of completion and wholeness. In the sand paintings four figures are placed either in a row or more often at the cardinal points. Newcomb says: "Every sandpainting emphasizes the cardinal points, the four corners of the Earth, where stand the four sacred mountains, four parts of the day, and four seasons of the year. There are four or eight sacred plants, four water monsters, four thunder, and four, eight or twelve prayersticks erected around the border of the painting after its completion" (1956: 10). There are numerous other ramifications. Human life has four stages; each person who needs a ceremony should have it repeated four times in his lifetime; when a question is asked or a demand made four times, it must be definitively answered. A great quaternity of heroic powers is at the center of the Shooting Chant: Holy Man, Holy Boy, Holy Woman, and Holy Girl.

In order to express an increase of power, four is often multiplied in the paintings. In the Night Chant painting of the Fire God (P11#9), he is shown as a figure repeated sixteen times around a central ear of corn. In the sand painting of the Mirage People (P12#4), there is a square of darkness in the center surrounded by eight mirage people. In the Bead Chant paintings the hero is carried to the upper world after his last dance by twenty-four or forty-eight hawks and eagles (P19#6). There is no change in meaning, only an increase in power by multiples of four.

Three, or its triangular form, is an active number and associated with those elements that move freely between the earth and upper land. It is used to portray birds, rain, clouds, and winds. Newcomb mentions that there are always three roots for every plant, three tips on a cornstalk, three sides to a rain cloud, three tassels on each side of a dancing kilt (to symbolize rain), and three bindings for an arrow (1956: 12). Many of the shorter ceremonies last three days or nights.

Five is often the number of minor elements in the sand paintings. Thunders are represented with five waterspouts, Monster Slayer and Child of the Water may carry five lightnings in their hands, and flint armor is shown with five points on the front and back. Five alternates with four as a major unit in the repetitions of the prayers. Usually in a unit of five there are four similar items and a fifth that is different. Also, in the sand paintings five may include four figures in the four directions and a special one in the center. In the myths there may be four brothers and a fifth who becomes a medicine man.

Beyond five, Navaho numerical symbolism becomes less extensive. In Indian ceremonialism there are six directions— east, west, north, south, up, and down—but these cannot be shown in the sand paintings. If the center is included as a directional place, then there are seven. Ten and eleven do not seem to play important roles. Eight is usually a multiple of four, extending its power, as are sixteen, twenty-four, and forty-eight. Nine is the number of nights in the longer chants, but it is broken up into four days of preparation, four days of identification with the healing powers of the sand paintings, and one final night of recapitulation.

Twelve has special significance for holiness and completion. There is a sand painting from Blessing Way, called the Twelve Holy People (Oakes, 1943: 55), which has twelve rectangular panels, each standing for a principal power. There is yellow Earth, blue Sky, black Darkness, white Dawn, and yellow Sunlight. Then comes Sun, Talking God, Calling God, Male Corn, Female Corn, Corn Beetle Girl, and Pollen Boy. The medicine man Jeff King said this painting was very holy and would give man a special blessing (*ibid.*).

There are twelve-word formulas associated with the chants which are very sacred and not often recorded. They are repeated only at certain moments in the ceremony. Reichard (1950: 272) gives one of these for the Hail Chant as follows: Earth, Sky, Mountain Woman, Water Woman, Darkness,

Dawn, Talking God, Calling God, White Corn, Yellow Corn, Pollen Boy, and Corn Beetle Girl. These must be repeated in exact order.

Thirteen has dark, evil connotations. In the story of Changing Bear Maiden she has twelve brothers and herself, the evil sister. Also in the Navaho calendar there are twelve lunar months and a thirteenth irregular one belonging to Coyote, which is inauspicious.

SAND PAINTINGS OF THE HAIL CHANT

The Hail Chant is a good example of the use of the symbolism of the sand-painting mandalas to control the strongest and most dangerous natural forces. The primary purpose of the chant is to defend against, then mollify and finally transform the great power of Winter Thunder to be used for healing. The name of the chant itself probably derives from the harmful effects of hail, and from its origin in the white storm clouds of winter (Winter Thunder).

In the myth, part of which was analyzed in Chapter Three, Rain Boy was driven out by his family because of his habitual gambling. In his wanderings he was first seduced by Winter Thunder's wife and then blasted to bits by the jealous husband. The other great powers of nature came to his aid and attempted to restore him. There was a great war between the beneficent powers of nature and the irascible Winter Thunder. Changing Woman and her warrior sons refused to participate in this battle, but White Thunder was finally subdued. In the final peace conference he was even persuaded to officiate as medicine man in the final great ceremony given to cure Rain Boy of his illness and exhaustion, and to restore him to harmony with nature.

This was still very precarious because Winter Thunder, even though he agreed to heal Rain Boy, still remained unpersuaded in his heart, and planned to kill Rain Boy during the ceremony. But Rain Boy was warned by his guide, and during the singing he substituted the words "We are in great peace" for the words in Winter Thunder's version: "We are in great danger." Winter Thunder was ashamed when he heard these words and knew that his intentions had been discovered. He whirled about in frustration, holding his powerful obsidian knife, but now he could not harm Rain Boy, so he completed the curing ceremony (Spencer, 1957: 101).

The original ceremony given by Winter Thunder to cure Rain Boy is the prototype for all Hail Chant ceremonies given since that time. The sand paintings and much of the detailed ritual are described in the longer versions of the myth, and these were followed as closely as possible in the actual ceremonies. Hosteen Klah was said to be the last medicine man to know the full version of the Hail Chant.

In the original ceremony, given in the Sky World, the paintings were made on permanent scrolls of cotton and unrolled for each performance. These scrolls were not entrusted to men because they were too sacred for careless handling, so they had to be committed to memory and reproduced each time in the medium of sand. After each ceremony they were destroyed. When a chant falls into disuse or is forgotten, many of its sand paintings are lost. When its last singers die, the chant disappears forever.

One of the sand paintings of the chant shows Winter Thunder's house (P2#3). This is made from a description given in the original myth. Winter Thunder himself is seldom portrayed in sand painting because he is too powerful to be controlled; his house is shown instead. The center shows the whirling seat of Winter Thunder made in the shape of a swastika. Around it in the four directions are four oblong shapes in four colors, representing parts of Winter Thunder's house made of clouds, water, fog, and moss. The guardian of the painting is a duck with a white bill, and there are different birds in the four directions.

In another powerful painting from the Hail Chant, four Thunder People are shown standing in a row (P2#3). They are shown in four colors: Black Thunder with white lightning, Blue Thunder with yellow lightning, Yellow Thunder with blue lightning, and White Thunder with black lightning. These are the symbolic colors always associated with the four directions, so even though the painting shows the figures standing in a row, the idea of the circular mandala is preserved in the color symbolism.

Many other sand paintings showing the powerful forces of nature are part of the repertoire of the Hail Chant. This includes separate paintings of the Sun (P2#5) and the Moon (P2#6). The two paintings are considered a pair. There are also Wind People (P2#8), Storm People (P2#11), Cloud People (P2#15a), and Rain People (P2#10). Sometimes these people are pictured in rows of four and sometimes in the circular mandalic form.

On the last day of the ceremony, a particularly impressive painting called the Night Sky Painting is often made (P2#169). It has a large black square representing the night sky, on which the blue Sun and the white Moon are shown in a central position, surrounded by many star constellations. Above the northern and southern borders of the sky appear the masked heads of the Cyclone and Storm People, who make the heavens move. To the east are a mountain goat, a bluebird, and a bat. To the west are figures of the yellow-shouldered blackbird, the mountain bluebird, the yellow warbler, and the western tanager.

When this painting was made in the original ceremony, Rain Boy was called in to receive its power. Then the Sun magically caused his image to appear on Rain Boy's chest, and Moon appeared on his back. Streaks of black and white appeared on his body, starting at his hands and going up to his mouth. A blue band across the lower part of his face, and a yellow band across the upper, symbolized the rising and setting sun. Various kinds of pollen were sprinkled on his head. In subsequent ceremonies on earth, body painting is used to represent the magically appearing images of the original ceremony. The following ceremony was then performed on the sand painting, with Winter Thunder officiating:

> Winter Thunder dipped a curved prayerstick into the medicine bowls and touched the heads of the Cyclone People and the feet of the birds in the painting. Holding these prayersticks he led Rainboy to the center of the painting. Rainboy sat at the center and a sacred feather symbol was tied to his scalp. Braided wreaths made of bulrushes, cornstalks, spruce twigs, turkey feathers and medicinal herbs were placed over his shoulders and on his wrists. Rainboy swallowed an obsidian figure and drank herbal medicine. White Thunder pressed the prayersticks to Rainboy's body. Then White Thunder pressed his hands to various parts of the painting and to Rainboy's body. Rainboy left the hogan and, facing the Sun, inhaled four times. The spirit of Thunderbird shot arrows into his body. The painting was rolled up and Rainboy re-entered the hogan. He ate cornmeal mush from the corn pollen basket and drank from the "Bowl of Changing Colors." By all these means the powers of nature were transferred to his body and he was completely restored.
>
> (abstracted from Wheelwright, 1946a)

In this ceremony all the five senses are used to treat the patient. The visual images of the sand paintings and the body painting, the audible recitation of prayers and songs, the touch of the prayer sticks and the hands of the medicine man, the taste of the ceremonial mush and herbal medicines, and the smell of the chant incense—all combine to convey the power of the chant to the patient. Not only in the prototypical ceremony, but in every chant ceremony held since, all these means are brought into play. The chant is a total experience for the patient.

SAND PAINTINGS OF THE MALE SHOOTING CHANT

Some of the finest mandalic forms are found in the sand paintings of the Male Shooting Chant, one of the greatest in the chant series. It has many phases and branches, and a repertoire of more than forty-five sand paintings to use for its performances, many of which show animal images as conductors of healing power. It is said to be "first among the chants," and it was the chant studied most thoroughly by Gladys Reichard under the tutelage of her teacher Red Point, also called Miguelito.

The myth of this chant (Reichard, 1939) recounts the adventures of Holy Man and Holy Boy, associated with Holy Woman and Holy Girl. Together they form a quaternity which stands at the center of Navaho theology. The masculine and feminine elements are evenly balanced by the stronger and weaker pairs of both sexes. The myth of this chant is long and contains many of the common themes of Navaho mythology. There is, for instance, a journey to Changing Woman's home in the west, and a journey by the heroes to their Sun-Father. But the main part of the myth recounts the heroic adventures of Holy Man among the Sky People and the Snake People, and Holy Boy among the Water People.

One of the most powerful sand paintings from this chant is called Taking Down the Sun (Reichard, 1939: 48, fig. 5). It is connected with that part of the chant myth in which Holy Man throws an eagle-feathered arrow at a painting of Sun. Sun refuses to swallow it, so Holy Man swallows it himself to show his power. Holy Woman, Holy Boy, and Holy Girl also show their power over divine beings. The center of this mandalic painting shows Changing Woman's house. In the four directions stand the members of the holy quaternity. To the east, Holy Man touches the horned figure of the Blue Sun with his bow; to the south, Holy Boy touches Black Wind; to the west, Holy Woman touches the horned White Moon; and to the north, Holy Girl touches Yellow Wind. This painting shows their power to control and "bring down" these divine beings that are so important to man's life. Each carries a basket in which to place the respective divine being after it has been captured.

In his journeys Holy Man came in contact with many kinds of Snake People. These are shown in several major sand paintings. One of these is called the Mountain That Fell Out (P4#8), which refers to a mountain not attached to a chain or ridge, where the Snake People live. At the center of the painting is a yellow mountain with a fire symbol on its top. Around it, seeming to come toward it, are several kinds of Snake People: Big Snakes, Crooked Snakes, and Arrow Snakes. Some of the snakes have markings symbolic of deer tracks, snake dens, and the phases of the moon. The emphasis in this painting is on the snake's control over animals used for food.

There is a painting of Endless Snake (P10A#2) in the form of a perfect mandala. This great black snake with many coils is in the center of the painting with his head facing east. Around him are four guardian snakes of different colors, facing inward toward the great central snake. Reichard (1939: 54) thought this was symbolic of all the Snake People. The black color indicates the darkness of the spirit world from which the Navaho emerged. The deer-hoof markings on the body stand for the paths of life, as well as plentiful game. The four smaller coiled snakes are guardians: the black one guards the sky, the white one the earth, the blue one the mountains, the yellow one the waters.

Snakes stand out as a predominant animal symbol in the Navaho chants. In Beauty Way they are in charge of moisture, rain, and fertility. Beauty Way has many sand paintings of snakes—Big Snakes, Crooked Snakes, Snake Pollen People, and Snake with No End (Oakes, 1957). Wind Way has paintings of snakes guarding the Sun and the Moon, and in one of these Sun is said to be clothed in snakes (Wyman, 1962). In Bead Way, snakes are shown as messengers who carry the hero over the threshold into the Sky World. Paintings such as these are made for various forms of contact with snakes, not only for bites but for sleeping where snakes live, seeing them unexpectedly, or dreaming about them. In some chants —Blessing Way, Night Way, and Hail Way—snake symbolism is minor or absent.

In North American mythology in general, the snake is associated with the sky and its phenomena—rain, rainbows, stars, and lightning. Paradoxically, it also stands for the underworld, darkness, and death. It is a symbol of renewal that governs life as well as death (Astrov, 1962: 50). This is abundantly borne out in Navaho myths and sand paintings. There the snake is associated with the ability to move from one world to another. In the Male Shooting Chant the snake is usually found on the earth's surface, whereas in the Bead Chant he inhabits the Sky World, and in the Beauty Chant he lives underneath the earth. The snake is connected with secret knowledge, healing, fertility, lightning, and rain. He protects, teaches, transports, and transforms, but he is dangerous and must be approached with caution.

In another part of the Male Shooting Chant myth, Holy Man was captured by the Thunder People because he disregarded ceremonial instructions. One of the sand paintings in mandalic form shows him surrounded by Thunder People and being carried away by them (Reichard, 1939: 58, fig. 6). Zigzag lightning binds him to Black Thunder, and at his feet is a dark circle symbolizing a lake. In the myth this lake opened up into the entrance to Big Thunder's house. At the bottom of a ladder of zigzag lightning sat Big Thunder. When he saw Holy Man he was angry, but when he was told about Holy Man's parentage and purposes, he agreed to teach him until his deficiencies in ceremonial knowledge were corrected. There is also a sand painting of Big Thunder (Reichard, 1939: frontispiece) standing alone with his wings outstretched, while waterspouts and lightning dart from underneath them. Four smaller Thunders are shown down the center of his body. His tail is rain and the sound of thunder. Jagged lightning surrounds the painting, and the guards are Big Fly and Bat.

Meanwhile the second hero of the chant, Holy Boy, went on his own adventures. His way led to the underworld of water, instead of the sky world of the Thunder People. At the top of a hill he came across a large lake. In the center was a cornstalk, with two eagle feathers floating nearby. Holy Boy reached for the feathers but could not quite touch them. When he reached from the east for the second time, he lost his footing and fell into the lake. He was swallowed by Big Fish, who was waiting there, and taken down to the Whirling Waters. Holy Boy remembered that he had a string of flint points with him, so he cut his way out of the fish. Then he used healing herbs to cure the wound. When he met the chief of the Big Water People, Holy Boy found him very angry. But when he found out about Holy Boy, he agreed to teach him offerings, prayers, songs, and paintings.

There is a large double sand painting called Sky-Reaching Rock (P4B#6). It is two mandalas combined. The one to the north shows Holy Man in the power of the Thunders; the one to the south shows Holy Boy surrounded and captured by the Fish People. All the places and animals that figured in these adventures are shown in the sand painting.

When the proper offerings were made and the teaching was finished, Holy Boy was free to return to his home. He was given a sand painting to use for people who had an accident or illness due to water. This painting shows a central lake around which are four black mountains. On each mountain is the figure of a dragonfly, the symbol of pure water. In each of the cardinal directions are a Thunder Person, a Water Ox, and a Water Horse. The four sacred plants are between them. All these mythical creatures are surrounded by special symbols connected with the power of water (Reichard, 1939: fig. 8).

On the way home, riding on zigzag lightning, Holy Boy

visited the homes of the Monster Fish Maidens, the Water Horses, and the Turtles. They all gave him something to use in the chant. Then he went to the surface of the water and on to Whirling Mountain, where Changing Woman and her people were searching for him. After all these adventures Holy Man and Holy Boy were wan and exhausted; a complete ceremony was held for them with many sand paintings.

Afterward Holy Man went on one more adventure, this time to the Buffalo People. The buffalo is a special symbol to the Navaho because of his hump, which confers power. The Navaho went on hunting parties to obtain buffalo, but it was mainly for medicinal purposes, not for food. The horns, the tail, the skin around the shoulder, the dried heart, and the skin from the nose all had special medicinal magic. The warmth and perspiration from the buffalo's body were thought to make medicinal herbs grow overnight.

Holy Man saw a group of these animals and followed them a long way, until they revealed themselves to him as Buffalo People. They taught him their prayers and paintings so they might be included in the ceremony. They also gave him two of their women for his wives. Holy Man had intercourse with the buffalo women, and because this broke ceremonial restrictions he became ill, but the Buffalo were able to heal him with their magic herbs.

The buffalo women were wives of the great Buffalo-Who-Never-Dies, who was on his way to avenge the indignity. That night was very long; when Holy Man called for the dawn, it came in a red glare instead of the usual white light, indicating the greatest danger. Buffalo-Who-Never-Dies saw Holy Man and made a mighty charge, but Holy Man with his two wives escaped to one of the sacred mountains and waited there. Each time he charged, Buffalo-Who-Never-Dies was able to demolish part of the mountain, but Holy Man was always able to move to another part; as he did so, he shot a powerful arrow into Buffalo. On the fourth charge the arrows took effect and Buffalo-Who-Never-Dies rolled over and died. Since he embodied the life of all the Buffalo People, they all died with him except the two wives of Holy Man. With their encouragement, Holy Man set about restoring the great Buffalo to life. He pulled out the arrows with prayers and rituals. This took much effort, but finally Buffalo-Who-Never-Dies began to move. When he was completely restored, he recognized Holy Man's superior power and relinquished all claim to his wives. Holy Man stayed with the Buffalo People for some time, learning more of their lore. Then, with all that he had learned, he made his way back to those who were waiting for him at Whirling Mountain.

Several important sand paintings show the magic buffalo. One of the most powerful depicts the restoration of Buffalo-Who-Never-Dies (Reichard, 1939: Plate XXIV). This shows again the stability and power of the central quaternity of the Male Shooting Chant. A sacred lake is in the center, and around it are the sacred mountains on which Holy Man stood to defy the charging Buffalo. In between the mountains are four different kinds of healing herbs used by Holy Man in the restoration. To the east is the figure of Holy Man, pulling an eagle-feathered arrow out of Black Buffalo. To the south is Holy Boy, pulling a yellow-feathered arrow from Blue Buffalo. Holy Woman in the west pulls an eagle-feathered wand from White Buffalo, and Holy Girl in the north pulls a red-feathered wand from Yellow Buffalo. This shows the control of the Holy People over the great powers of fertility and healing that are symbolized for them by the buffalo. The directional colors are slightly different from the standard ones—as often in the chants, if some specific reason requires it. Here black is to the east, blue to the south (which is standard), yellow to the north, and white to the west.

After Holy Man returned from his adventures with the buffalo, a final healing ceremony was performed and the Holy Ones prepared to depart. They gave their last instructions to their relatives, the Animal People, and empowered them to represent the Holy People on earth. Then they embraced the

Animal People warmly, rose into the sky, and vanished, nevermore to be seen on earth.

The animals of the Male Shooting Chant are not the only ones to be seen in Navaho sand paintings. If a thorough inventory were made, all the animals, insects, and birds of the Navaho country would be found to possess some symbolic significance. None is too large or too small to be left out, and each plays a part in the mythical drama of the heroes and gods. In many of the sand paintings they are the symbols that are brought into contact with the patient through the medium of the sand. The Snake People, the Eagle People, the Fish People, the Buffalo People, and many others contain reservoirs of healing power. The mythical animals—the Water Horses, Water Oxen, and Thunderbirds—are indistinguishable from the natural ones. One and all they are part of the great symbolic mandala that is incorporated into the sand paintings. They define and give meaning to the Navaho universe, and they transfer that meaning—and its secret power—to the patient.

The sand paintings themselves are a unique and specialized art form. With balance and careful symmetry, conventionalized symbolism, traditional form and style, and a flat, hieroglyphiclike appearance based on fourfold repetition, they have an immediate appeal. Great simplicity and subtle symbolism combine to produce a profound and stimulating effect on the viewer. As symbolic art they are peerless.

THE POLLEN PATH

Besides the mandalic round of birth, death, and seasonal change, there is, as its complement, a life pathway with a mystical goal: the Pollen Path. Matthews said of it: "Pollen is the emblem of peace, of happiness, of prosperity, and it is supposed to bring these blessings. When in the Origin Legend one of the war gods bids his enemy to put his feet down in pollen, he constrains him to peace. When in prayer the devotee says, 'May the trail be in pollen,' he pleads for a happy and peaceful life" (1897: 109).

Pollen is an integral part of the Blessing Way because "the pure, immaculate product of the corn tassel is food eaten by gods and man. Pollen, the beautiful, is a fit gift for the gods" (Wyman, 1970: 30). It is often sprinkled on the head or put in the mouth to bestow blessing. Frequently during the all-night sing of Blessing Way the pollen bag is passed around to everyone. Corn is the Navaho staff of life, and pollen is its essence. Both are often personified—corn as White Corn Boy and Yellow Corn Girl, and pollen as Pollen Boy and Corn Beetle Girl. "Corn beetle" here refers to a small insect that lives in corn pollen, and is called "the ripener," a symbol of fertility, happiness, and life itself (*ibid.*, p. 31).

The following excerpt from a Blessing Way prayer about the mating of corn shows the great importance of pollen in identifying the patient with White Corn Boy and his supernatural nature.

> White Corn Boy at the center of wide cornfield,
> His pollen feet become my feet,
> His pollen legs become my legs,
> His pollen body becomes my body,
> His pollen mind becomes my mind,
> His pollen voice becomes my voice,
> His pollen headplume becomes my headplume,
> Because of pollen he is an invisible one, therefore I become an invisible one,
> Pollen which rises with him is rising with me as I say this,
> Pollen which moves with him in bulk moves with me as I say this,
> Pollen by which blessing radiates from him radiates from me as I say this, etc.
>
> (Wyman, 1970: 204)

Ordinary pollen is shaken from corn, but the concept is extended to many other things. Real pollen is the pollen from cattail rushes, and blue pollen is the ground petals of larkspur. Reichard finds that associations with pollen are extended to "include glint or sheen as an essential part of an animal, object or person, a quality represented by pollen" (1950: 250–51). Yellow powder that collects on the surface of water is called water pollen. Animals may be sprinkled with pollen, and then dusted off to obtain the peculiar life quality of that animal—snake pollen for instance, or bird pollen. Animals to be killed for ceremonial purposes are smothered in pollen to absorb their life force. The symbol of pollen is concerned with essence. Pollen is a "living" component which can be seen as a haze or sheen around natural forms.

The great power of pollen can be invoked to keep peace and ward off enemy attack, as in this song, which is sung to an approaching enemy to pacify him:

> *Put your feet down with pollen.*
> *Put your hands down with pollen.*
> *Put your head down with pollen.*
> *Then your feet are pollen;*
> *Your hands are pollen;*
> *Your body is pollen;*
> *Your mind is pollen;*
> *Your voice is pollen;*
> *The trail is beautiful.*
> *Be still.*
>
> (Matthews, 1897: 109)

When asked if he could tell about the Pollen Path and what it meant, Natani Tso commented: "It's the pollen from all kinds of beautiful plants. The wind blows the pollen along the trail and you travel on it. It is everywhere, not only on the reservation. Your body is holy when you travel over that trail. If you take no heed of these things then it affects your life, you get sick and everything is of no use. The Pollen Path leads to the restoration of harmony and beauty. It is blessed above it and all around it, blessed is my voice to describe it. More than that I don't know." At the time of this discussion, some attempt was made to draw a distinction between the Pollen Path as a symbol and as an objective reality. But Natani Tso made no such distinction. He insisted that the Trail was "there" and you could find it any time you wanted it: "you can see it and travel on it and that's all you need to know."

He also said that all this leads up to *Sa'ah naagháí bik'eh hozhóón* (approximate rendering), an untranslatable pair of concepts at the core of Navaho religion. Their esoteric meaning is often withheld by the chanters, and is given only in old age as a last teaching to their students. Father Berard's informants said that the two meant something like "long life and happiness which follows long life." It may also imply perfect contentment. After long deliberation, Reichard thought the closest English rendering to be "according-to-the-ideal may-restoration-be-achieved." Since the chanters themselves do not discuss these concepts openly, many of them may never have learned the full scope of their meaning. According to another of Father Berard's informants, these ideals are also personified as a young man and woman who became inner forms of the earth, and were the parents of Changing Woman.

Natani Tso said that *Sa'ah naagháí* meant "you observe things, you look at them, you open your eyes," and that *hozhóón* meant "holiness," so that the whole concept would mean something like "to see holiness" or "to see according to holiness," which could be the ultimate teaching of symbolic healing.

CHAPTER TEN

The Navaho Synthesis

To understand the development of Navaho healing, it is helpful to place it in the spectrum of Southwestern Indian culture. The Navaho position between the hunting-oriented, nomadic tribes to the north and the agriculturally based communities to the south has been of the greatest importance in the formation of Navaho healing, with its own peculiar blend of borrowings and influences from neighboring tribes. The Apache, in close contact with the Navaho on the east, have a healing system more akin to the vision-quest religion of the plains Indians, while the Pueblo communities to the south and east have a more communally oriented healing system closely controlled by the priests and medicine societies. A brief overview of the healing procedures in these two neighboring cultures will show the Navaho position in clearer perspective and reveal some of its origins.

APACHE HEALING

The Apache arrived in the Southwest a little later than the Navaho. They are of the same stock and speak a closely related Athapaskan language. They have not been so long or so intimately associated with the Pueblos as their Navaho cousins, and their life style, religion, and healing methods still retain much of the nomadic, visionary style. The Apache differ greatly among the widely scattered divisions of their tribe, and generalizations about healing rites are for the most part difficult to make. But usually the Apache place a greater emphasis on the individually acquired vision than do the Navaho. For the healing descriptions given here, I will use Opler's reconstruction from the accounts of aged informants of Chiracahua Apache life in the nineteenth century (Opler: 1965).

Their pantheon is similar to the Navaho one, though less extensive. Above all the gods is a remote power called Life-Giver (Ysun), who intercedes little in human affairs. Coyote is present from the beginning, and it is he who steals fire, looses night and darkness upon the world, and makes death inevitable for mankind. White Painted Woman has much the same qualities as Changing Woman. She is impregnated by water or lightning, and gives birth to Killer of Enemies and Child of the Water. In the Apache myths, Killer of Enemies is variously represented as her son, her brother, or her husband. In contrast to the Navaho version, Child of the Water is the most important culture hero. He slays the monsters, establishes the girls' puberty rite, and in some versions creates people out of mud or cloud stuff. Two other sets of supernatural beings, the Mountain People and the Water People, are important in the cause and cure of illness.

Many of the Chiracahua healers did not acquire their ceremonies by diligence and learning, but by the acquisition of power through direct experience. Opler says:

No matter how eager a man is to acquire a ceremony, the first gesture is always attributed to the power, for power requires a man for its complete expression and constantly seeks human beings through whom to work. . . . The source of power may approach in a dream or if the person is ill or overwrought, in a vision. . . . Power first makes its presence known by the spoken word, by some sign, or by appearing in the shape of some bird or supernatural. Whatever its first guise, it later assumes a human-like shape and converses with the chosen individual. If the person is responsive, the details of the ceremony which he is thereafter to conduct are revealed to him, usually at the supernatural home of the power, within or near some well-known landmark.

(ibid., pp. 202–4)

Under some special conditions an Apache ceremony may be learned by one person from another, but the power must be willing and the recipient prepared for it.

As with the Navaho, illnesses that do not quickly yield to herbal therapy are ascribed to contamination by certain animals, ghosts, or witches. The most important of the infectious animals are the bear, snake, coyote, and owl. The first three, as we have seen, are each representative of a whole chant complex among the Navaho. The owl too has strong connections with the Night Chant, and is closely linked with ghosts. Owl sickness is thought to be a form of ghost sickness.

Apache dreams are generally regarded as warnings or prophetic signs. If a dead person is seen in a dream, that is the cause of terrible affliction. If one accepts food from a dead person, that is worst of all—a sign of imminent death. The Mountain People (called Gan) help to cure illness, but they also cause it if their rituals are not performed correctly.

Even though they are based on individual visions, Apache healing ceremonies have a common form. They usually last four days and nights; the nights are reserved for public events. Every shaman has his own paraphernalia, but objects in regular use include pollen, paints, herbs, a drum, and possibly eagle feathers.

When everything is ready the shaman rolls a cigarette and blows smoke in the four directions. Then he intones a prayer calling upon his power for aid. The shaman marks the patient and himself with pollen or some other sacred substance, then sings and prays. His songs are accompanied by the pottery drum or rattle, and they are addressed to his guardian spirit. If his appeal is granted, he sees a vision or hears a voice telling him what he must do to cure the patient. The prescription may call for special medicinal herbs, or the extraction of a witch object from the patient's body. If the power informs the shaman that the disease is due to witchcraft, the songs and prayers are kept up with great intensity to defeat the witch. At a dramatic moment, usually on the last night, the shaman sucks the pathogenic object out of the patient and spits it into the fire, where it pops loudly. That is the witch's "arrow," which was causing the trouble.

Sometimes a ground drawing is made, but the Apache paintings are rudimentary compared to the Navaho sand paintings. After the main performance the shaman imposes some behavioral or dietary restriction on the patient, and presents him with a protective amulet to prevent further illness. Before he leaves, the shaman receives the agreed payment. The supernatural powers are well pleased if the payment is generous, and are more likely to put forth energetic efforts on the patient's behalf.

In comparing these ceremonies with the Navaho ones, it should be remembered that the Navaho also pray and sing, using the rattle and the drum. They use pollen and sacred medicine objects, and impose restrictions on the patient. They give the patient an amulet, the chant token, and expect generous payment. But they do not have guardian spirits or hear spirit voices. They see no visions telling them how to treat the patient and they do not suck out the disease object.

The main part of the Apache ceremony described here is the shaman's vision given him by his guardian spirit. For this he has to undertake a personal journey into the lands of the supernaturals. Because of the close similarity with the traditional journeys of the Navaho heroes in the chant myths, I will cite some details of an account of a visionary experience given to Opler by the son of a prominent bear shaman (*ibid.*, pp. 289–91).

The informant explains that in the vision his father went across the White Sands until he came to a place at the foothills called Hot Springs. He slept and was awakei.ed by a silver-tip bear. The bear spoke as a human and ordered his father to get up and follow him. He promised his father something precious. His father went with the bear right through a door in the rocks, and the bear took on human shape. Together they went through the clashing rocks and other perilous passages without any trouble. They went through gates guarded respectively by two big bears, two big snakes, two timber wolves, and two wild geese.

Then they crossed a dangerous bridge of moving logs and came to a beautiful place called the Home of Summer. They crossed a spiderweb bridge and came to another place even more beautiful, called Medicine's Home, where many healing herbs were growing. There was a series of such places: one contained creatures in human shape who tried to show him supernatural things; another, girls dressed like Painted Woman who showed him the girls' puberty ceremony. In the next place he heard drums beating and saw the mountain spirits; he was offered their power, but he declined because he wanted something more. Several times his father declined power offered to him. Finally he came to another man who was shining with yellow light, so that it seemed the wind was blowing pollen from the trees all around him. His father did not stop here either, but the man gave him a wagon with two yellow horses with white tails.

Then the informant said: "My father got in the wagon with a guide and they came to a gate, a big white gate. Everything was as white as could be, even the trees and fruit. Even the faces of the people there shone and before him he saw all kinds of things. He bowed down four times, and the fourth time he was before a man in a big white chair who had a white staff in his right hand. This man was the last one. This man asked my father how he got in and such things as that. My father told him all. . . . So he listened and said 'Yes' to everything my father asked him. Everything my father wanted, he got. . . . This man sang and performed what was given my father. And it raised him as though he had wings. There was nothing but clouds around him. Before him everything shook and there was lightning and thunder. Much was shown my father, terrible things (witchcraft) and how to stop them. The man handed him a staff. 'You'll always have this. It will speak itself. It must never be lost.' He told him what was best. And this, they say, was the power of bear" (p. 290).

This man's father became a famous bear shaman, well known among his own people and neighboring tribes. An example of his healing by means of the bear ceremony was described in the case of a young girl severely ill with pneumonia. The ceremony lasted four days. First he sang songs to the bear to find out what was to be done. His power told him that a certain mixture of herbs had to be given right away. It was prepared and given to the girl in four doses. This was repeated and the shaman took the right front paw of a bear and put it on her chest where the pain was greatest. He took a bowl, put it to her chest, and sucked. Blood and pus foamed out freely. This same procedure was done several times, always under direction of the bear spirit. After the fourth day of treatment the girl was looking better; gradually she regained her strength.

PUEBLO HEALING

At the other end of the healing spectrum in the Southwest, among the Pueblo, curing is a function of the clans or medicine societies. There are some individual medicine men who use herbs and other simple remedies to cure minor ailments, but it is the members of the important societies who deal with all major afflictions. Among the Hopi, the great clans each have a certain time of the year in which their special ceremony is performed. They are powerful priesthoods, and the only hope of help from the gods comes through them. These priesthoods ceremonially control the rain and the harvest, and cause disease and can cure it. If a sick person applies to the society, one of its members may suck out the disease, or a particular ceremony is performed for the patient. There is no need for individual visionary experience (Underhill, 1965: 209).

Among the Zuñi, the rain-bringing functions and curing functions are separate. The curing societies suck out the cause of illness, or perform wonderful feats of handling or swallowing fire to encourage the patient. All the ceremonies are traditional and handed down in the societies. Sometimes a small sand painting is made on the medicine altar. There also is placed a bowl of sacred medicinal water, a bear paw, and effigies of sacred animals. The animals are summoned from the directions with which they are associated. This is done for a different animal in each direction. All the animals bring their particular medicine for the supplicating patient.

In these curing ceremonies, traditional as they are, there is still some shamanistic influence. This is seen on the last night of the winter solstice, when each society calls upon its members to become "one person." This results in spirit possession, in which the men of the society strip to the breechcloth and perform sucking cures for anyone who wants it. Then wonders are performed such as stick-swallowing or fire-handling. In some societies the members put bearskins over their hands and rush about growling and behaving like bears. At this one time shamanism expresses itself fully (Underhill, 1965: 220).

Among the eastern or river Pueblos, the curing is also done primarily by the priests or members of the curing societies.

In a study of the Cochiti Pueblo, J. Robin Fox (in Kiev, 1964: 174–99) found two kinds of psychiatric illness prevalent in the Pueblo, and two distinct types of curing ceremonies for them. The first kind, thought to be caused by witches, was accompanied by paranoid fear and acute anxiety, as well as other symptoms. It was cured in some cases by a dramatic shock rite. Fox thought that Pueblo society was preoccupied with controlling and repressing aggression, and with stressing co-operation and friendliness only as a further block to aggression. He presents a picture of a society that creates or enhances this kind of illness, and then at a peak point provides a dramatic, culturally approved means for its expression and cure (*ibid.*, p. 180).

The patient requests that the cure be undertaken by a medicine society. If the request is accepted the doctors prepare by spending four days in seclusion, chanting and abstaining from food and sleep. Witch phenomena increase in the village during that time. Then the doctors go to the patient's house and increase the intensity of their performance for another four days. Fox describes the last night:

> The monotonous rise and fall of the chant, the near-darkness with the flickering fire, the hideous make-up, the cries in the night and rappings at the door and windows, the elaborate precautions—all these elements build up until the doctors, worked into a controlled frenzy, dash from the house to do battle. Patients describe how they have been nearly mad with fear by this time, unable to move or cry out and convinced that they are to die. Then comes the terrible battle in the darkness. The doctors claim that, although of course they do a lot of the "business" themselves, it is the witches who get "inside them" and make them do it. They do indeed roll in convulsions and lacerate themselves. . . . Those in the house are by now at screaming point. "Sometimes we think the witches have got them (the doctors) and that they will come for us." The doctors reappear and enact the ultimate horror. They come in the semidark-

ness huddled together fighting with something in their midst that screams horribly. It is the witch who stole the heart. Then, by the firelight, the war chief shoots it, and it disappears. The effect on the patient can be imagined. The incredible relief and tears of joy and gratitude leave him "feeling like all the badness has gone out." The "heart" is returned to the patient. Then, almost nonchalantly, the doctors and people eat stew and drink coffee. Life returns to normal; the universe is on an even keel again.

(pp. 185–86)

Here the management of evil is effected to an extraordinary degree.

The Navaho medicine man handles these matters with more dignity and restraint. He has learned to use prayers and sand paintings, instead of these frightening scenes. Even the orderly Pueblos have not gone as far as he in the regulation and control of spirit possession through symbols.

The Pueblos recognize another less drastic type of illness and cure which is intimately bound up with the clan system. Clans in Pueblo society are extremely important, and are given more weight than among the Navaho. They center around matrilineal descent, so that one of the most terrible things that can happen to a child is to lose its clan mother. In such a case illness may occur. Fox (pp. 186–94) describes a patient who had pains in her stomach and was unable to eat. She talked to herself and acted frightened. These anxiety symptoms had been present since the death of her mother when she was twelve, and continued until the time of the curing ceremony when she was in her early thirties.

The cure was a calm, dignified ceremony in which she was adopted into another clan. Announcements were sent out four days in advance, and all the members of the patient's old and new clans gathered and conducted her to the curer's house. There her head was washed in amole suds, a symbol of adoption into the new clan. Everyone brought presents for her and enough food for a copious banquet. The patient was given a new name and thenceforth she could regard the members of the new clan as her "mothers." The new clan could give her many considerations and benefits that the old clan could not. The patient gained a new dwelling and security. All informants agreed that after the curing ceremony the symptoms that had plagued her for so many years decreased remarkably. Obviously, the cure depended less on the use of symbolism and more on the social factor, although symbols were still employed. In general, the social factor in the cure of illness looms much larger among the communally oriented Pueblos than among the Navaho.

SYMBOLIC SHAMANISM

The Navaho synthesis consists primarily of borrowing elements of healing from these adjacent cultures and creatively integrating them into a thoroughly unique healing system. The Navaho took much of the structure of Pueblo religion, and filled it with the visionary, wonder-working myths and symbols of the northern tribes they encountered on their long southward migration. If inferences can be made from the religions of other Athapaskan tribes who "dropped out" along the way, when the Navaho entered the Southwest their religion must have been simpler. Probably they had no masked dancers, no large ceremonials, and no specialized techniques like the sand paintings and ritual prayers, but probably did have sucking doctors and magic-working shamans. They must have feared witches, as do all the tribes, and their ceremonies were doubtless connected with visionary experiences and dreams, and concerned mainly with rites of passage (Underhill, 1965: 225).

As they came into close proximity with the Pueblo culture, they developed a more traditional ritual structure. It was now unnecessary to seek visionary experiences, but they still centered all the ritual action around the patient, and kept the time and place of the ceremonies fluid and adaptable to his needs. But they borrowed freely from the Pueblo cere-moniés. Even the Navaho term for some of their gods, the Yei, is taken from the Zuñi word for spirits. The figures on the sand paintings and the ceremonial dancers bear marked resemblance in costume to the Pueblo katchinas. Both danc-ers and katchinas wear kilts and sashes, a form of dress not found among the Navaho, and the masks in both cases must be made of unwounded buckskin. In the ceremonies a time pattern of eight days of secret rites and a ninth day of public spectacle is common to both cultures. Also, in both Navaho and Pueblo ceremonies the main participants must observe four extra days of restriction and seclusion. The major Nav-aho chants have adopted all the ceremonial forms of the Pueblo medicine society initiations: bathing, emesis, body painting, prayer-stick offering, meal strewing, sand painting, and payment for services (*ibid.*, p. 235).

But the great chant myths—except for the origin myth, which is also of Pueblo derivation—are really visionary tales. The basic idea of journeys to upper and lower worlds is es-sentially a shamanistic one. Eliade (1964: 259) tells us that a most important part of shamanistic technique is the ability to move from one cosmic region to another: from the earth to the sky world or underworld. The shamanistic universe is conceived as having these three levels connected by a central axis, and only the shaman knows the secret of the break-through plane. In some Siberian cosmologies the number of levels is increased to five or six or nine, but the threefold functional division remains basic.

The Navaho myths reveal much the same cosmology. In the chantway myths the heroes and heroines visit a sky world or spirit land above the earth, and an underworld reached by an underground passage or through a lake. Thus Holy Man, the hero of the Male Shooting Chant, is taken against his will to the home of the Thunder People, who teach him chant lore. Scavenger, the hero of the Bead Chant, is taken to the sky home of the Eagles. Glishpáh, the Snake Woman of Beauty Way, goes down a ladder to the underground home of the Snake People, while Holy Boy, the second hero of the Male Shooting Chant, falls into a lake and is carried down to the home of Big Fish. But the animals of the Navaho chants are no longer the guardian spirits of shamanism: they help or hinder the hero according to their nature, and the chiefs among them—Big Eagle, Big Fish, Big Snake—have become teachers and guides.

Both the Navaho heroes and the old shamans meet supernatural women on their journeys. A Goldi (Siberian) shaman has given an account of such a meeting. He was asleep on his bed when a beautiful spirit woman approached him. She said, "I am the *ayami* of your ancestors, the Shamans. I taught them shamanizing. Now I am going to teach you. The old shamans have died off, and there is no one to heal the people. You are to become a shaman." Next she said, "I love you, I have no husband now, you will be my husband and I shall be a wife unto you. I shall give you assistant spirits. You are to heal with their aid, and I shall teach and help you myself. Food will come to us from the people." He tried to resist her, but she said, "If you will not obey me, so much the worse for you. I shall kill you" (Eliade, 1964: 72).

The chant heroes also meet powerful women. The Warrior Twins are helped in crucial ordeals by Sun's daughter, who recognizes them right away and adopts them as her brothers. She shields them from the brunt of Sun's anger. In Plume Way the hero has to fight his wicked father-in-law for the daughter's hand, but she helps him by giving him her father's secret name. Rain Boy is enticed by the seductive wiles of Winter Thunder's wife, and thus becomes embroiled in his great adventure. Many of the chant heroes and heroines marry sons or daughters of the Holy People, and thus not only obtain chant knowledge but become part of the family.

Death, dismemberment, and subsequent rebirth and transformation form one of the great connecting links between shamanism and the Navaho myths. This has already been described in Chapter Eight. The shamans see it as part of their initiation. With the Navaho heroes, on the other hand, it usually comes about almost inadvertently, as punishment for going astray or disobeying instructions; nevertheless, it leads to an increase in power.

There are still other remnants of shamanism in the Navaho ceremonials. The methods of the diagnosticians—hand trembling, star gazing, candle gazing, or just "listening"—are examples. Similarly, the use of the basket drum and the rattle to accompany the singing of others. The moment of "turning down the basket" to begin the drumming is a special point in the ceremonies. If some misadventure or ill omen should occur during a performance, or if the participants or spectators should create too much disorder, the medicine man may at any time "turn up the basket," bringing the ceremony to a halt.

On the last night of Mountaintop Way a great Fire Dance (or Corral Dance) is held (Haile, 1946). An enclosure of spruce and pine boughs is built inside which ceremonial dances and feats of magic are performed around a roaring fire. These wonder-working tricks, once the stock in trade of the shamans, induced in the audience a heightened state of belief without which the cure would not work. The Navaho Fire Dance is mostly to amuse the spectators, but it still retains some of its old power to amaze and awe. The first and most important part of this ceremony is the rewhitening dance performed by the Fire Dancers. They announce their coming with a long whistle and enter in single file. Their bodies are painted with white clay to represent mountain sheep. When they first enter they spread their legs, hop forward, and much to the audience's amusement, imitate animals copulating. They chase each other with their feathered arrows, poking and tickling, then hop on one another leapfrog fashion. This is comical, but it also invokes natural fertility powers which are beneficial to the patient and the spectators.

The next part is more serious. The dancers circle the fire, holding large feathered arrows toward the flames. When they see an opening in the fire they dart forward, thrust the arrow feather into the fire, and hold up the charred remains. Then by quick manipulation they make the white feathers appear in place of the burnt ones, and cry out, "I have made it white again." This part of the dance symbolizes the hope that the patient will be restored like the arrows and regain his health.

In the next act the dancers show their power over the sacred arrows by swallowing them. The arrows have been prepared beforehand so that one part of the shaft slides into the other, allowing the whole shaft to shorten. As they dance around the corral, the dancers hold the arrows high. They place the arrowheads in their mouths and seem to swallow them. By their motions they show how painful and difficult it is. They sink to their knees with their heads bent back; with the arrows still apparently in their throats, they leave the corral with short, jerky steps.

Mountaintop Way may include a dancer dressed as a bear or a "dance with fire." In the latter about ten dancers run in wearing only breechcloths, their bodies heavily coated with white clay. In their hands they hold firebrands, which they light from the great fire. Some of the brands they throw over the corral walls. With the others they run as fast as possible around the fire, applying the torches to their bodies and rubbing their bellies and backs with the fire. When one dancer catches up to another, he slaps the other's back vigorously with the burning brand. They actually wash themselves in fire. When the brands are burned down, they throw them on the ground and leave the corral with a loud yelp. The spectators then take up the brands and wash their hands in some of the remaining fire. Other dances and tricks are exhibited throughout the night.

These acts are of peripheral importance in the Navaho

ceremonials. They are only distantly related to the patient, and they seem to be mainly for the amusement of the audience through the long night. Although they are not true rituals, they nevertheless have a symbolic meaning which relates to the healing purpose of the chant. The rewhitening dance demonstrates the dancers' power to restore the whiteness of the arrows, as the chant restores the patient. The fire dance shows the dancers' ability to handle fire with impunity and expose their bodies to its revivifying effects. When the power has been tamed, the audience may do likewise. In the arrow-swallowing acts the dancers show their ability to take the powerful arrows into their bodies and make them part of themselves. In the myth the arrows were one of the most powerful gifts of the Sun to the Warrior Twins. By swallowing the arrows the dancers are imitating the power of these supernaturals.

The medicine man who is in charge of the entire ceremony takes no part in these performances. He spends the night chanting the proper song sequences inside the hogan with the patient and his assistants. He does not engage in sleight-of-hand tricks or magical shows to demonstrate his potency. Such shamanistic practices have been relegated to the dance performers on the final night.

It is important to recall here that in spite of all these remnants of shamanism found in their ceremonies, the Navaho medicine men are not true shamans as found in many parts of North and South America, Siberia, and other parts of the world. The methods of these true shamans have been described as, first, an appeal to auxiliary spirits, which are often animals; second, drum playing and dancing as preparation for a mystic journey; and third, the trance—real or simulated—during which the shaman's soul is believed to have left his body (Eliade, 1960: 61).

Except for his appeal to supernatural beings in his prayers and songs, the Navaho medicine man does none of these things. All these events—dancing; ascending or descending into other worlds; talking to supernaturals who often have the form of animals; initiation through many severe ordeals into a secret healing process; and the return to earth, bringing these powers back for the benefit of the people—are incorporated symbolically into the prayers, rites, myths, and sand paintings, as shown repeatedly in the preceding chapters. The scenario which the true shaman acts out in his person is projected by the Navaho medicine man into the contents of his myths and rituals, into the symbols of the chant. As the medicine men themselves said in Chapter Two, they need no special trance or ecstatic vision to enter the profession of healing, only the desire and patience to learn the vast amount of symbolic material. They have no guardian spirit and no special connection with the gods. What they do have is the ability to manipulate power by means of the symbols. Because the supernatural power once carried by the person of the shaman is now displaced to the symbols, this particular healing method may be described as *symbolic shamanism.*

CHAPTER ELEVEN

Symbolic Healing: Ancient and Modern

Navaho healing is a fully developed form of symbolic healing. Because of the accessibility and clarity of its symbols, it can be readily analyzed and compared with other cultural forms, such as those of the Apaches and Pueblos in the preceding chapter. In Chapter One symbolic healing was compared with scientific healing; fundamental differences between the two were noted in defining, diagnosing, and treating illness. Scientific healing—with its empiricism, reliance on the experimental method, ideals of strict objectivity, and intellectual understanding—seemingly has little in common with the intuitive, symbolic approach.

Recent research on brain function suggests that the two approaches may be mediated by different hemispheres of the brain (Ornstein, 1972). The left hemisphere, which is connected to the right side of the body, seems more specialized in the deductive, analytic approach, while the right hemisphere, which is connected to the left side of the body, is more intuitive and holistic. If this research turns out to be well founded, then scientific healing clearly would belong to the left hemisphere, and symbolic healing to the right.

It is less than a century since dynamic psychology became one of the medical disciplines. Now every psychological theory claims to be objective and factual, but for each school the facts seem different and the objectivity relative. The scientific method has been extraordinarily elusive when applied to mental healing. Apart from its purely organic or behavioral aspects, much of the psyche remains terra incognita, open to the most varied projections. Like the six blind men who examined the elephant, every school finds something different. There are behaviorists, organicists, gestaltists, existentialists, Adlerians, Freudians, Jungians, Kleinians, and Rogerians, as well as group therapists, family therapists, marital therapists, and many others. Even the operational guidelines on what constitutes health and healing, or what disease is and when it is cured, remain lost in the fog of interdisciplinary feuding. A generally acceptable theory of healing has yet to be found.

Solid, demonstrable proof of inner psychological dynamics that can be convincingly replicated seems not only difficult but impossible. Therefore each school of psychotherapy has been free to follow its own intuitive leads, and to shape its theory and practice accordingly. Kiev points out in his study of folk psychiatry (1964: 4–5) that many statistical studies show that 65 to 70 per cent of neurotic patients and about 35 per cent of schizophrenic patients improve after treatment, regardless of the type of treatment received. This is quite a respectable medical cure rate, and it does not imply that these treatments are invalid. It implies rather that the theoretical differences stressed in the literature are perhaps not the one that really make a difference. No matter to what school a therapist professes allegiance, there may be some common underlying principles that guide his practice.

In addressing himself to that idea, Ackerknecht said: "The therapeutic achievements of the psychogenetic movement do not necessarily depend upon real etiological knowledge of causal treatment. . . . It is quite possible that the therapeutic successes are essentially due to the same two basic mechanisms of *confession* and *suggestion* which are so little understood and which have been used with such success by the medicine men" (1959: 84, italics mine). This idea points to a new level of understanding of the healing process, but it takes into account only two of the mechanisms of healing. Confessions to the medicine man of broken taboos and other transgressions, and exposure to forcefully made suggestions by the shaman or medicine man, are important. But this is often done through culturally accepted symbolism. Not only is the symbol in tribal healing rites a function of suggestion, but it is invoked and transmitted to the patient by identification and other devices illustrated in the preceding chapters. The healing transformation—the cure—comes from the patient's inner recognition and interaction with the symbol as well as with the medicine man. The medicine man takes the patient back to the origins of his being, to renew his energy for the healing process. He listens to the patient's "evil" in the form of confession, and then deals with it through absolution, rectification, dispersion, or integration, until the patient's guilty burden is somewhat relieved. He mediates the renewal process through symbols of death and rebirth, then at the end of the process places the patient in a new, reconstructed universe. All this he does with the aid of symbols, working through transference.

In his account of the methods of Indian medicine men, David Villaseñor emphasizes the subjective element of symbolism, which a purely behavioral description would neglect. Without this element the use of symbols would seem to be a simplistic, mechanical affair, which it certainly is not. Villaseñor believes that the vibratory chanting and prayer patterns form an inner stimulus which raises the patient's consciousness to a higher plane—which is very different from suggestion (1963: 71). Without this inner response, symbols are dead—mere pictures in a book or monotonous chants droning on all night. Getting the response brings an immediate connection to an energy source. The analogy of connecting a plug in a wall socket comes to mind. The symbol lights up, and suddenly energy is available to perform feats that would otherwise be impossible.

Extremely important in making this connection is the patient's need. In discussing shamanistic practices among the Cuna Indians of Panama, Lévi-Strauss emphasized this and gave it the prominence it deserves:

> The cure would consist, therefore, in making explicit a situation originally existing on the emotional level and in rendering acceptable to the mind pains which the body refused to tolerate. That the mythology of the shaman does not correspond to an objective reality does not matter. The sick woman believes the myth and belongs to a society which believes in it. The tutelary spirits and malevolent spirits, the supernatural monsters and magical animals, are all a part of a coherent system on which the native conception of the universe is founded. The sick woman accepts these mythical beings or more accurately she has never questioned their existence. What she does not accept are the incoherent and arbitrary pains which are an alien element in her system but which the shaman, calling upon the myth, will reintegrate with a whole where everything is meaningful.
> (1967: 192–93)

He calls this process "psychological manipulation," which is much the same as the symbolic healing treated in this book: the use of culturally accepted symbols acting directly upon the patient's unconscious and causing changes in his psychic patterning.

It is at the unconscious intersection of the physical and the psychical, the dynamics of which are only dimly perceived, that the work of the symbol becomes potent. The symbol is primarily an intrapsychic agent, but it can engender patterns which become concrete and therefore physically effective. The connection which makes this possible is difficult to establish; the psyche is seldom open to such influences. It is not enough to look through a picture book of symbols or develop an intelligent interest in world symbology. Outer symbols are dead until they contact and energize their inner potential counterpart. That is why ceremonies of symbolic healing are long and repetitive: they repeat the desired pattern over and over again, until the connection is made and the same symbolic pattern "lights up" in the patient's psyche. The ritual procedures and the sand paintings or other visual devices make the pattern visible and real. The myths, songs, and prayers relate the pattern to the mythological system which the patient has known since childhood and, as Lévi-Strauss said, "never questioned." The laborious task of identification with mythological deities is performed over and over again in such scrupulous detail that the psyche is driven into a state of receptivity. Then, by the grace of the gods, the transformation may occur, and if the symbol that impresses itself upon the receptive psyche is potent enough, the effects could be permanent.

ANCIENT CONCEPTS OF SYMBOLIC HEALING

The development of healing symbols capable of mediating such profound effects is a slow, intuitive process. Culture exerts a strong influence and provides a wide range of variability, but it has definite limitations. The origin of a symbolic idea must come like a stroke of lightning in exactly the right place. Only a few such ideas have survived the centuries. In a world-wide survey of concepts of symbolic disease causation among tribal cultures, Clements (1932) found only five.

If more advanced cultures are included, there are probably a few more. The five he perceived were (1) object intrusion, (2) spirit intrusion, (3) witchcraft, (4) soul loss, and (5) breach of taboo. Each of these etiological factors is associated with a corresponding concept of symbolic healing. The data suggest that each of these concepts developed only once or twice in world history, and spread by slow cultural diffusion. In this manner they spanned the length and breadth of continents. All of them, while clearly symbolic, are logically consistent. All are capable of great flexibility to suit varying conditions, but certain clusters of related traits have remained remarkably stable from culture to culture.

The simplest and oldest method of symbolic healing is object removal. It is based on the idea that an offending object —bone, hair, splinter, bloody worm, small animal, etc.—has entered the body, and is causing symptoms that are usually localized at the point of entry. The offending object may be removed by massage or bleeding, but most often it is done by sucking through a tube, or with the mouth alone, at the painful place on the patient's body. Then by sleight of hand the sucking doctor produces the offending object, ostentatiously exhibits it to the patient and his relatives, and quickly disposes of it. This procedure can be elaborated into a lengthy ritual with songs, prayers, and strenuous exertions on the part of the doctor. But the result is simple and concrete, and the symbolic object can be seen by all.

This method has been found throughout the New World, and in widely scattered parts of the Old. Such a distribution suggests that it had a long, slow history of development and diffusion, possibly stretching as far back as Paleolithic times. Lévi-Strauss cites an example, taken from Boas, of a Kwakiutl shaman who had learned to cure disease by manipulating the patient's body and then sucking out a bloody piece of down, which he declared to be the cause of the illness. At first the young shaman, whose name was Quesalid, was skeptical of his own methods. He knew the bloody object was in his mouth all the time, but to his own surprise he had great success with his patients. His skepticism began to wane. Then he journeyed to a neighboring tribe and encountered another group of shamans who cured, not by producing a bloody piece of down, but by merely spitting saliva into their hands. Quesalid was outraged at this improper procedure; though just a beginner, he challenged the older shaman to a contest. With his own dramatic technique and superior insight, he triumphed; the older shaman had to acknowledge his power. Gradually he gained full belief in his own method because it worked so well (Lévi-Strauss, 1967: 169–73).

The young shaman had also grasped an important premise of symbolic healing: that the effect on the patient's psyche is due not to the removal of the object, but to the *symbolic action of removal*. The action, symbolizing the removal of pain and evil, has its own impact. In many tribes it is publicly known that the object itself is not the cause of the disease, but only a symbol of the spiritual essence which is thought to be the real cause.

The concept of object intrusion leads naturally to that of spirit intrusion or possession. Here the cause of the disease is no longer symbolized by a visible object, but by an invisible spirit which usually causes symptoms of mental derangement rather than localized bodily pains. The associated method of healing is exorcism, whereby the offending spirit is transferred into an animal (Old World), or into a plant or stone (New World). This concept by its very nature has to be an integral part of a mythology which includes spiritual influences and demonic beings. It probably had a somewhat later origin than object intrusion.

Such a phenomenon may extend to total possession, in which the spirit takes over the victim's body and speaks through his mouth. This is well developed in Siberian shamanism, and as part of that complex spread to the Arctic and the Pacific Northwest. Conditions arising from spirit intrusion or possession are behaviorally similar to the hysterical reactions described in textbooks of psychiatry. In modern psychological thinking they would represent intrusions or possession of the patient's consciousness not by outside influences, but by parts of his unconscious psyche.

The third concept of disease causation—sorcery or witchcraft—is truly universal in its distribution. It is found continuously in both Old and New Worlds, and in the most primitive as well as the most advanced cultures. Witchcraft is associated with an elaborate symbolic system, and usually involves the supposed intent of another person—the witch or sorcerer—to injure the patient by symbolic means. He may pierce or burn small images of the victim, or obtain some part of his body—toenails, hair, excrement—or his intimate possessions, and by bewitching these objects cause the victim to sicken or die. He may shoot foreign objects into the victim's body—a practice that is sometimes called "bean shooting"—where they lodge and cause distress. The witchcraft complex nearly always includes certain characteristic traits: animals that move about at night with incredible speed; the notion that illness and death can result from introducing some kind of noxious substance into the victim's body; and a connection with incest (Kluckhohn, 1960: 49). This extremely detailed set of beliefs may have existed as far back as the Paleolithic period, perhaps in conjunction with object intrusion.

The cure for witchcraft is countersorcery: the shaman or medicine man must exert all his powers to battle the witch, turn the evil power back upon him, and destroy him. Both the patient and the medicine man are thought to be in great danger, for the witch's power might be greater than that of the medicine man. This method of healing involves a strong social element; it often unites the entire tribe or village in an intense, passionate drama in which the witch is apprehended and made to confess. The cure may not be thought effective until the accused person is tortured and burned.

Witchcraft is an essentially paranoid phenomenon which

involves the projection of dangerous aggressive impulses onto someone else. It seems to have been a universal method for the control of aggression, and may have been a safety valve necessary for the development of communal life. Many anthropologists have seen witchcraft as a balancing force to relieve and contain the hate and suspicion within human society. There is some evidence that in societies where belief in witchcraft is especially strong, the level of interpersonal violence is considerably lower (Driver, 1969: 444).

In these first three concepts—object intrusion, spirit intrusion, and witchcraft—something pathogenic is symbolically introduced into the body and then symbolically removed. In the fourth concept, soul loss, something is removed from the body that must be symbolically restored. This concept, found in widely scattered areas throughout the world, can probably be traced back to Siberian shamanism, where it is most fully developed. Clements estimated that it originated sometime after the concept of object intrusion, but still during the upper Paleolithic.

The concept of soul loss is part of a whole complex of ideas which accompany it. These may vary according to the culture involved, but must include belief in a soul which may leave the body for lengthy periods of time, especially in dreams. When it is gone, there is felt to be a marked loss of vitality resulting finally in death. The soul's wanderings may be perceived in dreams, and when it returns to the body it enters through the top of the head. The main cause of loss of soul is sudden fright; children are especially susceptible. The bodily seat of the soul is located by various cultures in the heart, liver, kidney fat, or gall bladder. The cure for soul loss lies in the skill of the shaman. He must embark on an ecstatic journey to the higher or lower regions, where he fights and usually conquers the malign disease-causing spirits and forces them to restore the patient's soul.

Among the peasants in various parts of South America, loss of soul is called *susto* and is cured by the local medicine man. John Gillin (1948) describes how such an illness is manifested by depression, withdrawal, confusion, and temporary ego collapse. These symptoms are objectively apparent, but in that culture they are interpreted universally as caused by loss of soul.

Every one of the four concepts already mentioned involves a particular symbol whose presence or absence causes disease: the intruding object or spirit that must be removed, the dolls or body parts used in witchcraft, and the soul itself which must be returned. The fifth and most recently developed concept, breach of taboo, involves no discrete symbol but is associated with a well-developed symbolic system that includes supernatural beings who lay down sanctions and send punishment in the form of illness or death. The taboos may include special foods that can be eaten only at certain times or not at all; acts that may be performed only at certain times; and ritual observances that rigidly prescribe what may or may not be done. If this system proliferates unduly it can become obsessive, even pathologically so, and stifle creativity within the society. There is good evidence, for instance, that pottery and basket making were almost abandoned by the Navaho, because these activities were surrounded by so many taboos. One Navaho woman said, "There are so many things that I can't do when I make baskets that I don't know what I can do and what I cannot do any more" (Tschopik, 1938).

The idea of disease as a punishment for breach of taboo probably developed independently in several places: Middle America, the Arctic, southern Asia, and Oceania. It spread north from Mexico and Peru to many North American tribes: the Hupa, Pomo, Luseño, Mono, Yokuts, Navaho, Zuñi, Crow, Iroquois, Chickasaw, and others. It may have been a precursor of more elaborately organized religions. The cure is usually confession and expiation. Complex ceremonies may be necessary to gain the god's forgiveness or to right the imbalance of broken taboos.

It is a further testimony to their adaptive genius that every one of these concepts of disease is found, at least in vestigial form, among the Navaho. Punishment for breach of taboo is the most dominant. We have examined in Chapter Five how many taboos surround the care of the dead and avoidance of ghosts. Improper behavior at ceremonials, handling or even observing sacred objects, may be dangerous. The ceremonials are themselves an intricate network of carefully controlled rites, during which there is the ever present possibility of error. Taboos can be broken by the slightest lack of vigilance on the part of the medicine man, the patient, or even the on-lookers, and improprieties may even cause illness to a fetus still in the mother's womb. Before contact with Europeans, Navaho society was developing ever increasing numbers of taboos and restrictions. The long, expensive ceremonials needed to correct mistakes of even the ordinary Navaho man or woman were becoming too heavy a burden. Often there was an obligation to have the chant given not only once but four times in the patient's lifetime.

Witchcraft is also a well-developed cause of illness among the Navaho. Until recent times much attention and energy were expended on finding and exposing witches, but witch-hunting among the Navaho was never as savage and brutal as among other tribes. It was soon incorporated into the chant system in the form of evil-chasing chants, in which the evil power is turned back upon the witch. An example of an evil-chasing prayer as used by Natani Tso was given in Chapter Seven.

Spirit intrusion is important in the Navaho theory of disease. Among the main causes of disease are the many powerful animals, natural forces, and supernatural powers that cause illness by "infection," another variant of the more general "intrusion" mentioned previously. Some essence from these sacred beings enters the patient and makes him ill. Contact with foreigners and ghosts also causes infection. In Chapter Five I mentioned the study of Kaplan and Johnson

(1964) which showed that the main forms of mental illness among the Navaho—moth craziness, ghost sickness, and crazy violence—are probably forms of possession. This is brought about by the infection just mentioned, and is part of what happens when a taboo is broken. In a variable culture, the several concepts of cause and cure do not exist discretely, but are woven together in a living system.

Soul loss and its cure are usually thought to be absent among the Navaho, but even this concept exists in vestigial form. In the chant myths the heroes and heroines generally make their journeys not to save souls, but to gain knowledge. Nevertheless in the prayers of liberation, an example of which was given in Chapter Eight, the Warrior Twins make a perilous journey through many underworlds to rescue something like a soul-body of the patient lying in the land of death, which they return to the actual physical body lying in the patient's hogan. This is analogous to the soul rescued from the other worlds by the shaman. These prayers are the most important elements of the chant ceremonials, and are experienced intensely by both the medicine man and the patient. Thus the idea of soul loss and its return is still preserved in the most sacred parts of the chants.

Object intrusion was also long thought to be absent among the Navaho, which was surprising because it occurs almost universally among the North American Indians. Reichard mentioned that in all her work on the reservation she had never come across any reference to it. Yet when I asked Natani Tso about it, he said: "Yes, Curtis Brady on the other side of Sweet Water performs sucking. I never saw that, only heard about it. There are no chants. He's got one of those crystals and puts it all over the patient's body. He finds out what's the cause of his illness, then he sucks it out. There are no prayers."

Both Berard Haile (1950) and Kluckhohn (1967) confirm that there once was a Navaho ceremony called Sucking Way. According to one of Kluckhohn's informants, this was given for foreign objects shot into a person by a witch. When the regular chant practices became powerful among the Navaho, sucking came to be regarded as an evil practice too closely associated with the witches themselves to be safe, so it was no longer tolerated. A few people may still practice it, but when the Navaho feel they need that kind of treatment, they visit sucking doctors from other neighboring tribes—Pueblos, Utes, and Apaches.

From this brief survey of ancient theories of the cause and cure of disease, some of which reach back to the Paleolithic era, a curious finding emerges. All the causes of disease are due to outside agents; none are due to the patient's own inner bodily processes. Object and spirit intrusion are from outside. Witchcraft is due to the hostile actions of another person. The soul is stolen by supernatural beings, who have to be persuaded or tricked into giving it back, and breach of taboo is punished by higher powers. In symbolic terms disease is never due to natural causes, but is always a product of error, punishment, or malicious intentions.

Theoretically, if all these causes could be rectified, the errors or imbalances righted, and the witches overcome, one could live forever or at least to a very advanced old age. I do not think that tribal man actually believed this—he was far too good an observer of natural fact. I think rather that this premise was always an integral part of the symbolic process. One idea running through all mythological systems is that life goes on forever and is constantly subjected to renewal; death is only a regrettable interlude. Such an idea underlies the custom, observed since earliest times, of providing the dead with food, possessions, and even animals and servants for the afterlife. In many places there was the custom of reddening bones to imbue them with the blood color of life. Such beliefs are not, or need not be, directly connected with ideas of an afterlife that involves reward or punishment. They are merely the deep-seated archetypal belief in the continuation of life. This notion transcends any thought of personal salvation.

TRANSFERENCE

In 1907 Jung and Freud met for the first time in Vienna. Their joy in discovering each other was so great that they talked for hours. Part of this conversation that Jung remembered all his life, and reported in his autobiography, was Freud's sudden question: "And what do you think about transference?" Jung answered that he thought it was the alpha and omega of the analytic method, whereupon Freud said, "Then you have grasped the main thing" (Jung, 1954: 172).

If members of the most varied and conflicting modern schools of therapy were to come together, the thing most of them would agree upon is the power of transference. It is a phenomenon of modern psychology that undercuts doctrinal differences. The relationship between the Navaho medicine man and his patient also has important transference implications. Because of the great cultural differences, we cannot simply equate the two, but they are structurally analogous.

Transference is usually defined as the projection of split-off or unintegrated parts of the patient onto or into the analyst. These parts are usually unconscious emotional attitudes, characteristic of infancy and childhood, that are transferred to the therapist because they were not adequately satisfied in the patient's early years. But this phenomenon does not always remain within the sphere of the personal. Many times in analytical treatment the feelings and attitudes directed toward the therapist bestow on him the amplitude of a god or godlike being. There is often a time when the patient is like the helpless victim lying in the land of the dead, while the analyst is like the powerful hero who must rescue him. The transference becomes suprapersonal and archetypal, whether the analyst wants this or not (Jung, 1953).

In Navaho symbolic healing the whole process revolves around this kind of transference, but there are many built-in safeguards. All the activities of the first few days revolve around ceremonies of purification in which both patient and medicine man take part. They are ritually cleansed both within and without. Also the long periods spent in making the invitations and offerings for the gods prepare the participants for the central event of the chant—the identification of patient and medicine man with the supernatural beings. In the songs, sand paintings, and prayer litanies, which the patient and the medicine man repeat in unison, the medicine man does not hesitate to identify himself and the patient with the most powerful supernatural beings. In a prayer from the Night Chant quoted in Chapter Eight, the patient becomes the subject or protagonist of the prayer, and the medicine man takes on the roles of the heroes, Monster Slayer and his brother, who go through many layers of the underworld to find the patient, rescue him from the land of the dead, and return him to his familiar hogan. There are many examples of such prayers of identification, as for instance this one from Blessing Way, called Changing Woman's Prayer.

> *I am the Dawn Young Man [repeat four times].*
> *I am Dawn Talking God, I am Dawn Calling God [repeat].*
> *I am Dawn Pollen Boy, I am Sunrise Cornbeetle Girl [repeat].*
> *I am old age, I am happiness, I have become blessed again [repeat four times].*
> *I am the child of the inner form of Changing Woman.*
> *I am her grandchild.*
> *I have become blessed again.*
> *I have become blessed again.*
>
> (Wyman, 1970: 186)

As the prayer continues, in successive stanzas, the speaker declares himself to be the grandchild of the inner form of the Earth, the Sky, the Sun, the Moon, the Dawn, and the Dusk.

There are still other ways in which the attitudes of the medicine man are similar to those of the modern psychotherapist. The medicine man relies on knowledge, not trance phenomena or magical effects. The chant work is a restrained and dignified procedure, and for the most part the medicine man represents for the patient a stable, dependable leader who is helper and guide until the work is ended. The medicine man must undergo a long period of training and apprenticeship, and he must be prepared to pay a considerable sum for it. He must also undergo the experience of being a patient in the chant he is studying, preferably four times, which enables him to endure its power without faltering.

Kluckhohn and Wyman confirm that the chanter is expected to bring all his concentration to bear on the ceremony, as is the patient. He should not quarrel or gossip, and is expected to remain in the ceremonial hogan most of the time (1940: 19–20). During the progress of the chant he takes the position of surrogate parent to the patient. He may have informal talks with him in the interval between regularly scheduled ceremonial events. He may give the patient advice or he may just listen. Where there is a question of selecting the right chant, the patient must confess all his "errors" to the medicine man, or the wrong chant may be chosen.

Medicine men do not like to sing over close relatives, especially their wives. If a chanter sings over his wife, their relationship becomes one of a man and woman belonging to the same clan. Kluckhohn confirms that when a singer in the Ramah district did perform a ceremony for his wife, the marriage was permanently dissolved (1962: 98). Furthermore, a medicine man must not marry a woman who has at any time been his patient. It is a less serious matter for the medicine man to sing over his children or the children of his siblings.

The medicine man, like his modern counterpart, charges a considerable fee, without which his therapy cannot be expected to succeed; but the fee is often scaled down for poorer patients. The singer will seldom fail to respond to a really urgent summons. Medicine men are held in great esteem by

the community, but they are carefully watched. If they engage in peculiar activities or invite suspicion in any way, they
may be accused of misusing their power—as in witchcraft—
and so may be feared and condemned.

These similarities to modern psychotherapy are not just
fortuitous: they are the phenomena of transference. They
strictly define the position of patient and therapist during
the performance of a symbolic procedure which renders both
vulnerable to intense inner forces. The chant swiftly induces
a strong, archetypal transference in which patient and medicine man are intimately involved. At certain moments they
are totally identified with each other and with supernatural
(archetypal) forces. The medicine man leads the way, and
the patient follows, into a confrontation with symbolic imagery of such power that it may be dangerous as well as
curative. The effect is expected to be forceful, impressive,
and transforming.

MODES OF SYMBOLIC HEALING

In order to compare symbolic healing in vastly different cultures, it is necessary to keep in mind the relationship between the doctor (medicine man, shaman, etc.), the symbolic system, and the patient. The material previously presented in this book supports the idea that there are differing
modes of relationship between these three.

The first is the mode of the shaman. He enacts the symbolism in his own person through periods of ecstatic trance. He
alone is the carrier and focus of symbolic power; the patient
is only a passive participant who must go along with him.
This can be more clearly visualized in a scenario of shamanistic healing witnessed by Jochelson among the Koryak, a
Siberian tribe (1905: 49): "Suddenly the shaman com-
menced to beat the drum softly and to sing in a plaintive

voice; then the beating of the drum grew stronger and stronger, and his song—in which could be heard sounds imitating the howling of the wolf, the groaning of the cargoose, and the voices of other animals, his guardian spirits—appeared to come, sometimes from the corner nearest my seat, then from the opposite end, then again from the middle of the house, and then it seemed to proceed from the ceiling. . . . The wild fits of ecstasy which would possess him during his performance frightened me." The shaman is the main hero and his journey is thought to be real.

The Navaho, as usual, occupy a borderline position. The Navaho medicine man does not act out the symbolism in his own person. He remains impassive and reserved, and the main focus of symbolic action is presented to the patient through the songs, prayers, and sand paintings. The medicine man draws upon a vast body of traditional symbolism, but he does not live it out. The mythic hero is the protagonist of the chant, and his journey occurs in the myth. The sand paintings alone—of which originally there were more than a thousand—comprise a major school of American Indian art. They combine a remarkable purity of style with great simplicity and emotional depth. They are, as Frank Waters said, "abstractions as pure as any known" (1950: 257). The Navaho have fallen heir to a great body of symbolism passed down through the centuries from northern shamanism. These images have been stored in the memories of the old Navaho medicine men and passed from generation to generation in their traditional forms. Now the myths are being written down, the songs recorded, and the sand paintings reproduced in permanent mediums. They are being made available for all to experience, but there will be no more.

The third mode of symbolic healing is found in modern psychotherapy. In this mode the doctor is comparatively passive. There are not only no ecstatic journeys, but no dancing, singing, sand painting, or any of the other culturally prescribed activities of the first two modes. There is no large traditional body of symbolism for the doctor to draw upon for the benefit of the patient. The main focus of symbolic action is from the patient himself. He must produce the symbols from his own dreams, fantasies, and personal visions. These might be expressed verbally or even in paintings, poems, or clay sculpture. The doctor's role is a catalytic one, mostly limited to reflection, interpretation, and encouragement. He listens to the patient, encourages him to explore his inner life, and through interpretation gives him a perspective in which to work. But the symbols, the basic material, must come from the patient himself. These three modes are summarized in Table IV. Transference, as mentioned before, is powerfully present in all three.

Dreams are handled in a different way in each of the three

TABLE IV

MODES OF SYMBOLIC HEALING

	Doctor's Role	Method	Patient's Role
Shaman	The shaman contains and carries the symbolism in his own person	and acts it out vividly and dramatically	for the passive, receptive patient.
Navaho Medicine Man	The Navaho medicine man draws upon	a fixed traditional body of symbolism (sand paintings, prayers, songs)	and presents them to the patient, who must actively co-operate in the ritual.
Psychotherapist	The modern psychotherapist receives the symbols	from the verbal and visual productions	of the patient, who actively produces them from his own psyche.

The circle designates the locus of greatest symbolic power, and the arrow represents the direction of its action.

modes of symbolic healing. In the early 1930s J. S. Lincoln (1935) collected dreams from several American Indian cultures which illustrate this point. The dreams he collected fell into two categories: culture-pattern dreams and individual dreams. Culture-pattern dreams were those whose manifest content was determined by the demands of the culture. As examples of these kinds of dreams, Lincoln cited Crow vision dreams, Ottawa puberty fasting dreams, and Yuma myth dreams. The contents of these dreams conform in all important respects to the mythology and expectations of their specific culture. They were sometimes obtained by fasting, going into seclusion, observing stringent taboos, or even mutilating the body. Individual dreams, on the other hand, were dreams without any specific cultural content. They sometimes contained elements of cultural importance, but these were always handled in an individual manner.

In cultures of the shamanistic type, where many of the members were encouraged to have ecstatic experiences and personal visions, dreams of the culture-pattern type were most prominent, almost to the exclusion of individual dreams. These dreams were sought not only for purposes of healing, but also to control the weather and originate new rituals for the tribal welfare. They all conformed to a stereotyped cultural pattern. A supernatural being, sometimes an animal, appeared and conferred power on the dreamer. Among the Blackfoot, a powerful Plains tribe, one person dreamed that an old man with white hair appeared and gave him a shell necklace which let him make clear weather. One Blackfoot medicine man had an especially powerful dream on the fourth morning of his fast. He dreamed that Sun Man and Moon Woman and their son, Morning Star, appeared. The Sun Man gave him his body and said, "You will live as long as I." The Moon Woman gave him power over rain. The Morning Star gave him eagle plumes for his hat, and tail feathers from a magpie that gave him power over the weather. Another Blackfoot medicine man dreamed he heard an owl singing.

The owl invited him into his tepee and sang a song four times whose words were: "Where you sit is medicine." This gave him the power to cure many people (*ibid.*, pp. 259–61).

Among the Navaho, where the symbolic mode is of the second type, the case was completely different. There were no culturally prescribed requirements for dreaming, and consequently no culture-pattern dreams. The dreams Lincoln collected from them were regarded as important, but they were all individual. Some of the dreams were thought to be prophetic: Hosteen Klah's mother dreamed when she was a young girl that she would live to be an old woman, and she did (p. 214). Often dreams were a sign that the dreamer needed a chant or a Blessing Way ceremony. One medicine man dreamed that the gods came after him and dragged him off toward the mountains. The dream recurred, and he felt it indicated that the medicines and masks of the Night Chant which he was handling were too strong for him. He felt that unless he had a healing ceremony sung over him, they would soon kill him (p. 218).

As might be expected from our previous observations about the fear of possession, the worst dreams were about ghosts and the dead. One medicine man had the following dream:

"I was going on horseback. Somebody was standing in front, I didn't know who. Then I said to the little girl who was on the back of the horse with me, 'What is that over there, my little mother?' My little mother didn't know what the thing was standing in front of us. So I left the horse and the little girl and went to see what the thing was. I walked towards it. As I got closer it was sinking. Finally I got to the spot where the thing was and it disappeared. There was a hole covered with a bunch of sticks and there was a Navaho sitting in the hole. His head was black and his body was grey. I think it was a '*chindi*' [corpse, ghost, evil spirit]. So I turned back towards my horse and the little girl was crying: 'Come back, my uncle, come back, my uncle.' So I got to the horse and tried to get on the horse but I couldn't. I had one leg on top of the saddle and I said to my little mother, 'Let's go, let's go.' The horse wouldn't go and I had my leg half way up the saddle. Then the *'chindi'* got hold of my leg and pulled me off the horse. The *'chindi'* got hold of my neck with his hand and his hand was cold like ice. He got me by the throat. So I fought with the *'chindi.'* I fought him hard and got loose from him. That's the end."

(pp. 231–32)

This is the worst possible kind of dream and puts the dreamer in danger of his life. Although the *chindi* is part of the Navaho cultural myth, the action of the dream is not culturally prescribed and takes on individual form.

In modern society, dreams have long been neglected; there is no culture pattern of any kind. Dreams are not even regarded as of special importance. All the great values of symbolism have been almost forgotten, except for a small body of persons engaged in psychotherapy. It remained for Freud, the great medicine man of our time, to appreciate once more the importance of dreams. When he said that dreams were the royal road to the unconscious he was rediscovering, in a different cultural context, an ancient heritage. He was restoring to modern man a great fecundating force—the dream symbol—that can draw upon the inexhaustible resources of the unconscious to give meaning once more to our scientific techniques of healing.

He was the pioneer and Jung was the prophet. Jung looked deeper and saw that the dream symbol revealed not only individual contents, as do Lincoln's Navaho dreams, but also bits and fragments of archetypal contents that echo the symbolism of ancient myths. By watching the patterns of a long series of dreams, he also saw that occasionally a big dream would occur, analogous to the vision-quest dreams. Today, however, such a dream would not be regarded as divine and "true," but rather as a product of that individual's unconscious processes, and meant mostly for him alone. Through these modern attitudes we are gradually becoming aware of the cultural and individual relativity of dream interpretation. Without imposing the rigid restraints of cultural dogmatism, we can then encourage the individual through association and amplification to find his personal meaning for his dreams and visions.

MODERN SYMBOLIC HEALING

This study of the theory and practice of Navaho chant healing has raised several important possibilities that only further research, and comparison with symbolic systems from other cultures, can confirm or negate. It has also given a new perspective on symbolic healing as a healing modality in its own right, quite distinct from other modalities such as scientific healing, empirical herbal medicine, and social healing, though it is often mixed with these. One can then distinguish a few basic principles that underlie its operation in ancient or modern times. These principles have served the main healing function for the entire human race over a period of time that can only be measured in millennia. They are archetypal forms and as such function outside the sphere of conscious intent, giving rise in every age to new intuitive adaptations to an ever-changing cultural environment. They are also to be found, as we have seen, in modern psychotherapy.

The first of these is the return to the origin or source. In mythological terms this means return to the creation of the world, and the evolution of mankind as revealed in the tribal origin myths. Eliade has reminded us that all myths are origin myths, telling how things began in that mythic place outside of time and space that is inhabited by the ancestors or supernatural beings—a place where all things are done and experienced in the original and proper way. Healing is always part of that paradigm. Eliade has said of it: "The *return to origins* gives the hope of rebirth. . . . We get the impression that for archaic societies life cannot be *repaired*, it can only be *re-created* by a return to sources. And the 'source of sources' is the prodigious outpouring of energy, life, and fecundity that occurred at the Creation of the World" (1968: 30).

For the modern individual in psychotherapy, more particularly in analytical therapy, this means a return to the origin of his individual life. Almost all forms of psychotherapy look backward to the patient's childhood to examine the familial and cultural influences on his illness. Sometimes this even extends back to birth, the "place of emergence" for modern psychology, and the very earliest mothering experiences. In this way important psychic images are activated, bringing about the transference of old distorted parental relationships to the therapist, and the gradual working through of repressed childhood emotions. What the Navaho medicine man does with myths, prayers, and sand paintings—returning his patient symbolically to the source of tribal energy—we do with memories, dreams, and fantasies. In psychotherapy we return the patient to the beginning of his life, and to the original shaping of his energy.

The second archetypal principle is the management of "evil." In archaic methods of healing this is done by symbolizing the evil as a small object or spirit that intrudes into the patient's body and must be ostentatiously removed. When the symbol is removed, the evil goes with it. Often the object is thought to have been placed there by a witch, so that the cure takes the form of a dramatic struggle between the medicine man and the witch, hopefully ending with the destruction of the witch. In the Navaho evil-chasing chants the evil is brushed, blown, cut, frightened, or prayed away.

In modern psychotherapy the therapist and the patient must also confront whatever is "evil" for that particular patient. The content of that evil is important to the patient in his particular life situation. But the underlying principle of the objectification and management of this evil—regardless of its content—with the assistance of the therapist, may be more important still.

The content of the "evil" will vary from culture to culture, and will be in accord with the patient's and the therapist's cultural expectations. Together they must call it forth and deal with it. There is probably always a time in intense analytic work when the therapist must actually take on the projection of the patient's evil, before it can finally be even partially integrated. There will always be a residue that must be neutralized or "exorcised."

This process was foreshadowed in the Navaho prayer already quoted in Chapter Seven, in which the medicine man temporarily identifies himself with the evil in order to exorcise it. Jung described the modern counterpart to this prayer in a case history stemming from a patient's dream. The patient, a middle-aged woman, said to him one day: "Sometimes you seem rather dangerous, sinister, like an evil magician or a demon. I don't know how I ever get such ideas —you are not a bit like that."

Jung recognized this as an unconscious projection of the patient's feeling onto the therapist. He also knew that she would never accept this explanation. She would much prefer to see the demon or evil magician in the therapist than in herself. Of this Jung said: "She is right: it is preposterous to transfer such things to her. She cannot accept being turned into a demon any more than the doctor can. Her eyes flash, an evil expression creeps into her face, the gleam of an unknown resistance never seen before. I am suddenly faced by the possibility of a painful misunderstanding. . . . Yet it is only a passing moment. The expression on the patient's face clears, and she says, as though relieved, 'It's queer, but just now I had a feeling you had touched the point I could never get over in relation to my friend. It's a horrible feeling, something inhuman, evil, cruel. I simply cannot describe how queer this feeling is. It makes me hate and despise my friend when it comes, although I struggle against it with all my might' " (1953: 39–91).

The third basic form of symbolic healing is the theme of death and rebirth. We have seen it repeated in the Navaho myths of the hero's journey, and experienced by the patient and the medicine man in the solemn recitation of the prayer litanies (Chapter Eight). This symbolic theme is found whenever there is an initiatory experience, whenever a psychic threshold is reached and crossed. Since in our society there are no clear ritual processes of initiation to guide the individual from adolescence to sexual awakening, from young adulthood to full maturity, and thence to the wisdom of old age and the mysteries of death, these are often dealt with in psychotherapy. This is often shown in patients' dreams in which the symbolic mood of death is experienced, leading to a resurgence of life in a new form. The mood of death occurs in connection with perilous ordeals, painful sacrifice, or separation from one's past life.

Joseph Henderson, a Jungian analyst who has studied these processes of psychic initiation (1967), gives as an example the dream of a middle-aged patient who had never been really "initiated" into manhood.

> Dream: My guide explains the theme to me. It is the ordeal of a young sailor who is exposed both to the wind and to being beaten up. I begin to object that this white monkey is not a sailor at all; but just at that moment a young man in black stands up and I think that he must be the true hero. But another handsome young man strides toward an altar and stretches himself out on it. They are making marks on his bare chest as a preparation to offering him as a human sacrifice. Then I find myself on a platform with several other people. We could get down by a small ladder, but I hesitate to do so because there are two young toughs standing by and I think they will stop us. But when a woman in the group

uses the ladder unmolested, I see that it is safe and all of us follow the woman down.

(Henderson, 1964: 115–16)

The guide is the therapist, and the figures in the first part of the dream all represent parts of the dreamer who are going through the initiation process. The dreamer is searching for the true hero, and finally a "handsome young man" stretches himself out to be sacrificed. We cannot see from the dream whether the sacrifice of this handsome youthful self takes place. Only a detailed report of the analysis would tell us whether it took place in the life of this patient, but the last part of the dream suggests that it is time for him to get down from such a high perch in life. The young toughs are part of his shadow self which still might prevent him from doing so, but the last part suggests that a relationship with a woman might lead the way. As in all dream analysis, these are mere suggestions that must be further borne out in the patient's associations and life. But the theme of symbolic death is clearly shown.

In a report on a series of initiation dreams (Sandner and Jongeward, 1967), one young male patient dreamed as follows:

> I was with a man. We went into a large building, either an apartment or a strange temple. He waved the guards aside and we climbed straight up. Now he looked like my father. We climbed a rafter straight up into a huge unfinished building without floors. We got to the top and there was a brightly lit bar with tiles and glass sticking up in triangular shapes. On either side were men in Aztec costume with jagged designs tending fires at various points. It was some kind of club. Some were naked to the waist and had great gashes in their sides. People got mutilated here.

This is the typical temple of initiation; the guide is the therapist or the patient's father. The unfinished building suggests the unfinished parts of the young man's life. The theme of the club suggests the initiatory motif, and death is symbolized as an ordeal in which there is danger of bodily injury or castration. Such rituals are still part of the initiation ceremonies of many primitive tribes. In the dream there is reference to the ritual sacrifices of the Aztecs on the top of their temple pyramids. The outcome is not given in this dream, but the mood is strongly expressed.

In another dream of this type from a young man in his twenties, the setting of the dream goes back to the period of high school, the natural time for adolescent initiation.

> Dream: I leave with the coach of our high school team. He has to arrange an athletic match. We climb into a mountain. Inside the mountain is a dressing room, and we meet the other coach. The visiting team is always beaten. In the game we must traverse some difficult moving path. If you lose you fall into an abyss with water at the bottom. There seems to be two ways to do it. I ask which is the best way and the coach says one way no one has ever succeeded. I take the other. Now it becomes a movie called Test of Manhood. Then I seem to wake up in bed with four other young men. I can't stand the closeness so I leave. I felt I had won the game.

Only by listening to the advice of the older man, the coach, does the dreamer know the right path. The risk of death is associated with athletic competition, which is often part of adolescent development. At the end another facet comes to light. The whole initiatory process is primarily a homoerotic activity in the wide sense of the term, and it intensifies the emotional solidarity between men. But as one of its consequences, it also tends to free the initiate from the physical manifestations of homosexuality and propel him toward heterosexual union as one of his manly prerogatives. As it occurs in the course of therapy, this is usually a complicated process, but it is suggested cogently in this dream. The dream also strongly hints of a successful conclusion.

Eliade viewed initiation in its broadest sense when he said:

"Initiation lies at the core of any genuine human life. And this is true for two reasons. The first is that any genuine human life implies profound crisis, ordeals, suffering, loss, and reconquest of self, 'death and resurrection.' The second is that, whatever degrees of fulfillment it may have brought him, at a certain moment every man sees his life as a failure. This vision does not arise from a moral judgment made on his past, but from an obscure feeling that he has missed his vocation; he had betrayed the best that was in him. . . . The hope and dream of these moments of total crisis are to obtain a definitive and total *renovatio*, a renewal capable of transmuting life" (1958: 135).

Finally, the restoration of a stable universe is a necessary part of any symbolic healing process, including psychotherapy. The regression must be reversed; the transference must be resolved; the patient must be put squarely back into his own life, just as the Navaho patient in the prayer litany (Chapter Eight) is brought back to his hogan restored in mind and body, and surrounded by his possessions and familiar cornfields. Sometimes patients will dream or see images of mandalic forms similar to those shown in the Navaho sand paintings, which indicate that the world is in place and all things are in order. Patients' mandalas may indicate various degrees of attainment of this goal, but they will not be as complete or as fully worked out as the Navaho ones.

The Navaho healing process at times goes beyond the symbolic work we are able to achieve in modern psychotherapy. It does this through its approach to nature as a vital, harmonious entity alive in every part and able, through its inexhaustible power, to resolve individual conflicts. This is no mastery of nature, such as adherents of the scientific discipline seek to acquire, but a striving for unity with natural forces. The Navaho does not relate to "raw" nature as science sees it, but to a highly refined symbolic nature which is intensely alive and imbued with an inner form of radiant beauty. At the core of this mystery is Changing Woman. She is the archetypal symbol of the natural cycle of birth, death, and rebirth. Contact with her through the chant ritual, especially in Blessing Way, fills the patient with joy and peace and brings about renewal, much as Changing Woman renews herself with every round of the seasons, or with the round of the directions in her magical house. Contact with her in the chant practice can bring a long, blessed life and a state of harmony within and without.

The life goal of "walking the trail of beauty in old age" is very different from the goals of Christian mythology. The Navaho does not look forward to personality survival after death. There is a vague idea of an afterlife in an underworld located to the north and reached by a trail down a sandy cliff. Generally it is thought that the unsatisfied or evil parts of a man may linger on as a ghost or spend a restless time in a dingy underworld (Wyman, Hill, and Osana, 1942). The greatest good is to live a long, harmonious life, and then be taken back into nature as part of her indivisible unity. This is the goal envisioned in the myths of the chant heroes and poignantly illustrated in a song from Mountaintop Way. After the hero has returned to earth from his perilous adventures, and imparted the sacred knowledge he has won from the Holy People to his younger brother, the gods beg him to return to them. Finally one day when he is off hunting with his brother, the gods come for him. He sings one last song for his brother and then departs:

Farewell, my younger brother.
From the high, holy places
The Gods have come for me.
You will never see me again.
But when the showers pass over you,
And the thunder sounds,
You will think:
There is the voice of my elder brother.
And when the harvests ripen,
And you hear the voices of small birds·of many kinds,

And the chirping of the grasshoppers,
You will think:
There is the ordering of my elder brother.
There is the trail of his mind.
(Matthews, 1887: 467)

The Navaho religion is a profound meditation on nature and its curative powers. Through the centuries their visions have crystallized into living symbolic units like the prayers and the sand paintings, which are easily reproducible and may be transmitted from one generation to the next. It all revolves around a great secret—an open secret, to be sure—which we all know but want to hear again and again. Reichard put it in these words: "Navaho dogma connects all things, natural and experienced, from man's skeleton to universal destiny, which encompasses even inconceivable space, in a closely interlocked unity which omits nothing, no matter how small or how stupendous, and in which each individual has a significant function until, at his final dissolution, he not only becomes one with the ultimate harmony, but he is that harmony" (quoted by Wyman, 1965b: 344). On that foundation the Navaho have constructed an edifice of symbolism that can take its place among the great healing systems of the world.

Bibliography

Note: *Where more than one title is listed for the same author or authors the entries are arranged in chronological, not alphabetical, order.*

Aberle, David. *The Peyote Religion among the Navaho.* Chicago: Aldine, 1966.
Ackerknecht, Erwin H. "Problems of Primitive Medicine." *Bulletin of the History of Medicine* 11 (1942): 503–21.
Appel, K.; Myers, J. M.; and Sheflin, A. "Prognosis in Psychiatry: Results of Psychiatric Treatment." *Journal of Consulting Psychology* 16 (1952): 319–23.
Astrov, Margot. "The Concept of Motion as the Psychological Leitmotif of Navaho Life and Literature." *Journal of American Folklore* 63 (1950): 45–56.
———, ed. *American Indian Prose and Poetry: The Winged Serpent.* New York: Capricorn Books, 1962.

Begay, Beyal; Hatrale, Yohe; and Wheelwright, Mary. *Eagle Catching Myth and Bead Myth*. Santa Fe, N.M.: Museum of Navaho Ceremonial Art, 1945.

Bergman, Robert. "A School for Medicine Men." *American Journal of Psychiatry* 130 (1973): 6.

Bierhorst, John, ed. *In the Trail of the Wind: American Indian Poems and Ritual Orations*. New York: Farrar, Straus and Giroux, 1971.

———. *Four Masterworks of American Indian Literature*. New York: Farrar, Straus and Giroux, 1974.

Black Elk. *Black Elk Speaks*. Transcribed by John G. Niehardt. Lincoln: University of Nebraska Press, 1961.

Blofeld, John. *The Tantric Mysticism of Tibet*. New York: E. P. Dutton and Co., 1970.

Brower, Kenneth, ed. *Navaho Wildlands*. San Francisco: Sierra Club, 1967.

Brugge, David M. *Navaho Pottery and Ethnohistory*. Window Rock, Ariz.: Navaholand Publications, 1963.

Bunzel, Ruth L. "Introduction to Zuñi Ceremonialism." *47th Annual Report of American Ethnology* (1932).

Burland, C. A. *The Four Directions of Time*. Santa Fe, N.M.: Museum of Navaho Ceremonial Art, 1950.

Campbell, Joseph. *The Hero with a Thousand Faces*. New York: Bollingen Series XVII, Pantheon Books, 1949.

———. *The Masks of God: Primitive Mythology*. New York: Viking Press, 1959.

Carter, Robert Brudenell. *On the Pathology and Treatment of Hysteria*. London: John Churchill, 1853.

Cassirer, Ernst. *The Philosophy of Symbolic Forms*, 3 vols. New Haven and London: Yale University Press, 1953.

Clements, F. E. "Primitive Concepts of Disease." *University of California Publications in American Archaeology and Ethnology* Vol. 32, No. 2 (1932).

Coomaraswamy, A. K. "Symplegades," in *Studies and Essays in the History of Science and Learning Offered in Homage to George Sarton*. New York: 1947.

Coulehan, John L. "Navaho Indian Medicine: A Dimension in Healing." *The Pharos* 39 (1976): 93–96.

Densmore, Francis: *Healing Songs of the American Indians.* New York: Ethnic Folkways Library, Album No. FE 4251, 1965 (original manuscript, 1943).

Driver, Harold E. *Indians of North America.* Chicago and London: University of Chicago Press, 1969.

Eliade, Mircea. *The Myth of the Eternal Return.* New York: Bollingen Series XLVI, Pantheon Books, 1954.

———. *The Sacred and the Profane.* New York: Harper & Row, Harper Torchbooks, 1957.

———. *Rites and Symbols of Initiation.* New York: Harper & Row, Harper Torchbooks, 1958.

———. *Myths, Dreams and Mysteries.* New York: Harper & Row, Harper Torchbooks, 1960.

———. *Shamanism: Archaic Techniques of Ecstasy.* New York: Bollingen Series LXXVI, Pantheon Books, 1964.

———. *Myth and Reality.* New York and Evanston, Ill.: Harper & Row, Harper Torchbooks, 1968.

Erikson, Erik H. *Childhood and Society.* New York: W. W. Norton and Co., 1950.

Foster, Kenneth. *Navaho Sandpaintings.* Window Rock, Ariz.: Navaholand Publications, 1964.

Fox, Robin J. "Witchcraft and Clanship in Cochiti Therapy," in *Magic, Faith and Healing,* Ari Kiev, ed. New York: Free Press of Glencoe, 1964.

Frank, Jerome D. *Persuasion and Healing: A Comparative Study of Psychotherapy.* Baltimore and London: Johns Hopkins University Press, 1961.

Freud, Sigmund. *An Outline of Psychoanalysis.* New York: W. W. Norton and Co., 1949.

Frisbie, Charlotte Johnson. *Kinaaldá.* Middletown, Conn.: Wesleyan University Press, 1967.

Fromm, Erich. *The Sane Society.* New York: Holt, Rinehart and Winston, 1955.

Furst, Peter, ed. *Flesh of the Gods.* New York and Washington: Praeger Publishers, 1972.

Geertz, Clifford. *The Interpretation of Cultures.* New York: Basic Books, 1973.

Gillin, John. "Magical Fright." *Psychiatry* 11 (1948): 387–400.

Goddard, Pliny Earle. "Navaho Texts." *Anthropological Papers of the American Museum of Natural History* 34 (1933).

Haile, Berard. "Navaho Chantways and Ceremonials." *American Anthropologist* Vol. 40, No. 4 (1938a): 639–52.

———. "Origin Legend of the Navaho Enemy Way." *Yale University Publication in Anthropology* 17 (1938b).

———. "Origin Legend of the Navaho Flint Way." *University of Chicago Publication in Anthropology* (1943a).

———. *The Navaho Fire Dance.* Saint Michaels, Ariz.: Saint Michaels Press, 1946.

———. *Navaho Sacrificial Figures.* University of Chicago Press, 1947a.

———. *Prayer Stick Cutting.* University of Chicago Press, 1947b.

———. *Legend of the Ghostway Ritual in the Male Branch of Shootingway and Suckingway, Its Legend and Practice.* Saint Michaels, Ariz.: Saint Michaels Press, 1950.

Hallowell, A. "Fear and Anxiety as Cultural and Individual Variables in a Primitive Society." *Journal of Social Psychology* 9 (1938): 25–47.

Henderson, Joseph. "Ancient Myths and Modern Man," in Carl Jung, ed., *Man and His Symbols.* Garden City, New York: Doubleday and Co., 1964.

———. *Thresholds of Initiation.* Middletown, Conn.: Wesleyan University Press, 1967.

Hester, James. "Early Navaho Migrations and Acculturation in the Southwest." *Museum of New Mexico, Papers in Anthropology* 6 (1962).

Hill, W. W. "The Hand Trembling Ceremony of the Navaho." *El Palacio* 38 (1935a): 65–68.

———. "The Status of the Hermaphrodite and Transvestite in Navaho Culture." *American Anthropologist* 37 (1935b): 273–79.

———. The Navaho Indians and the Ghost Dance of 1890." *American Anthropologist* 46 (1944): 523–27.

Hill, W. W., and Hill, Dorothy. "Navaho Coyote Tales and Their Position in the Southern Athabaskan Group." *Journal of American Folklore* 58 (1945): 317–43.

Horney, Karen. *The Neurotic Personality of Our Time.* New York: W. W. Norton and Co., 1937.

Jochelson, Waldemar. "Religion and Myths of the Koryaks." *Memoir of the American Museum of Natural History* Vol. 6, No. 10 (1905–8).

Jung, Carl, *Two Essays on Analytical Psychology.* New York: Bollingen Series XX, Pantheon Books, Vol. 7, 1953.

———. "Psychology of the Transference," in *The Practice of Psychotherapy.* New York: Bollingen Series XX, Pantheon Books, Vol. 16, 1954.

———. *Symbols of Transformation.* New York: Bollingen Series XX, Pantheon Books, Vol. 5, 1956.

———. *The Archetypes and the Collective Unconscious.* New York: Bollingen Series XX, Pantheon Books, Vol. 9, i, 1959.

———. "A Review of the Complex Theory," in *The Structure and Dynamics of the Psyche.* New York: Bollingen Series XX, Pantheon Books, Vol. 8, 1960.

———, ed. *Man and His Symbols.* New York: Doubleday and Co., 1964.

———. "The Spirit Mercurius," in *Alchemical Studies.* New York: Bollingen Series XX, Princeton University Press, Vol. 13, 1967.

Kaplan, Bert, and Johnson, Dale. "The Social Meaning of Navaho Psychopathology," in Ari Kiev, *Magic, Faith and Healing.* New York: Free Press of Glencoe, 1964.

Kelly, Roger; Lang, R. W.; and Walters, Harry. *Navaho Figurines Called Dolls.* Santa Fe, N.M.: Museum of Navaho Ceremonial Art, 1972.

Kiev, Ari. *Magic, Faith and Healing.* New York: Free Press of Glencoe, 1964.

Klah, Hosteen. *Texts of the Navaho Creation Chants.* Collected and translated by Dr. Harry Hoijer. Cambridge, Mass.: Peabody Museum of Havard University, 1929.

Klah, Hosteen, and Wheelwright, Mary. *Tleji or Yehbechai Myth*. Santa Fe, N.M.: Museum of Navaho Ceremonial Art, 1938.

——. *Navaho Creation Myth*. Santa Fe, N.M.: Museum of Navaho Ceremonial Art, 1942.

——. *Wind Chant and Feather Chant*. Santa Fe, N.M.: Museum of Navaho Ceremonial Art, 1946.

Kluckhohn, Clyde. "Recurrent Themes in Myth and Mythmaking," in Henry Murray, ed., *Myth and Mythmaking*. New York: George Braziller, 1960.

——. *Culture and Behavior*. New York: Free Press, 1962.

——. *Navaho Witchcraft*. Boston: Beacon Press, 1967.

Kluckhohn, Clyde, and Leighton, Dorothea. *Children of the People*. Cambridge, Mass.: Harvard University Press 1946.

——. *The Navaho*. Cambridge, Mass.: Harvard University Press, 1946; revised edition, Natural History Library, 1962.

Kluckhohn, Clyde, and Spencer, Katherine. *A Bibliography of the Navaho Indians*. New York: J. J. Augustin, 1940.

Kluckhohn, Clyde, and Wyman, Leland. "Navaho Classification of Their Song Ceremonials," *Memoirs of American Anthropological Association* 50 (1938).

——. "An Introduction to Navaho Chant Practice." *American Anthropologist* Vol. 42, Supp. No. 53 (1940).

La Barre, Weston. *The Peyote Cult*. Hamden, Conn.: Shoe String Press, 1938 and 1964.

Ladd, John. *The Structure of a Moral Code*. Cambridge, Mass.: Harvard University Press, 1957.

Laney, John. "The Peyote Movement: An Introduction," in *Spring, An Annual of Jungian Thought*. New York: Spring Publications, 1972.

Langer, Susanne K. *Philosophy in a New Key: A Study in the Symbolism of Reason, Rite and Art*. Cambridge, Mass.: Harvard University Press, 1942.

Leighton, Alexander, and Leighton, Dorothea. "Elements of Psychotherapy in Navaho Religion." *Psychiatry* 4 (1941): 515–24.

Lévi-Strauss, Claude. *Structural Anthropolgy*. New York and Garden City, N.Y.: Doubleday and Co., Anchor Books, 1967.

Lincoln, J. S. *The Dream in Primitive Culture*. Baltimore: Williams and Wilkins Co., 1935.

Lommel, Andreas. *Shamanism: The Beginnings of Art*. New York and Toronto: McGraw-Hill Book Co., 1967.

Lowie, Robert. *Indians of the Plains*. Garden City, N.Y.: Natural History Press, 1954.

————. "Shamans and Priests among the Plains Indians," in William Lessa and Evon Vogt, *Reader in Comparative Religion, An Anthropological Approach*. New York, Evanston, Ill., and London: Harper & Row, 1958.

Matthews, Washington. "The Mountain Chant: A Navaho Ceremony." *Fifth Annual Report of the Bureau of American Ethnology to the Secretary of the Smithsonian Institution*, 1883–84, Washington (1887): 379–486.

————. "The Prayer of a Navaho Shaman." *American Anthropologist*, Old Series 1 (1888): 147–70.

————. "Songs of Sequence of the Navaho." *Journal of American Folklore*, Vol. 7, No. 26 (1894b): 185–94.

————. "A Vigil of the Gods: A Navaho Ceremony." *American Anthropologist*, Vol. 9, No. 2 (1896).

————. "Navaho Legends." *Memoirs of the American Folklore Society* 5 (1897): 299.

————. "The Night Chant: A Navaho Ceremony." *Memoirs of the American Museum of Natural History* 6 (1902).

————. "Navaho Myths, Prayers and Songs with Texts and Translations." *University of California Publications in American Archaeology and Ethnology*, Vol. 5, No. 2 (1907).

McAllester, David, and Wheelwright, Mary. *The Myth and Prayers of the Great Star Chant and the Myth of the Coyote Chant*. Navaho Religion Series, Vol. 4. Santa Fe, N.M.: Museum of Navaho Ceremonial Art, 1956.

Middleton, John, ed. *Magic, Witchcraft and Curing*. Garden City, N.Y.: Natural History Press, 1967.

Moon, Sheila. *A Magic Dwells: A Poetic and Psychological Study of the Navaho Emergence Myth*. Middletown, Conn.: Wesleyan University Press, 1970.

Morgan, William. "Navaho Dreams." *American Anthropologist* 34 (1932): 390–400.

Morgan, William, et al. "Coyote Tales." *Bureau of Indian Affairs, Navaho Life Series* (1949).

Newcomb, Franc. *Hosteen Klah, Navaho Medicine Man and Sand Painter.* Norman, Okla.: University of Oklahoma Press, 1964.

———. *Navaho Neighbors.* Norman, Okla.: University of Oklahoma Press, 1966.

———. *Navaho Folk Tales.* Santa Fe, N.M.: Museum of Navaho Ceremonial Art, 1967.

Newcomb, Franc, and Reichard, Gladys A. *Sandpaintings of the Navaho Shooting Chant.* New York: J. J. Augustin, 1937.

Newcomb, Franc; Wheelwright, Mary; and Fisher, Stanley. "A Study of Navaho Symbolism." *Papers of the Peabody Museum of Archaeology and Ethnology,* Harvard University Vol. 32, No. 3 (1956).

Neumann, Erich. *The Origins and History of Consciousness.* New York: Bollingen Series XLII, Pantheon Books, 1954.

Niehardt, John G. *Black Elk Speaks.* Lincoln: University of Nebraska Press, 1961.

Oakes, Maud; Haile, Berard; and Wyman, Leland, eds. *Beautyway: A Navaho Ceremonial.* New York: Bollingen Series LIII, Bollingen Foundation and Pantheon Books, 1957.

Oakes, Maud; King, Jeff; and Campbell, Joseph. *Where the Two Came to Their Father: A Navaho War Ceremonial.* Princeton, N.J.: Princeton University Press, Bollingen Series I, 1943.

O'Bryan, Aileen. "The Dîné: Origin Myths of the Navaho Indians." *Smithsonian Institution, Bureau of American Ethnology, Bulletin* 163 (Washington, D.C., 1956).

Opler, Morris Edward. *An Apache Lifeway.* New York: Cooper Square Publishers, 1965.

Ornstein, Robert E. *The Psychology of Consciousness.* San Francisco: W. H. Freeman, 1972.

Parsons, Elsie. *Pueblo Indian Religion,* 2 vols. Chicago: University of Chicago Press, 1939.

Radin, Paul. *The Trickster: A Study in American Indian Mythology.* New York: Philosophical Library, 1956.

Reichard, Gladys A. *Spider Woman.* New York: Macmillan Co., 1934.

———. *A Navaho Shepherd and Weaver.* New York: J. J. Augustin, 1936.

———. *Dezba, Woman of the Desert.* New York: J. J. Augustin, 1938.

———. *Navaho Medicine Man.* New York: J. J. Augustin, 1939.

———. *Prayer, the Compulsive Word.* Seattle and London: University of Washington Press, 1944b.

———. *The Story of the Navaho Hail Chant.* New York: J. J. Augustin, 1944c.

———. "Distinctive Features of Navaho Religion." *Southwestern Journal of Anthropolgy* 1 (1945): 199–220.

———. *Navaho Religion: A Study of Symbolism.* New York: Bollingen Series XVIII, Pantheon Books, 1950; 2nd edition in one vol., 1963.

Reichard, Gladys, and Newcomb, Franc. *Sandpaintings of the Navaho Shooting Chant.* New York: J. J. Augustin, 1937.

Sandner, Donald. "Healing Symbolism in Navaho Religion," in *Spring, An Annual of Archetypal Psychology and Jungian Thought.* New York: Spring Publications, 1972.

Sandner, Donald, and Jongeward, David. " Initiation Symbolism in Primitive Rites and Modern Dreams," paper read at American Psychiatric Association, 1967.

Sapir, Edward, and Hiojer, Harry. *Navaho Texts.* Iowa City, Iowa: Linguistic Society of America, 1942.

Schaafsma, Polly. *Early Navaho Rock Paintings and Carvings.* Santa Fe, N. M.: Museum of Navaho Ceremonial Art, 1966.

Spencer, Katherine. "Mythology and Values: Analysis of Navaho Chantway Myths." *Memoirs of the American Folklore Society, Philadelphia* 48 (1957).

Stephen, Alexander. "Navaho Origin Legend." *Journal of American Folklore* 43 (1930): 88–104.

Stevenson, James. "Ceremonial of Hasjelti Dailjis." *Annual Report of the Bureau of American Ethnology* 8 (1886): 229–85.

Terrell, John Upton. *The Navahos, the Past and Present of a Great People.* New York, Evanston, Ill., San Francisco, and London: Harper & Row, 1970.

Tschopik, Harry, Jr. "Taboo as a Possible Factor in the Obsolescence of Navaho Pottery and Basketry." *American Anthropologist* 40 (1938).

Tucci, Giuseppe. *The Theory and Practice of the Mandala.* New York: Samuel Weiser, 1969.

Turner, Victor. *The Forest of Symbols: Aspects of Ndembu Ritual.* Ithaca, N.Y., and London: Cornell University Press, 1970.

Underhill, Ruth. *Red Man's Religion.* Chicago and London: University of Chicago Press, 1965.

Veith, Ilza. *Hysteria, the History of a Disease.* Chicago and London: University of Chicago Press, 1965.

Villaseñor, David. *Tapestries in Sand, the Spirit of Indian Sandpaintings.* Healdsburg, Calif.: Naturegraph Co., 1963.

Vogel, Virgil J. *American Indian Medicine.* Norman, Okla.: University of Oklahoma Press, 1970.

Waters, Frank. *Masked Gods: Navaho and Pueblo Ceremonialism.* New York: Ballantine Books, 1950.

Wheat, Joe Ben. *Prehistoric People of the Northern Southwest.* Grand Canyon, Ariz.: Natural History Association, 1955.

Wheelwright, Mary. *Tleji or Yehbechai Myth.* Santa Fe, N.M.: House of Navaho Religion, Bulletin No. 1, 1938.

———. *Myth of Sontso (Big Star).* Santa Fe, N. M.: Museum of Navaho Ceremonial Art, Bulletin No. 2, 1940.

———. *Navaho Creation Myth.* Santa Fe, N.M.: Museum of Navaho Ceremonial Art, Bulletin No. 2, 1942.

———. *Atsah or Eagle Catching Myth and Yohe or Bead Myth.* Santa Fe, N.M.: Museum of Navaho Ceremonial Art, Bulletin No. 3, 1945.

———. *Hail Chant and Water Chant*. Santa Fe, N.M.: Museum of Navaho Ceremonial Art, 1946a.

———. *Nilth Chiji Bakaji (Wind Chant) and Feather Chant*. Santa Fe, N.M.: Museum of Navaho Ceremonial Art, Bulletin No. 4, 1946b.

———. *Myth of Mountain Chant and Myth of Beauty Chant*. Santa Fe, N.M.: Museum of Navaho Ceremonial Art, Bulletin No. 5, 1951.

Wheelwright, Mary, and Haile, Berard. *Emergence Myth According to the Hanelthnayhe or Upward Reaching Rite*. Santa Fe, N.M.: Museum of Navaho Ceremonial Art, Navaho Religion Series, Vol. 3, 1949.

White, Leslie A. *The Science of Culture*. New York: Grove Press, 1949.

Wyman, Leland. "The Female Shooting Chant." *American Anthropologist* 38 (1936a): 634–53.

———. "Navaho Diagnosticians." *American Anthropologist* 38 (1936b): 236–46.

———. "Origin Legend of Navaho Divinatory Rites." *Journal of American Folklore* 49 (1936c): 134–42.

———. *The Windways of the Navaho*. Colorado Springs, Colo.: Taylor Museum, Colorado Springs Fine Arts Center, 1962.

———. *The Red Antway of the Navaho*. Santa Fe, N.M.: Museum of Navaho Ceremonial Art, 1965a.

———. "The Religion of the Navaho Indians," in Vergilius Ferm, ed., *Ancient Religion*. New York: Citadel Press, 1965b.

Wyman, Leland, and Bailey, Flora. "Navaho Upward-Reaching Way." *University of New Mexico Bulletin* 389 (1943): 1–47.

———. "Idea and Action Patterns in Navaho Flintway." *Southwestern Journal of Anthropology* 1 (1945): 356–77.

———. "Navaho Striped Windway: An Injury Way Chant." *Southwestern Journal of Anthropology* 2 (1946a): 213–38.

———. "Two Examples of Navaho Physiotherapy." *American Anthropologist* 46 (1946b): 329–37.

———. "Navaho Indian Ethnoentomology." *University of New Mexico Publications in Anthropology* 12 (1964).

Wyman, Leland, and Haile, Berard. *Blessingway*. Tucson, Ariz.: University of Arizona Press, 1970.

Wyman, Leland; Hill, W. W.; and Osana, T. "Navaho Eschatology." *University of New Mexico Bulletin* 377 (1942).

Index

▶▶▶▶